Gillian Whiteley is a curator and lecturer in Critical and Historical Studies at Loughborough University School of the Arts. Her publications include *Assembling the Absurd: the Sculpture of George Fullard* (1998) and the co-edited *Telling Stories: Countering Narrative in Art, Theory and Film* (2009). Her exhibitions include *Radical Mayhem: Welfare State International and Its Followers* (Burnley, UK, 2008) and *Pan-demonium* (AC Institute, New York, USA, 2009), an ongoing project which forms part of her research into bricolage and improvisatory techniques and practices (www.bricolagekitchen.com). She is Associate Editor of the Intellect journal, *Art & the Public Sphere.*

JUNK

ART AND THE POLITICS OF TRASH

Gillian Whiteley

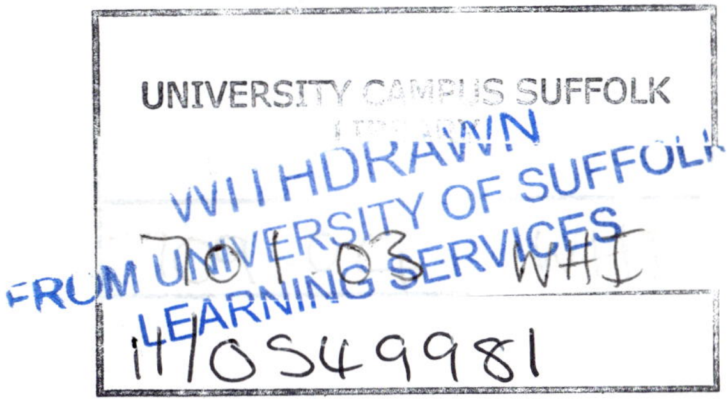

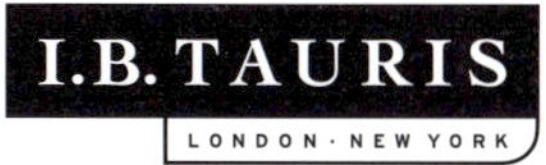

Published in 2011 by I.B.Tauris & Co Ltd
6 Salem Road, London W2 4BU
175 Fifth Avenue, New York NY 10010
www.ibtauris.com

Distributed in the United States and Canada Exclusively by
Palgrave Macmillan
175 Fifth Avenue, New York NY 10010

ISBN: 978 1 84885 412 3 (hb)
ISBN: 978 1 84885 413 0 (pb)

A full CIP record for this book is available from the British Library
A full CIP record is available from the Library of Congress

Library of Congress Catalog Card Number: available

Typeset in Utopia by MPS Limited, a Macmillan Company
Printed and bound in Great Britain by TJ International Ltd, Padstow,
Cornwall

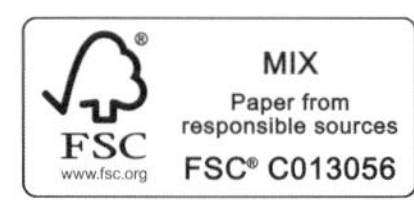

CONTENTS

LIST OF ILLUSTRATIONS

conservation lab at San Francisco Museum of Modern Art in 2006. Photograph by the author, reproduced with permission of San Francisco Museum of Modern Art and Gallery Paule Anglim.   *p. 73*

ACKNOWLEDGEMENTS

I would like to thank many individuals and organisations for their generous financial, intellectual and personal support and for giving time, energy and enthusiasm to my project over the past few years.

With particular thanks to Tony Adams; Art Gallery of New South Wales; Bancroft Library, University of California, Berkeley; Peter Boswell; Stuart Brisley; British Academy; Bruce Conner Family Trust; Michael Cataldi; Centre Georges Pompidou, Paris; Lorraine Connelly-Northey; Tony Cragg; Sarah Crellin; Dianne Tanzer Gallery; Jane England; Clive Evatt; Fondation Dubuffet; Irena Fullard; Gabrielle Pizzi Gallery; Gallery Paule Anglim; Elizabeth Gower; Henry Moore Institute, Leeds; Leonora Howlett; Hauser & Wirth; Carole Itter; Chris Jordan; Clay Lucas; Ash Keating; Bruce Lacey; Colin Lanceley; Sophie Matthiesson; Marsha Meskimmon; Michael Kohn Gallery; Kendragh Morgan; Musée d'Art Moderne et d'Art Contemporain (MAMAC) Nice; Museum of Modern Art, New York (MoMA) archives and library; National Gallery of Australia; National Gallery of Victoria; National Library of Australia; Al Neil; New York Public Library; Kajal Nisha Patel; Lucy Puls; Ben Read; Jasia Reichardt; Ronald Feldman Fine Arts; San Francisco Museum of Modern Art; John Scanlan; Joy Sleeman; Kathryn Spence; Clinton R. Starr; Stephen Wirtz Gallery; Lynn Thomson; Tate Library and Archive; Jane Tormey; Mierle Laderman Ukeles; University of Liverpool Special Collection; Frank Watters; Jon Wood; Bill Woodrow. With special thanks to Ash Keating for the book cover image.

Finally, I owe gratitude to my ragpicking ancestors, without whom this book would never have been started, and also to my closest family – Alex, Danny and especially Geoff, 'one of the roughs' – without whose emotional support, encouragement, intellectual and cultural sustenance this project would never have been finished.

Gillian Whiteley
www.bricolagekitchen.com

PREFACE: THE RAGMAN'S GRANDDAUGHTER

Any old iron? Any old iron? Any, any old iron?[1]

There is an element of embodied history in this exploration of junk, art and politics. Growing up in the 1950s and 1960s in a mining village on the edge of the Derbyshire coalfields on the outskirts of Sheffield, with its landscape of steel mills, billowing chimneys, scrapyards and pit-tips, I lived amongst the detritus of 'heavy' and 'light' industries. Walls commonly incorporated coke-oven waste and paths were often made from clinker and ashes.

Besides growing up with the postwar 'make-do and mend' mentality of the Northern working class, I was also subject to a particular familial resistance to 'the new'. Our pantry was a storeroom for rubbish awaiting recycling: shopping bags were stuffed with neatly folded used brown paper bags, jam jars jostled on the marble slab beside the 'meat-safe'; beneath, empty lemonade bottles were lined up ready for re-filling from the local 'beer-off'. Elsewhere, old jerseys were stored for unpicking and re-knitting, torn nylon lingerie was saved for use as cleaning cloths, cotton knickers were particularly prized for dishcloths. On the mantelpiece, old envelopes were stacked for writing shopping lists and flattened cereal boxes for making 'spills' to light the fire. The sewing machine housed a battered biscuit tin of old buttons, its drawers were crammed with broken zips, lengths of over-stretched elastic extracted from various garments. And so the list goes on. Nothing much discarded, everything collated, collected, stored and waiting for another use. Partly, this was the legacy of the 1950s' 'austerity', but it all made sound economic sense.

My father, a spring-smith in a Sheffield steel works, was an instinctive *bricoleur* who lived by a makeshift ethos. I remember watching him transform our mahogany upright piano into a rickety fablon-lined 'china cabinet'. Later, he fashioned miniature tools from hand-beaten old saucepans for a series of small concrete sculpted figurines. His wardrobe housed 'dead-men's suits' and second-hand brogues. His aspiration to 'go on the tramp' owed little to hobo culture or Jack Kerouac's Dean Moriarty – it echoed the leanings of his own father who, as a youth, had absconded with Irish travellers at Sheffield's annual Wicker fair, went 'AWOL' in Greece whilst in the army and returned to Sheffield during the desperate years of the 1930s to become a 'scrap-tatter', collecting old clothes around the backstreets with a horse and cart. My grandfather was not one of Sheffield's notoriously well-off scrap-dealers like the one in Alan Sillitoe's *The Ragman's Daughter*,[2] but he was a 'rag and bone' man with a horse and cart (Fig. 1). Collecting, sifting, sorting and weighing rags was one of the chief pastimes of my father's early life. Of course, for Walter Benjamin, like Baudelaire before him, the 'ragpicker' was a fascinating and symbolic figure.[3] The *chiffonier* had a worthy occupation which epitomised urban modernity – and a certain pride in that heritage has informed this research.

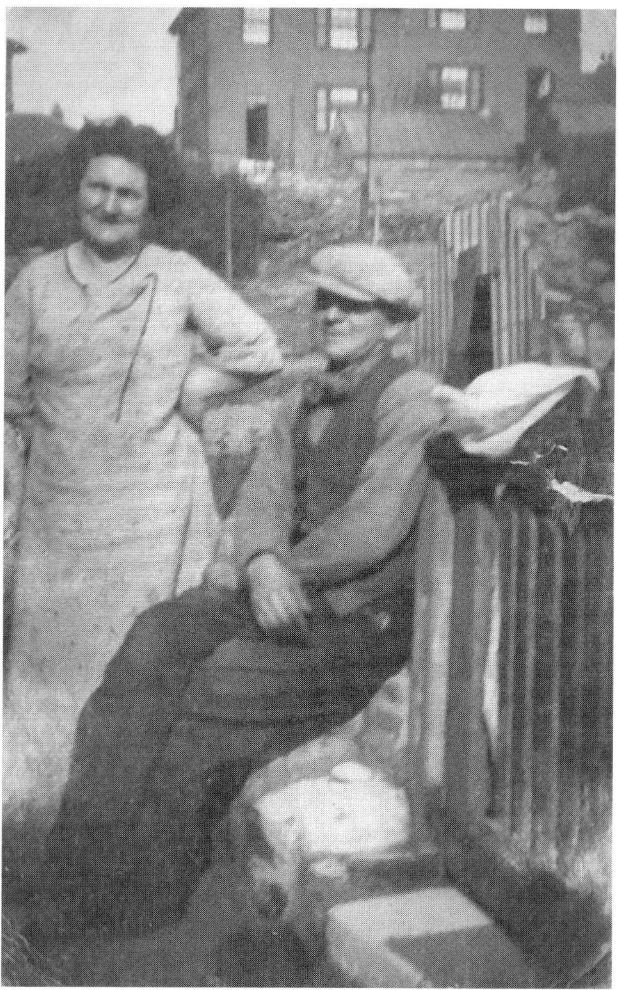

Fig. 1 An honourable heritage: my grandfather was a 'rag and bone' man during the 1930s in Sheffield. Photograph from author's family album.

Now, of course, with a fashionable rhetoric of sustainability, recycling makes ethical as well as economic sense – but the thrill of finding incongruous objects and the real and imagined narratives which they evoke is not diminished. Reclaimed materials and salvaged objects 'tell stories' in a way that new things do not.

This project, then, has been in incubation for many years although it has also developed through an academic journey, emerging from PhD research on assemblage and artists working with junk in the mid-twentieth century.[4] Additionally, devising and teaching *Assemblage–Collage–Bricolage*, as part of the postgraduate programme at the University of Leeds, facilitated a further exploration of some of the ideas and practices discussed in this book and I am grateful to all my students for their participation and contributions to related seminars, events and exhibitions. A British Academy Research Grant and the support of Loughborough University School of Art and Design, (now School of the Arts), have enabled all the strands of this project to come to fruition with this book.

Bricolage provides the perfect analogy for the haphazard and serendipitous nature of one's journey through life. A common working method for many artistic practices, it is important also as an alternative paradigm for research and writing. According to Denzil and Lincoln,

> ... the researcher-as-*bricoleur* theorist works between and within competing and overlapping perspectives and paradigms. The *bricoleur* understands process shaped by his or her personal history, biography, gender, social class, race, and ethnicity, and those of the people in the setting ... [...] ... The product of the *bricoleur*'s labour is a bricolage, a complex, dense, reflexive, collagelike creation that represents the researcher's images, understandings and interpretations of the world ...[5]

Walter Benjamin's *Arcades Project* is seminal in its bricolage approach to material culture and to history. As Tina Kendall and Kristin Koster have noted, for Benjamin, the past as loss and degradation is not occluded by, but revealed through, the ragpicking work of cultural recycling.[6]

A bricolage approach is an essential counter to linear, sequential thinking, narratives and practices. This book offers a study of a personally selected collation of art production and practices which have employed trash at particular times and in particular contexts. It also reflects a pressing need to consider art's uses of trash within a global setting and, whilst this book does not aim to offer a world survey, it does aim to consider the implications of a series of specific moments and incidences at the start of the eco-conscious twenty-first century. In Denzin and Lincoln's terms, it is a product of a bricoleur's labour: a bricolage of moments, understandings and interpretations.

Introduction: Culturalist Bricolage and Garbology

Bricolage Culture

It is mid-summer 2006 and I am sweltering in the clammy heat beneath the corrugated metal roof of Hauser and Wirth's vast Coppermill gallery in London's East End, amidst an enormous environment of rotting, dribbling matter created over many years by Dieter Roth.[1] Explaining that it was impossible to see where the artwork begins and ends in the gallery space, one reviewer described it as a 'begrimed indoor city'.[2] *Large Table Ruin* began by chance in the early 1970s when the artist found some tools stuck in solidified puddles of goo on his workbench. Over the next 20 years,

> the work took on a life of its own, and by a slow process of accumulation became a sprawling configuration of table-tops, out of which grew towering piles of lashed-together junk, until by the end it became a multi-layered agglomeration, its surfaces laden with rafts of debris, illuminated here and there by a wonky lamp ...[3]

The installation is a conglomeration of dust-covered objects, boxes, bottles, oozing filthy liquids, unidentifiable sticky substances, an accumulation of abject matter teetering on the brink of collapse. Roth's 'cacophonous agglomerations of found objects'[4] both invite and resist interpretation. His life's work consisted of a disparate assortment of activities – much of it literary and collaborative – ranging from writing poetry and composing symphonies to creating art objects from the pulped writings of Günter Grass. My encounter with Roth's work is a comic one – the preposterous tableaux provoke hilarity but they also initiate an inquiry into the fundamental nature of materiality and the fragility of human existence. Decomposition and entropy connotes the transition from unity to disunity, disintegration and chaos. Material dissolution can be a metaphor for political states, signifying social upheaval, anarchy and revolution.

In the cavernous Coppermill warehouse, the shambolic mess of Roth's installation is mildly distasteful but, deceptively, it is carefully curated (Fig. 2). The dribbling fluids remind me of the junk tableaux and assemblages made by Ed Kienholz in the 1960s and 1970s. A recent retrospective exhibition of the work of Ed and Nancy Redding Kienholz at the Baltic in

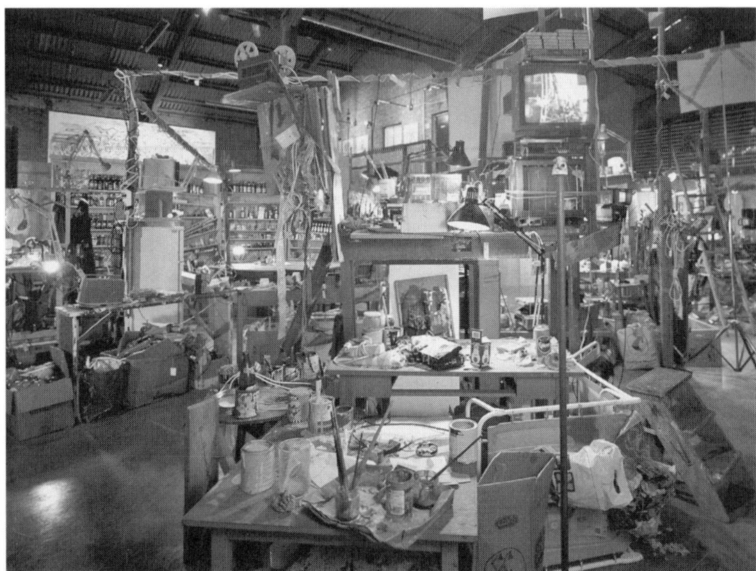

Fig. 2 Dieter Roth, Martin Kippenberger, installation view at Hauser & Wirth London, Coppermill, 2006. Courtesy the Estate of Dieter Roth and Hauser & Wirth.

summer 2005 brought together a series of installations and assemblages which presented a polemic on war, global poverty and social injustice.[5] There, the viewer moved out of the newly renovated space of the Baltic onto the Tyne riverside, an area once heaving with the industrial dirt and noise of the shipyards, but now a sterile place of neatly organised visitor centres and heritage sites – a homogenised, planned, controlled environment where nothing is intended to disturb the visitor experience. The message of the exhibition was annulled by the surroundings where a ubiquitous 'culture-led re-generation' has tailored any real sense of historical particularity and difference.

In contrast, I step out of the Roth into the jumbled material environment of the streets around Brick Lane, an area which seems to be eternally on the cusp of social and demographic transition. Here the ramshackle bric-a-brac of decaying stuff integrates into its surroundings. Thrift store stench segues into a rash of 'vintage' clothes shops which have sprung up around Spitalfields, racks of shoes and bags tumbling over and onto the pavement representing the contemporary shift into 'eco-chic', a greener brand of consumerism. Litter and edible leftovers spill onto the streets around the gallery. A bin is stuffed with congealed liquids oozing into each other and the physical matter in a state of flux reflects the historical layering of ethnicities and migrating cultures of the East End. Coppermill, once a factory, now an art gallery,[6] is situated in an area that is a palimpsest of cultural history, a vibrant anarchic environment where materiality meets social life in a messy tension of economic inequalities and cultural diversity. In her recent study of London as an archetypal 'world city', Doreen Massey relates it to the 'mixity' of lived practices and the criss-crossing multiple allegiances described by Saghal and Yuval-Davis in what Gilroy has termed 'a convivial demotic cosmopolitanism'.[7] Monica Ali's novel, *Brick Lane*, operates within this framework of criss-crossing 'mixity'. Nazneen, the Bengali heroine and narrator, captures the cultural and material paradoxes of the environment as she describes the sounds and smells, wandering through the streets

> ...stacked up with rubbish, entire kingdoms of rubbish piled high as fortresses with only the border skirmishes of plastic bottles and grease-stained cardboard to separate them ... '[8]

The surrounding urban environment at Coppermill can be experienced as Massey's 'mixity', as a *bricolage*[9] of heterogeneity, an array of objects and textures, social and cultural tensions, physical matter and architectural structures. The city itself is like a gigantic assemblage of junk continually being re-made and re-inscribed. My encounter with Roth's installation of trash in this particular location presents itself as merely one element of what Colin Rowe described in 1975 as a place of 'collisive fields and interstitial debris', as 'culturalist bricolage'.[10]

All confrontations with artworks are embodied experiences. They are *located* and *temporal* viewings: they need to be considered as *situated* encounters with stuff. Massey has emphasised the importance of considering this space/time dialectic in relation to 'place'. As Massey points out, 'in debates around identity, the terminology of space, location, positionality and place figures prominently' – she reminds us to be mindful of 'the politics of location' and not to forget to *politicise* the spatial.[11]

Mesmerised by the smashed bottles, oozing liquids and the claustrophobic heat inside Coppermill, I recalled that this specific moment was exactly a year since a young British Asian man had blown himself up in a carriage on the London Underground at nearby Aldgate East. In this moment, the vectors of place and materiality are inexorably political.

The Global Scrapheap

We head into the hills to see the biggest of the mega-city's rubbish mega-pits: the Changshengqiao landfill site – a giant reservoir of garbage, more than 30 metres deep and stretching over 350,000 square metres. The waste engineer, Wang Yukun, tells me the city produces 3,500 tonnes of junk every day. None of it is recycled. Some is burned. Here, it is layered like lasagne: six metres of rubbish, half a metre of earth, a chemical treatment and then a huge black sheet of high-density polyethylene lining. The site opened in 2003 and it already contains more than a million tonnes of rubbish.[12]

Waste is, of course, an adjunct of luxury. Junk, trash, garbage, rubbish, refuse – whatever we call it – is dependent on economic wealth and excess production. Industrialised hi-tech urban cultures produce and thrive on the market for new and disposable goods – in 1960, Vance Packard warned the rest of the world of the environmental consequences of American-style 'hedonism for the masses' and 'planned obsolescence' in his classic study, *The Waste Makers*.[13] Dealing with gargantuan amounts of rubbish is currently a key crisis management topic. Popular and scholarly accounts chronicle alarming statistics on domestic and industrial production of rubbish which suggest that we are in danger of being completely overwhelmed by its accumulation. As Girling warns us:

> Every hour in the UK we throw away enough garbage to fill the Albert Hall. A gathering tsunami of rubbish – organic and inorganic, active and inert, electronic, aural and visual – pours into our lives and out again, into a world no longer infinite.[14]

Recent figures on the production of garbage in the USA show Packard's warnings were not heeded and that trends have escalated. In her book, *Gone Tomorrow, The Hidden Life of Garbage*, Heather Rogers demonstrates how the USA, the wealthiest country in the world, leads in the production of trash – in 2003, almost 500 billion pounds of paper, glass, wood, food, metal, clothing, dead electronics and other refuse were burnt, dumped at sea or 'buried under a civilised veil of dirt and grass seed'.[15] As she outlines:

> The United States is the world's number one producer of garbage: we consume 30 percent of the planet's resources and produce 30 percent of all its wastes. But we are home to just 4 percent of the global population. Recent figures show that every American discards over 1,600 pounds of rubbish a year – more than 4.5 pounds per person per day. And over the past generation our mountains of waste have doubled.[16]

With current concerns about climate change and the rapid growth of cities within and outside the West – Chongqing, Guangzhou and others in China, for example[17] – narratives about the global scrapheap have become

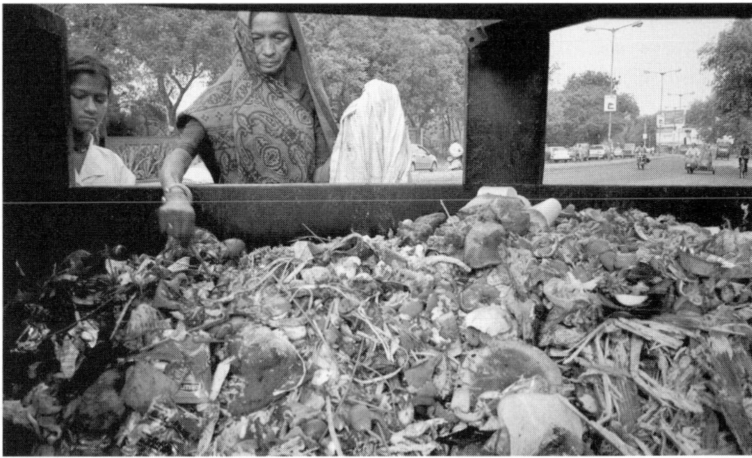

Fig. 3 Kajal Nisha Patel, *Even rubbish has a value*, photograph. Reproduced with kind permission of Kajal Nisha Patel, www.kajalpatel.com

apocalyptic.[18] The politics of geography creates abundance in some parts of the world and waste, scarcity and poverty in others – with the twenty-first century development of rapidly expanding 'global cities' though, these extremes are often, simultaneously, at their most visible (see Fig. 3).

Sustainability and 'thinking green' are increasingly fashionable in the economically rich West but working with trash, creatively or in any other way, has historical, cultural and social connotations which relate to hierarchies of materials at particular times and in particular places. Detritus has ideological, social, political contexts and associations. Anyone forced to work with other people's garbage – from office cleaners to sewage workers – recognises this. Everyone contributes to the domestic rubbish tip and landfill sites but the processing of waste is generally left to those on the social and economic margins. Besides having one of the world's fastest growing economies, India has become one of the largest dumping grounds for the rest of the world's toxic 'e-waste'. In Delhi, for instance, more than 10,000 people are employed in recycling activities, with little awareness of the health hazards and no control over working conditions; children dismantle the e-waste by hand to recover the valuable parts from the components contaminated with lethal toxins such as lead, cadmium and mercury.

The fumes get worse at night – sometimes it's hard to breathe, you feel like you're choking. A girl died here last year. She had asthma. And one night she choked. The people have argued with the workshop owners, but the police are bribed, so nothing changes … we're from Gwalior, in Madhya Pradesh, but there's no work there, so we can't afford to go back …[19]

Paradoxically, whilst the social outcasts and destitute children of India process lethal cyberjunk, in other parts of the world it is fashionable to work with trash. In the UK, local authorities are increasingly devising more elaborate recycling projects for household waste and every facet of everyday life and culture is subject to 'eco-spin'. Advertisements market products with promises to reduce or offset carbon footprints; retail stores have competed to limit their use of packaging and whole towns have declared 'plastic bag free zones'.[20] A plethora of exhibitions, such as *Well fashioned – Eco style in the UK*, have presented new green design approaches, incorporating re-using and recycling.[21] Trash and waste is currently being explored and researched from every perspective with the study of trash itself now regarded as a field of study in its own right – garbology – with William Rathje and Cullen Murphy its chief pioneers.[22]

For me, Justin Gignac's *NYC Garbage boxes* are the epitome of the contemporary cultural fascination with trash. Gignac has created a lucrative online business out of packaging and selling rubbish collected from New York City streets (Fig. 4). His exquisitely designed boxes appeal in a number of ways: visually and aesthetically in a Baudelairean sense, they convey the beauty of the ruin and have intimations of mortality; they are 'exotic' souvenirs which reference collective memory and a vicarious glimpse of 'other' lives. The minimal see-through cubes also give them a contemporary look which means they could just as easily be executive desk toys or ornaments for inner-city loft apartments. Disguised as ecologically sound purchases they are parasitic on a throwaway culture but they have the talismanic and fetishistic properties of the *objet trouvé* and promote a 'garbage aesthetic'.

> I sell garbage. I scour New York City streets picking up trash. After filling bags with subway passes, Broadway tickets and other NYC junk, I carefully arrange plastic cubes full of the stuff. Each box is unique and won't leak or smell. The cubes are then signed, numbered and dated, making them perfect for anyone who wants their own piece of the NYC landscape. Just get one now before they clean up this city.[23]

As Ella Shoat and Robert Stam have emphasised, it is imperative to acknowledge the complex nature of multifaceted economic development. They have identified the 'aesthetics of garbage' as just one of a range of alternative revalorisations which invert what has formerly been seen as

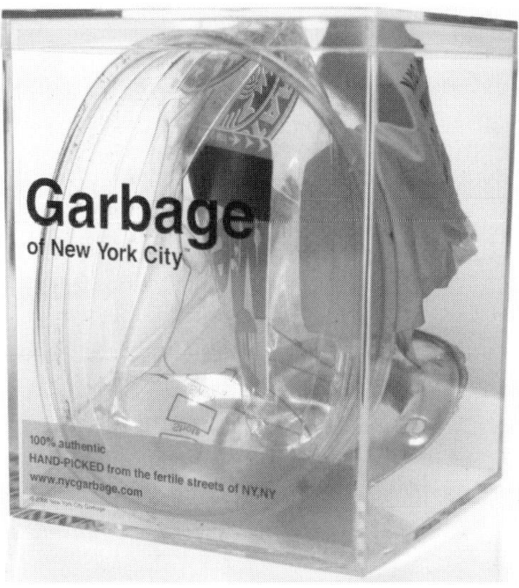

Fig. 4 *New York City Garbage.* Publicity image from website produced with kind permission of Justin Gignac, founder of New York City Garbage, www.nycgarbage.com

negative, especially within colonialist discourse. They note that the co-existence of pre-modern, modern and postmodern economies produces a series of interlinked, coeval worlds living the same historical moment but under diverse modalities of subordination and domination. As they point out, the recuperation of trash as art in West and Central Africa exemplifies a strategy of resourcefulness in a situation of scarcity.

> … The trash of the haves become the treasure of the have-nots: the dark and unsanitary is transmogrified into the sublime and the beautiful … as a diasporized, heterotropic site, the point of promiscuous mingling of rich and poor, center and periphery, the industrial and the artisanal, the organic and the inorganic, the national and the international, the local and the global: as a mixed syncretic, radically decentred social text, garbage provides an ideal postmodern and postcolonial metaphor.'[24]

If, as Shoat and Stam note, garbage is the ideal postmodern and postcolonial metaphor, then Gignac's NYC garbage boxes encapsulate a contemporary global obsession with waste and obsolescence. In Gignac's boxes, the 'dark and unsanitary is transmogrified into the sublime and the beautiful' – but in this case, the trash of the haves becomes the treasure of the haves. It symbolises an identifiable current trend of fascination, fetishisation and reification by Packard's 'waste-makers' for their own waste.

The histories, discourses and narratives of trash are multiple – from its associations with transgression and dissent to its appropriation as souvenir *kitsch* – but, importantly, its histories are no longer marginal or secret. Shifting beyond garbage as 'the ideal postmodern and postcolonial metaphor', trash has become *the* trope of the turn of the twenty-first century, with, as Nicolas Bourriaud has identified, the 'flea market' as an 'omnipresent referent'

> … since the early nineties, the dominant visual model is closer to the open-air market, the bazaar, the souk, a temporary and nomadic gathering of precarious material and products of various provenances. . . .[25]

With 'the nomadic gathering of precarious materials and products' using 'recycling (a method) and chaotic arrangement (an aesthetic)', the ragpicker and the bricoleur – both in the anthropological sense expounded by Claude Lévi-Strauss and as one of the makeshift strategies of everyday life outlined by Michel de Certeau[26] – present powerful models for recent and current artistic practice. Over the last decade, the Los Angeles-based artist, Tom Sachs, has explored the model of the 'make-do ethics of bricolage'[27] extensively in his own work and in curatorial projects. Sachs continually blurs the distinction between art and design, mixing idioms and re-contextualising trash, consumer products and mundane materials to create installations, sculptures and functional objects.[28]

Art and Trash

The motivations behind the ubiquitous theoretical and practical appropriations of trash are myriad. Art's use of trash needs to be read accordingly in diverse social, cultural and geographical contexts and situated within specific cartographies, chronologies and ethnographies.

Trash has been a central feature in a diverse range of art practices throughout the twentieth century. The *objet trouvé* was prized and fetishised by Surrealists but 'junk art' is primarily associated with the idiom of *assemblage* – a set of object-based practices which emerged in the mid-1950s and culminated in the seminal exhibition *The Art of Assemblage* in New York in 1961.[29] With its deployment of the ephemeral, the discarded and the filthy, it has been viewed as a disruptive, transgressive art form which engaged with narratives of social and political dissent, often in the face of modernist condemnation as worthless *kitsch*. Parallel techniques flourished in visual and literary culture in western Europe, the

USA and Australia. The idiom of assemblage and the continued re-use of found materials and objects have proliferated in art, popular culture and craft traditions all over the world with folk cultures reclaiming and re-using consumer objects in a range of ways.[30]

Since the 1960s, the employment of trash and found materials and the idiom of assemblage – with artist as *bricoleur* – have been particularly prevalent in global contemporary art practice and this book will explore some of those historical and contemporary moments of coalition. It does not aim to present a selective or exhaustive global survey of art's appropriation of trash. It does not address 'junk sculpture' which tends to be a genre associated with the welded scrap metal sculpture of artists such as Richard Stankiewicz, John Chamberlain and César.[31] Instead, it focuses on work which utilises 'rubbish' in the form of ephemeral and found materials and objects and explores some recurring themes such as the dialectic of poetics and politics. Is the use of trash inherently an act of dissent or is that notion historically grounded? Does the use of trash provide merely a frisson of transgression? Has the contemporary use of garbage and assemblage become an orthodoxy?

The locus of my research has been the identification of a range of discourses, narratives, chronologies and cartographies of trash. It seeks to understand the use of particular materials at a series of key moments and locations. As a contemporary examination of selective moments, it is also presented as experiential and subjective. Echoing Doreen Massey's terminology, it attempts to *situate* these moments of junk-based practice by politicising the spatial and looking at the cultural politics of location. It seeks to situate them within their place and time but is also mindful of their specific genealogies and legacies.

The project has focused around mid-century practices and contemporary legacies largely within the Anglophone world. It does so knowingly but with a conscious attempt to situate these practices within a framework of the kind of polycentric aesthetics which Shoat and Stam argue for. Utilising the notion of *bricolage* as a paradigm for research, it aims to contribute to a process of evaluating and re-contextualising art's historical and current appropriation of junk within an eco-conscious and economically diverse globalised culture.

Chapter One investigates histories, values and aesthetics of junk. It looks at its social-historical roots, the shift from cultures of disposability to sustainability and trash aesthetics. Chapter Two focuses on the cultural life of trash and investigates the deployment of the found object in art from its historical roots to the mid-twentieth century culminating in the seminal exhibition *The Art of Assemblage*, staged in 1961 at the Museum of Modern Art in New York. Chapter Three explores the poetics and politics of West Coast assemblage in the 1960s, its links to the notion of 'place', its narratives and legacies. Chapter Four addresses 'the comedy of waste' in relation to British artists working with trash in the mid-twentieth century and traces a continuing strand of artistic puns and humour within contemporary practice. Chapter Five explores the work of artists associated with the Nouveaux Réalistes and l'Ecole de Nice through a framework of philosophies of the quotidian. Finally, Chapter Six examines the junk installations of a small group of artists based in Sydney in the 1960s – the Annandale Imitation Realists – which had obvious parallels with West Coast assemblage and British Pop. However, their work had a good deal to do with the historiography of Antipodean modernism, with ethnic hybridity and cross-cultural encounters, and much less to do with the epiphany of the everyday or cultures of dissent. It looks at the relationship of their work to contemporaneous West Coast and European assemblage, indigenous art practices and the work of artists currently working in Australia and examines the issues raised in the context of an ethnographic and postcolonial discourse of trash.

CHAPTER ONE
Rehabilitating Rubbish: Histories, Values, Aesthetics

Introduction: Skip Raiders, Dumpster Divers and Tip Dwellers

Alf put a flashlight on a band around his head. He looked like a miner as we turned to where the bins stood, then I saw the other lights, and a large group of strangers. 'Bin raiders' said Alf. 'They all come out at night.' Some of them were immigrants from Eastern Europe, who had come to London to live the dream. A man from Poland had laid out five plump grapefruit on top of a wooden palette. 'Are very good,' he said. 'Not rubbish'.[1]

Feral scavenging provides a means of existence for skip dippers, dumpster divers and tip dwellers the world over – from Alf and the Freegans of Camden[2] to the *karang guni* of Singapore.[3] A few weeks ago, the *Financial Times* weekly 'pull-out' review of the investment industry featured a photograph of a group of people crawling over a pyramid of waste, tossing objects into their baskets on their backs. The caption read '… poverty stricken rubbish scavengers in Jakarta: the Asian financial crisis of 1997–1998 took its toll'. Their destitute existence does not provoke a sociological analysis of global economics; it is merely presented as 'illustrative material' for a short article advising investors on how best to 'soften the impact of financial crises on their portfolios'.[4]

I grew up in the late 1950s and the early 1960s, when the consumption of goods in working-class households was meagre and domestic waste didn't have today's high levels of packing materials and packaging. Then, people stigmatised the Council rubbish tip which happened to be at the edge of my village. Tips were dirty, smelly, unhealthy places. The odours wafting across from the nearby coke-processing plant and sewage works mingled with the smells of fusty clothes, rusted metal and the interminable smell of burning from incinerators. Then, the tip overseer directed carloads as they arrived, dumping everything into one large container, purloining anything worth 'weighing-in' for scrap – this, like the routine theft

of 'mullock', was a common practice and legacy of the area's steel industry. Now the rubbish tip has been rebranded as a 'recycling centre' and
the athletic sun-tanned supervisor oversees a thriving privatised business.
Domestic waste is sorted and categorised into containers marked glass,
metal, paper, electrical. Lines of open car boots are marshalled and skips
are neatly painted in vibrant colours. 'Dumping' has become anachronistic as the activity has become, at least superficially, part of the responsible
citizen's contribution to an ecologically aware community.

The trashcan and the cess pit have always, of course, provided staple
materials for archaeologists. More recently though, besides destitutes and
down-and-outs, rubbish dumps have attracted academics and writers
who have identified trash as a key social anthropological site for the examination of a range of discourses to do with local and global politics and economics. In December 2001, Jeff Ferrell resigned from his job as a tenured
professor in criminology at an Arizona University and embarked on an
eight-month stint of field research and 'free-form survival' as a feral scavenger in the urban neighbourhoods of Fort Worth.[5] Exploring and embracing the 'rhythms of urban scrounging', Ferrell drifted into a nether
world that he came to call 'the empire of scrounge'.

> ... a far-flung, mostly urban underground populated by... illicit dump-
> ster divers, homeless trash pickers, independent scrap metal haulers,
> activist recyclers, alternative home builders and outsider artists ...[6]

Ferrell offers a sociological examination of homelessness and poverty
and he outlines the resourcefulness of those who find themselves on the
economic margins – either through choice or through exclusion. It documents an ethnography of lost and found objects and presents a popular
critique of the hyper-production and consumption culture of American
society and the profligate waste which is generated by global capitalism.
He describes the squalid, unhealthy and dangerous aspects as well as the
meticulous processes of salvaging and re-assembling lost lives from tiny
fragments of shredded documents, fading photographs and discarded mementoes. He is seduced by the promised bounty which each dumpster
might yield.

In the 1990s, Ted Botha arrived in New York from South Africa and,
after furnishing his home with 'mongo' – a term coined in the 1980s to
describe goods and objects retrieved from skips and tips[7] – he realised
that he was part of a community of urban foragers (Fig. 5). In his study
published in 2004,[8] he portrays a range of street characters, outlining the
motivations and reasons behind their parasitic and erratic way of life. In
Manhattan, besides survivalists and anarchists he finds treasure hunters,
dealers and entrepreneurs who make a business out of sifting through

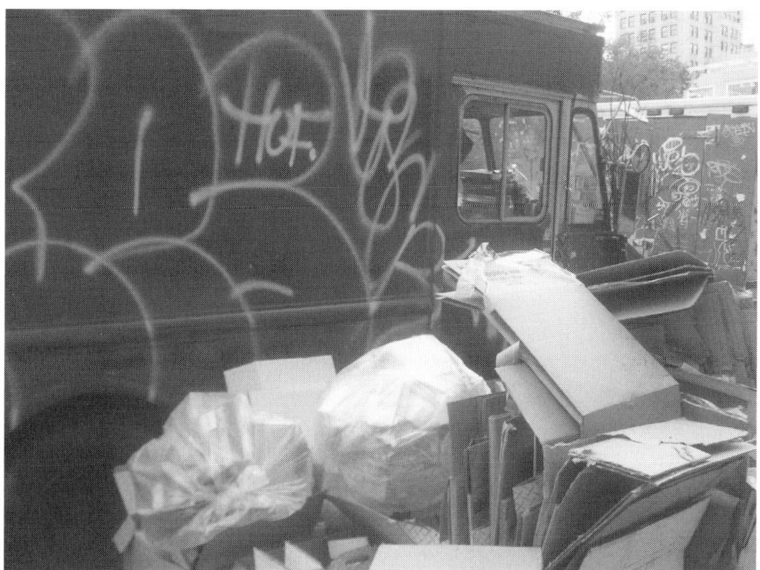

Fig. 5 Abandoned van crammed with cardboard and debris, Union Square, New York, September 2009. Photograph by the author.

rubbish. Botha's book reminds us that appearances can be deceptive – 'mongo' can be lucrative: even rubbish-scavenging in Jakarta can offer a good living.

Whilst Ferrell admitted he was not totally dependent on his daily pickings for survival or shelter, there are plenty of circumstances in which people rely on trash out of necessity. There is an insidious exploitation at work in a project such as Ferrell's which aims, overtly, to 'speak for' the destitute. As with the recent phenomenon of *favela* tourism in Brazil[9] – the comfortably-off always experience the poor as 'elsewhere' and 'other' – these encounters reveal how one part of society provides spectacle for another. The desperate plight of 'the other' becomes a voyeuristic object of tourism.

The documentary series, *The Tower*, broadcast by BBC television during 2007, exemplified a similar kind of *faux* social engagement. Lol and Nicky were two of the most compelling characters throughout. They met in a skip whilst looking for metal to 'weigh-in' for scrap to fund their heroin and alcohol habits. The film sensitively conveyed the social paradoxes and economic inequities inherent in the regeneration of a particular area of Thames-side Deptford but, at the same time, the aestheticisation of destitution has the effect of annulling any possibility of real empathy or impetus for social change. In perhaps the most extreme example, a Channel 4 TV 'reality' show took this further; in *Dumped*, the waste tip itself becomes the site of spectacle as participants were invited to 'survive' on the dump.[10]

Ferrell's project may be viewed as parasitic but it did show that, for some people, feral scavenging can be a purposeful lifestyle choice which is motivated by a personal ethical agenda, an anti-materialist gesture. In the UK, disillusioned by contemporary society's obsession with money and ownership, Alf and Martin gave up their possessions, to devote their lives to 'Freeganism'. Living in the back of a van, they go out at dusk searching supermarket skips and bins for food past its sell-by date. As Andrew O'Hagan points out, Alf and Martin's ethos is more 'soft utopianism than militant politics'. Their ambition is 'not to gather political forces but to replenish the spiritual motives of their generation'.[11]

This brings us back to Shoat and Stam's comment cited earlier regarding 'the co-existence of pre-modern, modern and postmodern economies producing a series of interlinked, coeval worlds living the same historical moment but under diverse modalities'.[12] The world of feral scavenging is paradoxical and polysemous – from the desperate poverty-stricken existence of the *gecekondu* slum dwellers living precariously on garbage mountains in Turkey[13] to the Freegans, skip dippers and mongo seekers of the developed world. As Susan Strasser points out,

> To the dumpster diver – as to the scavengers who live on the Mexico City dump, the ragpickers who fascinated bohemian Paris, and the Chinese immigrants who foraged on San Francisco streets at the end of the nineteenth century – what counts as trash depends on who's counting.[14]

From the *chiffoniers* of nineteenth-century Paris through to the retailers of recycled designer wear in Brick Lane, trash has undergone a lengthy rehabilitation. This chapter will consider some of the histories, definitions and shifting values of detritus in its diverse forms and the implications of all that for a subsequent consideration of 'junk art' within an aesthetic and anti-aesthetic context.

Trash Histories

Rags, Bones and Refuse

As excess matter resulting from industrialisation and urbanisation, rubbish is a relatively new phenomenon. The development of mass production of desirable commodities to satisfy and stimulate mass consumption is linked to the rise and expansion of capitalist economics in the wealthier

Western and 'developed' parts of the world. But 'excess' is not exclusively a capitalist or twentieth-century problem and landfill and rubbish tipping are not recent solutions to dealing with garbage.

As Richard Girling puts it, 'waste has always been a badge of affluence' – as early as 3000 BC, the Minoan palace at Knossos in Crete had its own refuse site layered with earth.[15] However, in pre-industrial cultures and even in early industrial societies, the contents of refuse pits, middens and rubbish bins tended to be organic and relatively benign.[16] It was primarily the proliferation of permanent settlements and urban concentrations that led to unprecedented quantities and new forms of waste – and a failure to deal with this in an organised way leads to epidemic disease and high mortality rates.

In Britain, the 'insanitary state' of fast-growing industrial urban centres was a major concern in the nineteenth century. At mid-twentieth century, Sheffield with its steel mills and engineering factories was one of the most polluted cities in the UK, but in Victorian times, its chief environmental problems were caused by organic effluence and human sewage.

> We have surveyed Birmingham, Stafford, Wolverhampton, Newcastle-upon-Tyne, Hull, Shrewsbury and other towns, but Sheffield in all matters relating to sanitary appliances is behind them all.... The rivers that water Sheffield so pleasantly are polluted with dirt, dust, dung and carrion; the embankments are ragged and ruined; here and there overhung with privies and often the site of ash and offal heaps – most desolate and sickening objects...[17]

In the most densely populated districts, zymotic diseases such as cholera were generally spread by insanitary conditions. Poorly ventilated housing, undrained courtyards, stagnant water, sewage, decayed carcasses and putrid animal matter from slaughterhouses all contributed. In a report for the Royal Commissioners for the Health of Towns in 1842, the overcrowded lodging houses were cited as 'dens of disease'; here, lodgers slept amongst piles of rags as a common occupation of the lodging-house keepers was rag-collecting.[18]

In the nineteenth century, living amongst filth was perceived as breeding poor morals, leading to licentiousness and laziness. Public health reports made this clear. In one of the Sheffield Borough Surveyor's reports, he noted a house where sewage had been amassing on the tenant's roof and advocated

> ... the strong necessity of appointing some person to see that they are regularly cleansed – for unless this be done, all the attendant evils of filthy habits and filthy houses must necessarily follow...[19]

The history of waste has been the history of separating organic human waste from the rest. Processing rubbish involves sorting and categorising forms of waste – whether human, organic or industrial – into sanitary and insanitary, toxic and non-toxic. As Susan Strasser points out – trash is *created* by sorting. She relates an early twentieth-century description of a factory that extracted useful products from bones:

> The first operation is that of sorting… several women are constantly engaged in separating rags, iron, beefy matter, hoofs, horns, etc. As they are sorted the bones are pushed to the mouth of the crusher…[20]

The trade in used goods and the reclamation of materials was an essential part of the early industrial system and it provided a living for many people. In his four volume study of the *London Labour and the London Poor*, published in 1861, Henry Mayhew documented the daily activities of a series of different categories of people who worked with refuse of one sort or another. As Girling indicates, dustyards employed 'entire dust dynasties' of dust*men*, dust*women* and dust*children*[21] with sifters, fillers-in, loaders and carriers-off. Mayhew also catalogued a range of street-collectors, describing the work of the rag-gatherers and bone-grubbers in some detail:

> The bone-picker and rag-gatherer may be known at once by the greasy bag which he carries on his back. Usually he has a stick in his hand, and this is armed with a spike or hook, for the purpose of more easily turning over the heaps of ashes or dirt that are thrown out of the houses.… The bone-grubber generally seeks out the narrow back streets, where dust and refuse are cast, or where any dust-bins are accessible. The articles for which he chiefly searches are rags and bones – rags he prefers – but waste metal, such as bits of lead, pewter, copper, brass, or old iron, he prizes above all.[22]

The grubbers and pickers sold their goods to itinerant ragmen and junk dealers. Rags and bones went for making paper and glue, metals went to make fastenings. Out of the dust, every retrievable object and scrap of re-usable material was reclaimed for re-use.

In nineteenth-century Paris, the *chiffonier* – the ragpicker – fascinated and inspired artists and writers and has subsequently been viewed as a symbolic figure of modernity. As Strasser points out, for Charles Baudelaire the ragpicker was an archivist, a cataloguer who sorted through everything that the big city has cast off, disdained and lost.[23] Baudelaire's city poems, in particular, are marked by an interest in marginal characters who live on the edges of society such as prostitutes, street cleaners and scavengers of various sorts. For Baudelaire, the *chiffonier*, 'stumbling like a poet lost in dreams', sifts through the everyday debris and discards of the city, searching for objects and materials to sell,

> … plagued by household cares,
> Bruised by hard work, tormented by their years,
> Each bent double by the junk he carries,
> The jumbled vomit of enormous Paris[24]

As Walter Benjamin later noted, Baudelaire adopts the *chiffonier* as an extended metaphor for poetic activity itself. Baudelaire positions himself as a poet firmly at the end of the cycle of the production, consumption, disposal and recuperation of material objects, a cycle that so deeply preoccupied nineteenth-century writers.[25] Benjamin's examination of Baudelaire's fascination with the writer-poet as ragpicker was, in turn, reflected in his own writings. In the introductory comments to a collection of Benjamin's essays published as *Illuminations* in 1970, Hannah Arendt comments on the working method Benjamin used in his notebooks whereby the systematic accumulation, collection and collation of quotations was not done to facilitate a further study but 'constituted the main work'.

> The main work consisted in tearing fragments out of their context and arranging them afresh in such a way that they illustrated one another and were able to prove their raison d'etre in a free-floating state, as it were. It definitely was a sort of surrealistic montage…[26]

Benjamin's predilection for collecting and assembling fragments is paramount in *The Arcades Project*, an enormous unfinished palimpsest-like work which presents quotes and snatches of text. Here, as Eiland and McLaughlin indicate, his methods are 'more akin to the nineteenth-century rag-picker'. For Benjamin, the object of study was

> … not the great men and celebrated events of traditional historiography but rather the 'refuse' and 'detritus' of history, the half-concealed, variegated traces of the daily life of 'the collective'[27]

It is interesting that Strasser has emphasised that the ragpicker was not similarly romanticised in the USA though. She argues that they did feature in urban literature through the nineteenth century but they were much more mundane. She cites, for example, 'the ragpicker with hook and bag' which appeared in *New York by Gas Light* (1850), a sensationalised portrait of brothels, saloons and slums. In Frank Norris' *McTeague* (1899), a novel set in San Francisco, they appear as part of the scenery:

> Across the flats, at the fringe of the town, were the dump heaps, the figures of a few Chinese ragpickers moving over them.[28]

Ragpicking never achieved the romantic status of the *chiffonier* in the UK either. Indeed, in the 1960s, the rag and bone business became the setting for one of the most successful sitcom series on British television in *Steptoe and Son*, a comic but poignant study of two rag and bone men who lived a meagre existence in their ramshackle yard in Shepherds Bush.[29]

So, since being viewed as the mythic, romantic figure of modernity, the *chiffonier* – in its various characterisations – has had a range of historical and cultural representations. Significantly though, the figure of the rag-picker has been resurrected and is omnipresent within contemporary visual and popular culture. In the repertoire of the contemporary pop band, *The White Stripes*, the 'rag and bone' trade offers another set of historical folk heroes which the singers adopt and ironise along with 'pearly kings and queens' on their album *Icky Thump* released in 2007:

> Well can't you hear we're selling rag and bone?
> Bring out your junk and we'll give it a home
> A broken trumpet or a telephone
> Come on, come on, come on, come on and give it to me
> Yeah
> Come on, come on, come on, come on and give it to me
> Rag and bone
> Rag and bone[30]

Moreover, rag-collecting increasingly appears as a global referent which resonates with a Baudelairean sense of finding beauty in the ruin but also articulates the disquiet and anxieties of the wealthy West. The cultural re-appropriation of ragpickers and their rubbish persists.

From disposability to sustainability

The twentieth-century transition from a thrift to a throwaway culture is, then, well-documented. However, on the brink of the hyperbolic consumption alluded to by Vance Packard in *The Wastemakers* in 1960, ethical and ecological approaches to design were emerging. There is a burgeoning history and historiography of the 'greening' of product and object design.[31] Early prototypes for re-using materials include the famous WOBO (WOrld BOttle) house made of special brick-shaped bottles designed by John Habraken, commissioned by Heineken partly because it was uneconomic to return lager bottles over certain distances but also as a way of providing cheap housing from recycled materials.[32] As Jonathan Woodham argues, countercultural lifestyles and subcultures in the 1960s, such as the 'hippy' movement and other alternative groups on the West Coast, articulated oppositional models 'to the conventional material and social mores of consumer society'.[33] Publications such as E. F. Schumacker's *Small is Beautiful*[34] with its promotion of 'Buddhist economics' rather than modern materialism and Victor Papanek's *Design for the Real World* advocated socially and morally responsible approaches to design and were widely read and highly influential in the 1970s. Papanek suggested that 'in an environment that is screwed up visually, physically and chemically', the best thing architects and designers could do for humanity would be 'to stop working entirely'.[35] His rallying call was for design to be 'ecologically responsible' and 'socially responsive', to be dedicated to

> ... minimum inventory for maximum diversity... doing the most with the least. That means consuming less, using things longer, recycling materials and probably not wasting paper printing books such as this...[36]

In her study of the intellectual and political history of ecology, Anna Bramwell argues that two distinct strands of late nineteenth-century 'ecologism' – an anti-mechanistic, holistic approach and 'energy economics' which focused on the problem of scarce and non-renewable resources – fused together in the 1970s to form a new ecological movement.[37] Writing in the late 1980s, with the phenomenon of ecologism itself a product peculiar to Western society, Bramwell notes that 'ecologists believe that society has taken a wrong path'. She argues that the emphasis was on finding salvation through a transcendental 'other' – at that time she argued that in England, Germany and North America, that idea followed the powerful Rousseauian narrative of a return to nature and 'the noble savage'. Interestingly, she indicates that, in contrast, among the German Greens and in aspects of American ecology, another transcendental strand is dominant – that of Lao Tzu and Buddha.[38] This strand of thinking might be linked directly to comments made by William Rathje, archaeologist and director of the large-scale Garbage Project, who talks of 'the wonder' of sifting through trash and insists that our garbage reflects a kind of 'truth':

> Sorting garbage is the ultimate Zen experience of our society... because you feel it, you smell it, you see it, you record it; you are in tactile intimacy with it. Some time or other everybody ought to sort garbage.[39]

The ecological agenda has moved on, beyond the 'New Ageism' of the 1970s and 1980s with its perception as quirky and alternative, to acquire

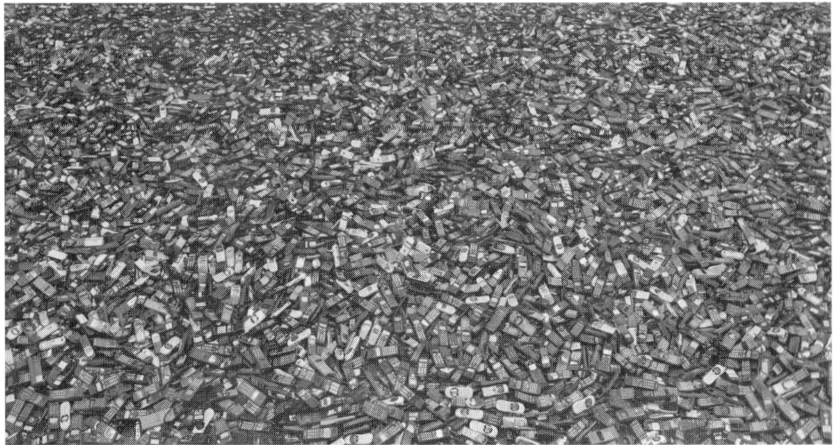

Fig. 6 Chris Jordan, *Cell Phones, Orlando*, 2004. Reproduced with kind permission of Chris Jordan, Paul Kopeikin Gallery.

considerable currency within mainstream culture. A prime example might be the Findhorn Community, set up originally around a set of spiritual beliefs in 1962 at Moray in Scotland, but also with the aim of demonstrating sustainability in environmental, social and economic terms. Its religious underpinnings aside, the ecological ethos and activities pursued in the establishing of its 'eco-village' have attracted international awards and have become something of a blueprint and inspiration for other projects.[40]

At the turn of the millennium, with transnational corporations controlling global economies, hyper-production and mass consumption continue to dominate. Strasser echoes Packard's 1960s' diatribe, arguing that America knows only a well-developed consumer culture based on a continual influx of products designed to be used briefly, then discarded (see Fig. 6).[41] She asserts that the topic of trash has been central to our lives generally, yet it has been silenced or ignored. She does also note, however, that this taboo has been 'toppled'[42] and that there has been an increasing public discourse about household trash.

Certainly, since the publication of Strasser's book in 1999, a further significant shift has taken place. There has been a flurry of literature on the topic at the turn of the millennium – the 'secret histories' and 'hidden journeys' of garbage have been 'outed'. Waste may still be profligate but it is no longer 'hidden'. Passionate warnings of crisis and scaremongering abound in the popular and serious press. The debate has become hyperbolic and apocalyptic.[43] *The Guardian*, the mouthpiece of the comfortably-off, left-thinking, socially responsible UK consumer, reflects the ecological mores and anxieties of its readership through its reportage, articles and photo-features:

> What a Load of Old Rubbish…every hour we throw away enough rubbish to fill the Albert Hall – and most if it ends up in overflowing landfill sites. But how much waste does each of us produce in 24 hours? And what we can do about it? Ada Edermariam asked the experts to analyse a day's worth of her own garbage – and that of a diverse group of Guardian readers…[44]

Waste consciousness has arrived, 'eco-warriors' have become 'eco-worriers'. Trash has become the trendy trope of the twenty-first century and acquired its own chic caché. Furthermore, in the UK, a range of government and local initiatives suggest that the transition from a culture of disposability to economies based on sustainability, at least in terms of popular rhetoric, is underway. There is daily evidence within the mass media that a new 'eco-rhetoric' is operating at a small business and corporate level as well as within popular culture. In marketing terms, new 'eco-segments' such as LOHAS (Lifestyle of Health and Sustainability)[45] are emerging. 'Lohasians' or 'conscious consumers' are categorised by the kinds of goods which will appeal to their ecological lifestyle – eco-tourism, organic/recycled products, environmentally-friendly appliances, houses built using renewable resources and energy, socially responsible investments, green transport. New marketing strategies are being devised to attract this significant group of consumers.[46]

With new ecologically orientated vocabulary referring to 'waste diversion' and 'carbon-offsetting', adverts place producers and suppliers in a benevolent environment-saving light whilst cleverly addressing individual consumer guilt. In an ironic twist, we are persuaded that *buying more* becomes *buying less* – as in this new line in 'Carbon Neutral Entertainment' from HMV:

Classic Albums

RE-RECYCLED

A range of classic artist albums re-presented in 100% biodegradable packaging – the CO_2 emissions generated in the making of this range are being offset by investing in renewable energy products around the world. Two for £10 – offer applies to stickered stock only for a limited period while stocks last. For more information, visit: www.carboneutral. com[47]

At local and sub-national level, public programmes are addressing the issues of waste on a collective and communal basis. Elizabeth Royte recounts a 'two-day recycling roundtable' to look at the problems in Manhattan, addressed by the charismatic Robert Haley, director of the recycling programme in San Francisco – 'a solid-waste utopia with trucks that run on liquid natural gas, a massive composting operation, and happy Italian American workers making thirty dollars an hour, plus triple time on twelve holidays a year' …

> San Francisco, Haley told the rapt audience during his powerpoint presentation, was aiming for 75 percent diversion by 2010. In a few months, the city council would revise that optimistic goal, aiming for Zero Waste by 2020.[48]

As twenty-first century global citizens, we are encouraged to take an ethical audit of our everyday activities and habits. There is a quasi-religious tone about the debate with talk of 'conversion', 'saving' and 'sacrifice'. Girling's warning that we need to do something urgently about the 'dirt on our hands'[49] feeds on an existentialist discourse of individual fear, anxiety and guilt.[50]

Individual human agency can curb waste levels but there is plenty of evidence to show that the only thing that will really make a difference is when the issue of environmental waste is adequately addressed politically – not just at a local public level but at a corporate-industrial level on a transnational, global scale. What has also become clear is that dealing with trash is an environmental and sustainability issue and, as such, it is part of the 'climate change' debate which is now being viewed by some as the *key* issue of contemporary global politics. In his introduction to a special 'Gobalisation and Biopolitics' issue of the *New Left Review* in June 2007, Malcolm Bull commented:

> Almost imperceptibly, globalisation has become bio-politics, the pivot between the two 9/11 and the global state of emergency known as the 'war on terror'.[51]

In the same issue, George Monbiot's latest publication, *Heat: How to Stop the Planet Burning*,[52] is debated. Monbiot campaigns against what he perceives as 'growth fetishism' in favour of a radical austerity. Monbiot argues that individuals need to make a psychological transition to purposefully curb their own profligate consumption. Clive Hamilton accuses Monbiot of relying on the 'politics of individual guilt' instead of focusing on a collective response to a collective problem within a global context. For Hamilton, the climate change debate is, above all, 'a clash of ideologies'.[53] Similarly, particular ideologies and discourses are at play in debates about the production and processing of trash.

With the profligate production of rubbish representing a contemporary 'moral panic'[54], all this shows what a complex issue we are dealing with at an individual, local, national and global level. In a balanced and rational re-viewing of their own *Garbage Project* ten years earlier, Rathje and Murphy point to some of the complexities at play. Noting that their book was published during an earlier periodic peak of 'garbage-crisis fervor', they attempt to set out and clear up some of the misunderstandings and myths that are affecting the debate currently. Recycling is useful but, as they point out explaining the 'percentage paradox', it is not the answer to all the waste-disposal problems.[55] The UK situation may be more critical in terms of landfill capacity,[56] but, according to Rathje and Murphy, the situation is very different in the USA. Despite previous fears that landfill space was running out, some authorities are currently raising 'the spectre of a "glut" of landfill space'.[57] Lohasions, Freegans and advocates of LOVOS (Lifestyles of Voluntary Simplicity) are all equally devoted to an ecologically sustainable lifestyle shaped by environmental awareness. As we all become 'eco-worriers', a much more critical attitude to consumerism is discernible. The journey of trash's rehabilitation has, indeed, been paradoxical and contradictory.

Trash Values

trash (n.) 'anything of little use or value', 1518, perhaps from a Scand. source (see O.N. *tros* 'rubbish, fallen leaves and twigs', Norw. dial. *trask* 'lumber, trash, baggage', Swed. *trasa* 'rags, tatters'), of unknown origin. Applied to ill-bred persons or groups from 1604 ('Othello'). Applied to domestic refuse or garbage in 1906 (Amer.Eng.). The verb meaning 'to discard as worthless' is 1895, from the noun; in the sense of 'destroy, vandalize' it is attested from 1970; extended to 'criticize severely' in 1975. *White trash* is from 1831, originally Southern US black slang. *Trashy* 'worthless' first attested 1620.[58]

I know you'll lay down and scream when you taste Loretta's Chicken Delight. And Tutti's Fruited Porkettes are fit for the table of a queen … I know you'll want to place this cookbook next to the Holy Bible on your coffee table (I know you've got a coffee table with Polaroid snapshots under the glass). And in the kitchen you'll become another Mrs. Betty Sue Swilley, in the true spirit of WHITE TRASH COOKING.

White Trash Cooking: it's a dream come true. I can just hear Raenelle and Betty Sue at every Tupperware party in Rolling Fork saying, 'Ernie went from white trash to WHITE TRASH overnight'.[59]

Bric-a-brac, cast-offs, crap, crud, detritus, discards, dross, dregs, garbage, junk, lumber, mongo, ordure, rammell, refuse, residue, riffraff, rot, rubbish, rubble, schlock, scrannel, scrap, spam, tat, waste. All these different terms for trash have their own specific linguistic origins, cultural and ethnic associations and social significations. The etymology of 'trash' has its own history, shifting from its Scandinavian roots as *tros*, relating to organic matter, to acquire characteristics associated with particular social and cultural values and contexts.

The idea that trash is merely 'matter out of place' is commonly referenced[60] and was used by the anthropologist, Mary Douglas, in her classic study, *Purity and Danger*. She discusses the point in relation to 'dirt' in a passage in which she examines 'dirt-rejecting' and 'dirt-affirming' philosophies and cultures.[61] All dirt is relative. Clearly, 'matter out of place' is 'trash' in one diverse modality of living – and treasure – or matter *in place* – in a different interlinked, coeval one. Generally, at the point of 'dislocation', stuff usually consists of leftovers or remainders – waste or unwanted material – from some activity or process. This is reflected in the origins and roots of many of the words used for dislocated stuff. *Refuse*, for example, comes from the Old French *refus*, with its use as 'outcast' and 'waste' dating back to the fourteenth century. Trash, generally, equates particular materials or objects with 'waste' – matter that is unwanted, of low value.

So attempts to define trash lead back to a fundamental link to systems of value which are time and place specific. There is no material which is intrinsically trash. Indeed, it is a social and culturally constructed concept – the word, like its physical manifestation, is in a continually shifting state of conceptual, symbolic and material flux. So, before going on to look at the different narratives and discourses which art that employs trash has engaged with at specific historical junctures and in different localities, I want to give some consideration to the shifting valorisation of trash both in its material form and in terms of its symbolic and cultural signification. I want to explore some of the kinds of value that have been attached to trash, from the lowest form of the throwaway – human defecation – through to common everyday stuff and to consider its rehabilitation not only as material, but also as a discourse from reclamation to celebration, from trash to treasure.

A Load of Shit

When you are cleaning out the henhouse, you're glad to take a deep breath of fresh air. Pig and human excrement, however, smell worst, because men and pigs are carnivores and their appetites are indiscriminate. The smell includes the sickeningly sweet one of decay.… And on the far side of it there is death.… The shit slides out of the barrow when it's upturned with a slurping dead weight. And the foul sweet stench goads, nags teleologically. The smell of decay, and from this the smell of putrefaction, of corruption. The smell of mortality for sure.[62]

What makes shit such a universal joke is that its an unmistakable reminder of our duality, of our soiled nature and of our will to glory. It is the ultimate *lèse majesté*.[63]

Clearing out the year's excrement from the outhouse at his home in a peasant community in the French Alps, John Berger ruminates on the nature of the operation. As he shovels the barrowloads into a grave-sized hole he has dug in the earth, he asks – why is shit so repugnant, so offensive? Shovelling the sticky substance, the pungent odours attack his senses. He is seized with an irrational anger and is compelled to name the very stuff which, in all languages, is a swear word of exasperation – shit! For this is something we always want to be rid of – it is the ultimate waste material.

There are good reasons for humans to have an aversion to their own faeces as medical evidence shows that contamination with raw sewage can lead to serious infectious diseases. There is also evidence, as Mary Douglas indicated, that aversion to faeces is not necessarily innate or inherent but, rather, it is a learnt social and cultural response.[64] All societies view excreta as dirty but there are cultural variations and different forms of taboo operate. Research has shown that, in the first few years of life, children do not have an innate faecal phobia – indeed they often play with their own stools. Cleanliness and hygiene is about re-ordering the environment with all the psychoanalytical implications of that activity. Dealing with waste and cleaning up has a scientific basis but there is also an equation with civilisation and modernity which reveals more complex connections. Anne McClintock's study of Unilever history shows how its advertising campaign for *Imperial Leather* soap – with its slogan, 'Soap is Civilisation' – conveyed the idea that imperialism literally washed away the dirt of 'primitivism'.[65] Here, clean is equated not only with order but with the 'civilisation' of colonialism and empire.

In his eccentric but seminal study, *The History of Shit*, Dominic Laporte deconstructs such narratives and myths about hygiene and challenges the drive to order, classify and eliminate waste.[66] As Rodolphe el-Khoury points out, Laporte ties the concept of the individual to the fate of human waste and, as he remarks, 'in a twist that Georges Bataille would have appreciated, the history of shit becomes the history of subjectivity'.[67] In a rumination on 'shit, soul', Laporte writes of the noxious aspect of the body's waste – of its perceived *wickedness,* which is not to do with it being inherently pernicious but 'only through its recent association with the flesh'.[68] The disgust and abhorrence of shit which Berger articulated whilst shovelling out his cess pit clearly reflects a whole range of underlying and complex emotive, psychological and cultural responses to the stuff. All flesh turns to humus in the end. As Berger suggests, we are uncomfortable with our own shit, not just because it relates to our own visceral bodily functions, but because we are uncomfortable with our own death – of which it is a daily reminder.

Besides presenting the self as cadaver, Kristeva indicates how, when faced with the usually internalised 'other' of shit, we also undergo loss of self:

> If dung signifies the other side of the border, the place where I am not and which permits me to be, the corpse, the most sickening of wastes, is a border that has encroached upon everything. It is no longer I who expel. 'I' is expelled.[69]

Kristeva's writings on the horrors of bodily waste and fluids as 'abject' are pertinent here. Repulsion and disgust is driven by our apprehension of filth and dirt as 'abject'.[70] There is also, as John Scanlan emphasises in his study, *On Garbage,* an underlying fear of the 'formless'.

> … what we might also say about traces of material disorder (for example, dirt, filth and dust) is that these become symbolic of garbage not simply because they represent displaced matter, but more precisely because of 'things' such as their formlessness (ie they may have been something once but are now nothing)…[71]

The concept of formlessness needs to be linked to Georges Bataille's writings. *La bassesse,* a kind of 'base materialism' – an area explored in his critical dictionary – was prized by the Surrealists in the 1920s as transgressive and a potential way of upsetting the status quo.[72] Anything which is shapeless, or uncategorisable by its form, has the capacity to defy our desire to pattern the world. As Bataille commented,

> The whole of philosophy has no other goal: to provide a frock coat for what is, a mathematical frock coat. To declare, on the contrary, that the universe is not like anything, and is simply formless, is tantamount to saying the universe is something like a spider or spittle.[73]

Waste is often unrecognisable. That bit of slimy sticky substance at the bottom of the rubbish bin terrifies us: it is the equivalent of Bataille's *spittle.* It offends our desire to categorise and classify the world which, of course, is one strategy for keeping the world under control. Classificatory systems have a role to play in ideological and political frameworks too. Hegemony is maintained by control and organisation whereas disorder and chaos is perceived as a threat to social stability. As Alexander Trocchi points out,

> For centuries, we in the West have been dominated by the Aristotelian impulse to classify. It is no doubt because conventional classifications become part of prevailing economic structure that all real revolt is hastily fixed like a bright butterfly on a classificatory pin.[74]

So, the unrecognisable 'formless' aspects of shit terrify us – we work constantly to remove dirt and human waste from our everyday lives. The fear and disorder unleashed when it seeps out is palpable. Shit can be a powerful political substance too. Jimmy Boyle found this when he covered his prison cell with it to protest at his inhumane treatment in Barlinnie[75]; in the 1970s, H block prisoners in Northern Ireland daubed their own faeces on the walls in their 'blanket protests'.[76] There may be nothing inherently transgressive about any substance or objects – shit included – but materials have and accrue cultural, social and political significance and associations at particular moments in particular places.

Trash Aesthetics

> I have always loved – it is a sort of vice – to employ only the most common materials in my work – those that one does not dream of at first because they are too crude and close at hand…I like to proclaim that my art is an enterprise to rehabilitate discredited values…[77]

Outside the Western sphere of influence and in other philosophical traditions, common materials have a different set of values. In Zen Buddhism, for example, worth is sought in the everyday and the mundane as part of a set of practices that raise awareness about worldly attachment to objects of conventional economic value. As Shunryu Suzuki, one of the twentieth-century's Zen masters, has commented, 'for Zen students, a weed, which for most people is worthless, is a treasure'.[78] In Mahayan Buddhism, the concept of *wabi-sabi* gives preference to the coarse, the unrefined and the imperfect. Ordinary everyday objects and materials – or the ones cast aside as worn out and valueless – can have an aesthetic beauty.[79] Jean Dubuffet's proclamation that his art would embrace only 'the most common materials' might be a leitmotif for this book as he constantly worked to rehabilitate and to re-value the lost, the discarded and the unwanted – both metaphorically and materially.

In a topsy-turvy world, one might say that Dubuffet's 'enterprise' has been fulfilled as the discarded becomes fetishised, and trash, in all its forms, is embraced by postmodern culture. With its polysemic, multiple and pluralist approach to phenomena and materials, postmodern culture has, at least superficially, appropriated and embraced the unthinkable and the incongruous. Parody, pastiche and *kitsch* have become key cultural components. A makeshift bricolage approach has been identified and examined as a key element of the postmodern.[80] Steven Connor comments on bricolage as

> the improvised juxtaposition of incompatible or heterogeneous fragments, often for ironic or parodic effect, as opposed to the principle of unity or 'match'.[81]

The colloquial use of 'trash' to denote 'worthless' has been extended more generally to a specific association with mass culture and all things denigrated as cheap, nasty and trivial. The term is routinely used to describe popular cultural production, including comics, cartoons, sci-fi, pulp fiction and 'B' movies, computer games and TV.[82] As a counterpoint to Greenbergian modernist aesthetics which denigrated the popular as *kitsch*,[83] we now have a kind of 'trash aesthetics' at play. Of course, *kitsch* is a problematic and relative concept and one which requires a psychological, sociological, historical and anthropological analysis rather than an aesthetic one.[84] But in its pluralist embracing of mass culture, postmodern culture took on *kitsch* and trash, often conflating the two.[85] In a curiously inverse aesthetic, trash has achieved primacy.

In an article published in the mid-1980s, John Roberts examined this new postmodern phenomenon. For him, contemporary culture's appropriation of the abject and lowly had affinities with 'Benjamin's allegorisation of the cultural fragment as the symptomatic ruin of modernity's shattered whole'.[86] Roberts surveyed the transition trash has made within the field of cultural analysis since the 1930s, commenting that

> The broken shell of the commodity lying in the skip, the mound of rotting rubbish and discarded household goods on the pavement, functions as part of a continuous, unconscious, permanent act of criticism of the culture.[87]

Roberts questions the assumption that rubbish is the ubiquitous 'other' of capitalist rationality and warns against the uncritical romantic approach to trash which, in his view, Julian Stallabrass articulates, arguing that it replays

… one of the most routinised aspects of early modernism's romantic-primitivism: the idea that the unformed, the grotesque, the anti-aesthetic can provide a utopian glimpse beyond the limits of capitalist order and linearity. Thus he appears to believe that every time we pass a rubbish dump (or for that matter a graffitied underpass) or every time the kitchen bin is full to overflowing we experience a moment of critical insight into the law of value.[88]

Roberts' comments reflect Pierre Bourdieu's sociological writings on taste whereby all aesthetic judgments must be understood as forms of cultural capital – as exercises in social power. These ideas are pertinent to any discussion of the use of rubbish in art because they bring us back to questions of political context and human agency. I am in accord with Roberts' view, that 'rubbish-as-a-site-of-consciousness raising becomes strangely hollow and compensatory' especially, as he asserts, if that is within a 'romanticised cultural politics in which an undifferentiated account of the "primitive" carries a universal utopian content'.[89] Trash is not – inherently – a conduit for the subconscious and neither is it a universal site of transgression or dissent. Working with trash as a raw material for art is not, *per se,* a political activity. As Jacques Rancière has implied in his exploration of the correlation between politics and art, meaning is usually dependent on an exterior state of conflict. There are no inherently politicised materials or art objects – there are only political 'contexts'.[90]

Trash as Art

The hygienist is a hero. He overcomes the most visceral repugnance, rolls up his short sleeves, and takes on the cloaca. He faces the foul unnameable and speaks of that thing of which no one else will speak.[91]

Mierle Laderman Ukeles has, perhaps, more than any other artist, focused on the idea of 'hygienist as hero'. From the *Maintenance Project* in the 1970s, through to her recent long-term collaborative project at Freshkills landfill site off Manhattan, her practice has focused on the devalued labour of sanitation and refuse workers. In the 1970s, her street-cleaning and step-scrubbing performances engaged with feminist perspectives,[92] but her work as Artist in Residence with New York Sanitation Department over the last 30 years has had a much broader political context. Her work with garbage and with refuse workers has drawn meaning from specific sociological contexts – trade union histories and the ethnic and cultural associations of particular occupations – rather than through the romanticisation of trash as a base material or as a conduit for deeper understanding (Fig. 7).[93]

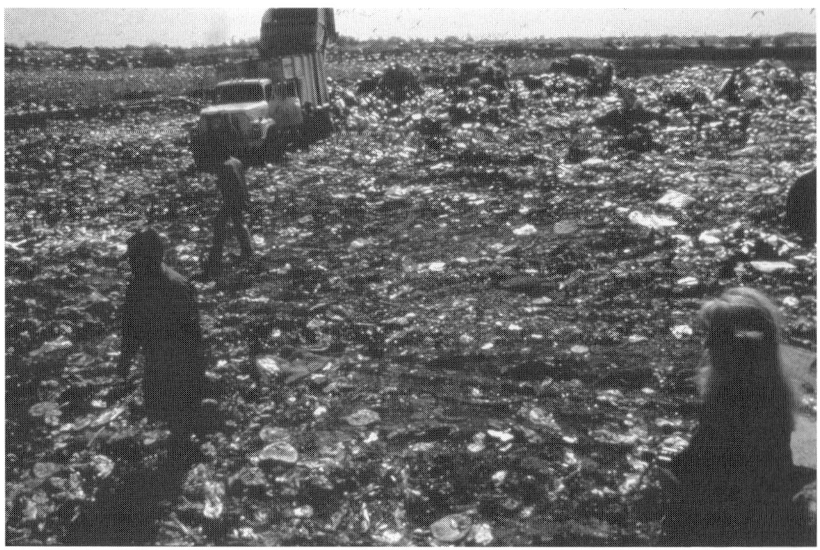

Fig. 7 Mierle Laderman Ukeles, *Touch Sanitation*, 1978–80. Courtesy Ronald Feldman Fine Arts, New York.

Various artists have worked with faecal matter in their work. Gilbert and George laugh, ironically, at the horror of it all. Piero Manzoni's cans of *Artist's Shit*, created in 1961, explore corporeal processes and the veneration of the artist as subject but their sale, and subsequent re-sale, has raised the aesthetic and economic value of shit. Even so, as Bernhard Hadolt has pointed out, human waste retains a 'symbolic infectiousness' which still operates.[94] In his examination of the controversy in Austria in 1998, in which Cornelius Kolig, an artist known for his use of blood, urine and shit, was potentially involved in working on government premises, he found that it was difficult to extract it from connotations of vulgarity, dirt and disgust – even within academic discourse.[95] He concluded that shit is still a 'risky business'.

So trash is no longer the secret or taboo it once was: in the twenty-first century celebrity detox makes televisual spectacle out of cloaca. Trash has undergone a rehabilitation in material terms as much as within the field of cultural analysis and aesthetics. However, it is important to keep in mind Roberts' points that there is no such thing as 'universal utopian content'. Whatever particular materials the artist as bricoleur has to handle – whether it is shit or plastic – are within a context and it is the particularities of history, location and culture that must always be considered in relation to the employment of trash in art.

CHAPTER TWO
The Cultural Life of Detritus: From *Objet Trouvé* to the *Art of Assemblage*

Introduction

Assemblage has become, temporarily at least, the language of impatient, hypercritical and anarchistic young artists... The vernacular repertoire includes beat Zen and hot rods, mescalin experiences and faded flowers, photographic bumps and grinds, the *poubelle* (i.e. trash can), juke boxes, and hydrogen explosions.[1]

Arjun Appadurai's seminal study of the relationship between commodities and culture, *The Social Life of Things*, marked a return to objects as a focus for anthropological study.[2] It focused attention on the varying commodity potential of all things, suggesting that the process was dependent on their 'social history' or their 'cultural biography'. Artworks, such as assemblages, which present and re-present found or pre-formed objects – whether fragments or complete – invoke the kinds of questions which Appadurai raised about the 'social life of things' and commodity fetishism. Found objects might be considered as relics, repositories, signs and texts. But do found objects have 'life' of their own? Do they have agency, can they *act*?[3]

In the catalogue for the exhibition, *The Art of Assemblage*, staged at the Museum of Modern Art in New York in 1961 (Fig. 8), William Seitz drew constant parallels and analogies between assemblage and Beat culture – making explicit links in terms of technique, the merging of life and art and the extensive employment of vernacular motifs and objects – particularly in the form of rubbish. As far as Seitz was concerned, trash assemblage 'spoke'. For him, it was an edgy, youthful, subversive idiom identified with radical politics – '... the language of impatient, hypercritical and anarchistic young artists ...'.[4] At the same time though, he argued that artwork which incorporated found objects had an aesthetic appeal as he constantly equated it with poetic rhetoric. He stated that his aim was 'to reveal the diversity, expressive power and beauty which has been

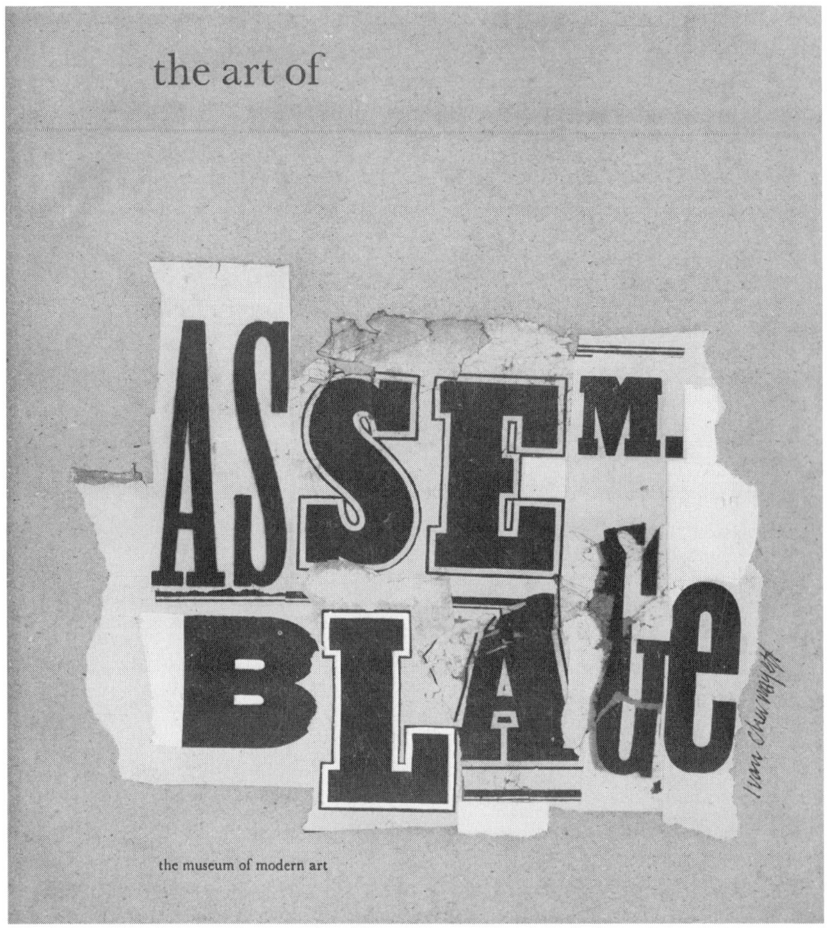

Fig. 8 Cover of the exhibition catalogue, *The Art of Assemblage*, held at the Museum of Modern Art (MoMA), New York in 1961. MoMA Library, New York, Acc. No. MS72 © 2009. Digital image, The Museum of Modern Art, New York/Scala, Florence.

achieved in these uniquely contemporary artforms…'.[5] Whilst some of the work had a purposeful anarchistic message, many of the artists featured were certainly not overtly exploring political ideas or events. To reiterate Jacques Rancière's viewpoint,[6] their art was politicised only because it was bound up with political contexts through the subjectivity of viewers and critics and dependent on the specificities of time and place for interpretation.

The term *assemblage* has generally come to refer to a technique in which an assortment of things, often found objects and discarded materials, are combined to create three-dimensional artworks. Assemblage has associations with other techniques in the visual arts such as *collage*[7] and *montage*[8] which involve the composition and juxtaposition of fragments of objects, materials or images. In cinema, montage is closely associated with the Soviet film director, Sergei Eisenstein who developed the technique of cross-cutting images to convey complex ideas. For him, montage was

> … any two pieces of a film stuck together inevitably combine to create a new concept, a new quality born of that juxtaposition …[9]

The idiom of assemblage has a host of connections with other media which rely on metaphor and juxtaposition to create layers of meaning. All language operates through the juxtaposition of words but there are particular parallels with both conventional and experimental forms of poetry. Examples might be the work of Futurist artist-poet, Filippo Tommaso Marinetti who produced visual and phonic images that combined vulgarity and nobility, Dada artists with their nonsensical assemblages of sounds or the idiosyncratic literary 'cut-ups' created by post-war 'Beat' writers, William Burroughs and Brion Gysin.[10]

In the mid-twentieth century, critics wrote of a 'collage explosion'[11] in the visual arts and the associated technique of assemblage expanded into the making of Environments and Happenings. In 1961, Seitz recounted Allan Kaprow's comments on his preference for using the debris of mass culture – 'the medium of refuse' – as part of a purposeful attempt to 'abandon craftsmanship and permanence'. Kaprow explained his wish to employ

> … the use of obviously perishable media such as newspaper, string, adhesive tape, growing grass or real food … so … no-one can mistake the fact that the work will pass into dust or garbage quickly …[12]

Since then, the use of ephemeral materials, the remnants of everyday life and the technique of assemblage have been effectively appropriated by every aspect of contemporary culture, embraced by a postmodern inclination towards 'sampling', multiplicity and *bricolage*.

However, it is significant that the term, *assemblage*, only really gained common currency after *The Art of Assemblage* in New York in 1961. Doré Ashton's regular 'New York Commentary' for *Studio International* in 1963, entitled 'High Tide for Assemblage', highlighted this, signifying the extent to which the 'new' idiom had permeated practice and had generated its own expanded market and audience:

> It is still high tide for the art of assemblage. Ever since the controversial exhibition at the Museum of Modern Art, the New York galleries have

ransacked the western world for new material. The season has begun with a spate of assemblage exhibitions and future schedules indicate an inordinate number to come.[13]

Furthermore, the show marked a culmination of activity as much as it marked a beginning – as it brought together an extensive range of artwork from the early twentieth century alongside contemporaneous work.

This chapter will explore the genealogy and incubation of that seminal exhibition through a consideration of some of the historical and early twentieth-century roots of the use of trash in art. It is concerned with narratives and art-historical 'roots' of assemblage – in terms of both 'high art' and 'low art' – and particularly its deployment of the throwaway and the ephemeral. Its relationship to collage is important and, of course, the 'readymade' is an essential part of the history: Seitz included both in *The Art of Assemblage* show.[14] Rather than providing a comprehensive survey of assemblage though,[15] I want to address the artistic traditions and cultural narratives of the found object and to consider what Margaret Iverson terms the 'elusive object'[16] – the *objet trouvé* and its metonymic nature as sign, fetish and souvenir, through to a mid-century preoccupation with urban detritus. Finally, as the new idiom of assemblage emerges, it is essential to examine the origins, curatorial strategies and presentation of the seminal exhibition, *The Art of Assemblage.*

Curiosities, Collections and Memorabilia

Although assemblage is generally associated with twentieth-century art, the fundamental process of collecting, sorting and arranging objects and paper-based ephemera has a long history in popular and folk cultures. Collage has diverse roots from twelfth-century Japanese text collages to German folk-art weather charms of the eighteenth century.[17] With the development and reproduction of the photographed image in the nineteenth century, the pasting of photographs and cuttings into scrapbooks and large hinged screens became a popular pastime. Images and objects acted as sentimental mementoes and nostalgic souvenirs. The custom of placing groups of precious objects near images and statues of deities predates the purposeful incorporation of real objects into sculpture. Many cultures have long histories of the incorporation of real objects and talismans in cultural and religious artefacts.

Importantly though, if we are to understand the concept of 'the object' and its collection, we must turn to the institution of the modern museum. Recognising the role of the museum in Western culture is central to the discourse of the collection. A number of museums developed from private collections of objects which resulted from the amassing of ethnographic or curious specimens from overseas expeditions: such as the Ashmolean Museum in Oxford, based on the collection of Elias Ashmole.[18] From the seventeenth century, collections of ethnographic objects and specimens of various natural and unnatural kinds were displayed in 'curiosity cabinets' or 'wonder-rooms'. The Jesuit Athanasius Kircher's *wunderkammer* included preserved and stuffed animals and mineral specimens alongside peculiar hybrid objects and mythical creatures.[19]

The systematic classification and categorisation of such objects was linked to the development of the museum as an institution. Objects, extracted from their cultural contexts, become defined by a range of imposed criteria such as chronology, shape, material and location. Subsequently, collections of objects and the ways in which these have been organised and re-presented have taken on a significant role in constructing collective memory and history.

Mark Dion has extensively explored the object collection and its classification through his artistic practices. The cabinet of curiosities, the archive and the museum have been central to a number of his projects.[20] Through a range of artistic interventions, Neil Cummings and Marysia Lewandowska have also explored the histories of these institutions. In *The Value of Things*, they examined the valorisation and commodification of objects through a study of the ideological role of the museum and its relationship to the department store.[21] Jeremy Deller took a social anthropological approach to popular culture with his *Folk Archive* project in 2005, similarly exploring and exposing cultural values as constructed and narrow.[22]

Deller's *Folk Archive* included collections of souvenirs. Whether manufactured *kitsch* or found objects, souvenirs can be repositories of personal, collective and cultural memory.

> In contrast to the souvenir, the collection offers example rather than sample, metaphor rather than metonymy.... The collection does not displace attention to the past: rather, the past is at the service of the collection, for whereas the souvenir lends authenticity to the past, the past lends authenticity to the collection.[23]

Susan Stewart's examination of the narrative of the souvenir can be related to the found object. Stewart comments on the capacity of objects to serve as traces of authentic experience. For her, this is exemplified by the souvenir. She explains how we need and desire souvenirs as perpetual reminders of experiences we have had as well as experiences we have not had. Souvenirs act as surrogate experiences and enable us to have a second-hand experience or encounter. As she says, the souvenir displays the 'romance of contraband'. The souvenir museum

> … speaks to a context of origin through a language of longing, for it is not an object arising out of need or use value; it is an object arising out of the necessarily insatiable demands of nostalgia.[24]

She relates her discussion of the souvenir and its generation of a narrative always 'beyond' and 'behind' the object itself to Sigmund Freud's description of the genesis of the fetish whereby a part of the body is substituted for the whole, an object is substituted for the part or, inversely, the whole body can become an object. Objects and parts or fragments of objects can, in this way, operate as substitutes or surrogates. According to Freud, the 'distance' may be experienced as loss, catastrophe or *jouissance*.[25] The souvenir is always a referent to some other experience, hence it is always incomplete and so, she argues that the object is metonymic: it operates as an allusion, not a model. Furthermore, the narrative of the souvenir is not related to the object, but to the possessor. Objects can be viewed as indexical of collective memory or as agents of imagined community but the subject rather than the object provides the narrative.

The discourse of the souvenir and the collection informs a reading of the early use of found objects in modern art. Picasso, often credited as one of the earliest users of found objects in art, explored their metonymic properties. Various artists, including Picasso and Jacob Epstein, were also avid collectors of ethnographic objects and artefacts. The narrative of the object as metonymic, its fetishisation as ethnic and cultural curiosity as well as a signifier of everyday life needs to be considered.

Early Modernity and the Found Object

The original wax version of Edgar Degas' *Little Dancer* of 1880–1, with its wig of human hair and satin ribbon, muslin tutu and ballet shoes, is commonly regarded as one of the precedents for assemblage in Western art. However, most of the earliest twentieth-century works which included real or found objects are only known through photographs, such as Umberto Boccioni's *Fusion of a Head and a Window* of 1911, a plaster and wood sculpture which incorporated a real window frame.[26] In the Futurist manifesto of 1912, Boccioni expressed profound disaffection with traditional materials:

> We must destroy the so-called nobility, wholly literary and traditional, of marble and bronze … […] … The sculptor may use twenty or more different materials if he likes … […] … glass, wood, cardboard, iron, cement, hair, leather, cloth, mirrors, electric light, etc …[27]

Around the same time, various artists, either independently or through association, were experimenting with the introduction of real objects and found materials into the picture plane.[28] Significantly though, the incorporation of everyday objects as signifiers of everyday life can be identified as a development of Cubist painting and collage. After the repeated references to a series of motifs of vernacular culture – newspapers, lettering, bottles – *actual* materials and objects were applied to the picture surface as verbal and visual puns. From around 1912, Georges Braque and Picasso developed *papier collé*, pasting decorative and printed papers and cardboard onto a two-dimensional ground. Whilst Picasso's *Still Life* of 1914, with its offcuts of ornate wood and upholstery fringe, remained wall-based, his first free-standing assemblage, six painted bronze versions of *Verre d'Absinthe* of 1914, was equipped with real silver spoons.[29]

An irrational anti-aesthetic use of objects and found materials informed Dada, the art movement which emerged from and through the chaos and madness of the First World War. Tristan Tzara, Richard Huelsenbeck and other Dada associates were as provocative in their deployment of objects in artworks as they were in cabaret, performances and poetry readings. Collage and photomontage lent itself to bizarre and disturbing juxtapositions of imagery for Club Dada artists Hannah Hoch and Raoul Hausmann in Berlin, who used the idiom to criticise every aspect of society and politics. In sculptural works such as *The Spirit of Our Time – Mechanical Head* of 1919–20, an assemblage of wood, metal, leather, cardboard and found objects, Hausmann dispensed with traditional materials and techniques to satirise nationalism and reveal the grotesque and brutal side of humanity.

Affiliated to Dada through technique rather than association, Kurt Schwitters is one of the most influential figures in the development of assemblage, using collage techniques with discarded objects, materials and found sound.

> I don't see why one shouldn't use in a picture, just as one uses colours made by the paint merchants, things like old tram and train tickets, scraps of driftwood, cloakroom tickets, ends of string, bicycle wheel spokes – in a word all the old rubbish which you find in dustbins or on a refuse dump.[30]

Inventing *merz* in 1919, he noted:

> The word *merz* denotes essentially the combination, for artistic purposes, of all conceivable materials, and, technically, the principle of the equal distribution of the individual materials…. A perambulator

wheel, wire-netting, string and cotton wool are factors having equal rights with paint…[31]

Paradoxically, the extensive body of collages and reliefs which Schwitters produced, whilst incorporating a plethora of found materials such as money, buttons and paper ephemera, often depended on aesthetic arrangements and formal composition to achieve their effects. John Coplans argued that much emphasis has been given to Schwitters' use of urban artefacts whereas, in his view, the most significant aspect of his work was his improvising with materials, 'spontaneous play'. For Coplans, Schwitters

> … made it possible for formal or intellectual play and the notion of spontaneous and automatically derived compositions to become part of the means of art…[32]

Arguably, Schwitters' most important contribution to the development of assemblage was the idiosyncratic fetishistic use of objects in the three *Merzbau* he constructed first in Hannover (destroyed by wartime bombs in 1943), then Oslo (destroyed by fire in 1951) and, finally, Ambleside in England (salvaged and reconstructed in 1965 at the Hatton Gallery, University of Newcastle on Tyne, England).[33] Schwitters employed ephemeral materials and found objects in these environmental assemblages, including bits of wood and metal, children's toys, old plaster casts, dried flowers, animal horns, newspaper cuttings and rags. The Hannover *Merzbau*, which occupied him for over 15 years, grew organically from a single phallic column to a series of free-standing structures which, eventually, became a chaotic but continuous 'cavernous maze'[34] of junk. A number of distinct grottoes emerged including the 'Goethe Grotto', the 'Lavatory Attendant of Life' and the 'Sex-Murder Cave'.[35] The 'Grotto of Great Love' was one of the largest, forming part of the column known as 'The Cathedral of Erotic Misery'. Schwitters' scatological choice of objects in some of these grottoes – samples of urine and shit, nail clippings, locks of hair – opens the *Merzbau*, as Bernard Vere has noted, to Freudian readings of fetishistic and coprophilic pleasure.[36]

Of the early modernists then, Cubists appropriated and incorporated found objects to signify the everyday realities of modern life, whereas Dada adopted a more conceptual approach, using objects playfully and provocatively. However, in the vein of Schwitters's *Merzbau*, in the 1930s, artists associated with Surrealism exploited the metonymic and associative properties of objects. They made extensive use of collage, montage and frottage techniques and their work was often concerned with the juxtaposition of unexpected images and found objects. A key strategy adopted, for example, by Man Ray[37] and Eileen Agar, was the juxtaposition of incongruous objects, epitomised by Lautréamont's oft-quoted 'chance encounter of a sewing machine and an umbrella on a dissecting table', the notions of 'compulsive beauty' and the 'exquisite corpse', both of which have been explored extensively since.[38] Aldo van Eyck summed up the method as one

> ... adopted from Lautréamont of provoking a casual meeting of two alien realities with a third alien to both, causing a shudder of unprecedented poetry...[39]

The movement's most important contribution to assemblage was the way in which the Surrealists extracted functional and found objects from their familiar surroundings and presented them as ludicrous and fetishistic realisations. For the Surrealists, it was the associative properties of objects which were most important. As Waldman argues, the Surrealist object – valued for the 'poetic and visual metaphors that it evoked' – came into its own in the 1930s.[40] The 'Surrealist Exhibition of Objects' in 1936, held in Paris, presented a bewildering range of objects, including

> ... natural objects, interpreted natural objects, incorporated natural objects, found objects, perturbed objects...[41]

As part of a recent resurgence of scholarship on Surrealism,[42] Margaret Iverson has attempted to reconfigure the distinctiveness of the Surrealist use of the found object. André Breton positioned found objects in the 'space of the unconscious', viewing them like 'visual residues' from past experience that turn up in dreams.[43] However, she writes of the way in which any interpretation of the Surrealist encounter with the found object must consider the subjective experience of the viewer. For her, a Lacanian subject is implied by the Surrealist found object which she refers to as the 'elusive object'. Hal Foster, in his book *Compulsive Beauty*, suggests that Breton's conception of the found object anticipates Lacan's *objet petit a* – the lost object which sets desire in motion and which, paradoxically, represents both 'a hole in the integrity of our world and the thing that comes to hide the hole'.[44] The Surrealist encounter with the found object and its subjective viewing might be considered in relation to Freudian notions of the fetish object but its elusiveness and capacity to evoke desire are central.

Found objects also have a place in the history of early modernist interiors where they were often placed alongside sculpted forms. The organic *objet trouvé* – particularly in the form of animal bones, pebbles, stones and driftwood – were of particular interest to British sculptors such as Henry Moore and Barbara Hepworth and this is reflected throughout their work. In 1952 at Kettle's Yard in Cambridge, Jim Ede, a Tate Gallery curator, brought together collections of sculpture and objects which he had accumulated since living in Hampstead in the 1920s and 1930s when his home had been a meeting place for Herbert Read's 'nest of gentle artists'.[45] Apart from art, furniture, glass and ceramics, Ede had been a keen collector of all sorts of natural objects such as shells and pebbles from remote parts of the world. Many of these became part of the permanent display at Kettle's Yard as Ede believed their presence would enhance the beauty of the works of art by juxtaposition and comparison.[46] The collection of artworks and found objects was based on a modernist aesthetic form, an aspect reflected in 1995, when Ian Hamilton Finlay described Kettle's Yard as the 'Louvre of Pebbles'.[47]

So, under early modernism, the cultural life of detritus was multifarious and diverse – whilst found objects could signify a social urban modernity, their metonymic properties were also exploited as functional fragments were incorporated into incongruous juxtapositions of playfulness and provocation. In other settings, the *objet trouvé* made a transition from being an idiosyncratic object of curiosity to something which – in a domestic environment – could make an aesthetic bridge to the organic abstract forms of the carved sculpture of Moore and Hepworth. At the 'Louvre of Pebbles', detritus was in harmonious accord with art.

Junk Culture

Junk Culture is city art. Its source is obsolescence, the throwaway materials of cities, as it collects in drawers, cupboards, attics, dustbins, gutters, waste lots and city dumps . . . [48]

The specific identification of the found object with the urban environment was particularly articulated in various contexts in the late 1950s and early 1960s. The linking of detritus with the city signifies Vance Packard's 'waste-maker' society founded on mass consumerism and the manufacture of goods with a short shelf life. Branded as 'junk', a term associated with narcotics,[49] urban rubbish then acquires a connection not only to the transgressive but, more specifically, to those existing on the outlaw margins of the city, the 'hustlers' and 'downbeats'.[50] Detritus, by association, becomes a signifier of urban alienation, disharmony with nature and social rupture.

In his article entitled 'Junk Culture', published in the *Architectural Design* journal in 1961, Lawrence Alloway used the term to refer to the work of artists like Richard Stankiewicz who utilised scrap metal and industrial debris. For Alloway though, 'junk culture' was a much broader concept which essentially connoted mass urban culture – a subject which he had explored extensively since the mid-1950s through his involvement with the Independent Group in London.[51] In his introductory essay on the important *New Forms – New Media* exhibition at the Martha Jackson Gallery the year before the *Art of Assemblage* show, Alloway made similar comments. There, he set out the contemporary characteristics of 'junk culture as a tradition', linking it to Dada and Futurism – not, he argued, to give it 'an art history' but to 'link it to a common source, the city'.[52] In his view, the essential thing about junk culture was that the kind of objects used resisted incorporation into a smooth aesthetic whole.

> Assemblages of such material come at the spectator as bits of life, bits of the city…[53]

In the 1950s then, urban refuse became a medium as artists worked with 'bits of the city'. Making artworks with detritus, often collected directly from city streets, provided an opportunity to, as Robert Rauschenberg famously commented, work in the 'gap' between art and life.[54] Ed Kienholz extended his junk sculptures into a series of gothic tableaux. With *The Street* at the Judson Gallery in 1960, Jim Dine and Claes Oldenberg expanded into real space and time; working with urban trash they blurred the boundary between artifice and social reality. Allan Kaprow, inspired by John Cage's activities at Black Mountain College, built murals, environmental structures and created Happenings, extensively documented in his seminal study, *Assemblages, Environments and Happenings*.[55] These multimedia actions and performances invited spectators not only to look but to participate and contribute too.

By the early 1960s, artists were physically engaging with 'bits of the city' to create junk sculptures, shamanistic performances and spontaneous events, sometimes exploring the formal, material and physical properties of objects for aesthetic and anti-aesthetic purposes or, exploiting their associative properties, to engage with issues of politics, gender and identity. Environmental and 'action' artforms usually involved the juxtaposition – the assemblage – of objects and materials.[56] Significantly, in his introduction to *New Forms – New Media*, Alloway specifically used the term assemblage – a term which only really gained common currency the following year after the major exhibition, *The Art of Assemblage*, was presented at the Museum of Modern Art in New York.

The 'Art' of Assemblage

> Assemblage is a method with disconcertingly centrifugal potentialities. It is metaphysical as well as physical and realistic … […]… The fabric of meaning woven by materials can cover the distant in time and space, awakening a romantic response to ruins, architectural and sculptural fragments and the evocative richness of old walls or ritual vessels. As element is set beside element, the many qualities and auras of isolated fragments are compounded, fused, contradicted so that – by their own confronted volitions as it were – physical matter becomes poetry.[57]

The exhibition, *The Art of Assemblage*, brought together an extensive diverse range of historical and contemporary assemblage, including works by Picasso, Schwitters, Duchamp and Dubuffet (Fig. 9). The exhibition and the accompanying symposium aimed not only to establish a genealogy for assemblage but also to develop a coherent theory or rationale.[58] Seitz recognised the multiple and polysemic potential which assemblage – as an artform which primarily used found objects and materials – offered both to the artist-maker and to the viewer-spectator. For Seitz, assemblage was not only a new artistic idiom but also one which linked to contemporary literary forms. On a critical level, the show represented a culmination of assemblage practice and generated a plethora of smaller exhibitions. Despite relatively little attention paid to it at various times since, it has been viewed by some as a seminal event.[59] Doré Ashton recognised the exhibition's significance not only at the time[60] but also in retrospect, commenting

> Seitz's serious appraisal of the breakdown of conventional categories cleared the way for increasing attention to genres of art that had previously been seen only in isolated contexts.[61]

But how important was it? Was it unique? Had there been other similar shows at different times and elsewhere? It is important to examine Seitz's claims by considering the origins of the exhibition, its organisation and curatorial strategies and the narratives it presented.

The exhibition was the specific project of two key figures, William Seitz[62] and Peter Selz,[63] both of whom had only recently taken up curatorial posts at the Museum of Modern Art, New York (MoMA). A shared enthusiasm for assemblage and a common vision ensured the show's success. Selz arrived from the West Coast in 1958,[64] with the idea of doing an exhibition which investigated collage and objects. Seitz, who had accumulated a collection of catalogues of collage exhibitions from Europe

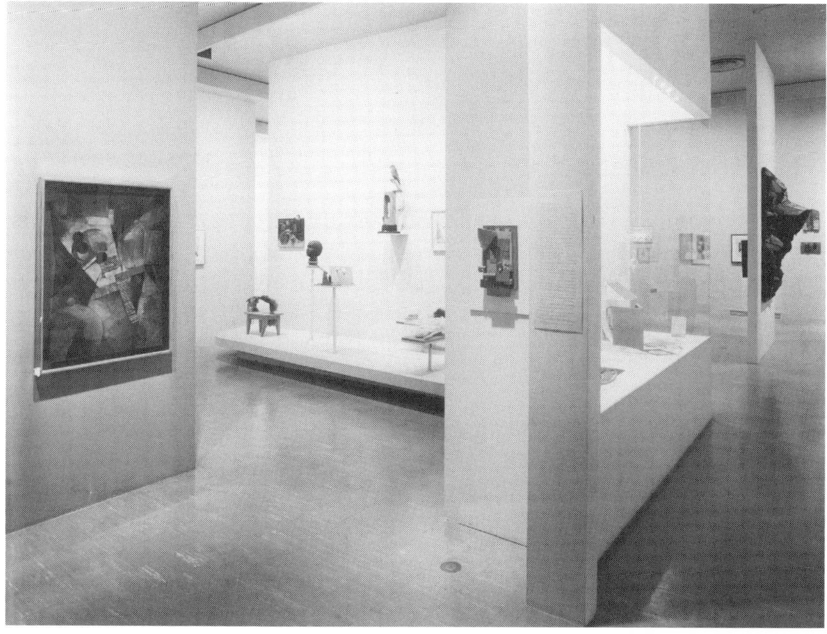

Fig. 9 Installation view of the exhibition *The Art of Assemblage*, Museum of Modern Art, New York. 4 October–12 November, 1961. IN695.20 © 2009 Digital image, The Museum of Modern Art, New York/Scala, Florence.

and the USA, was thinking on similar lines when he took up his post in 1960.[65]

> ... no book on collage and construction now exists... and unless one appears before 1961 (and it may do) this will fill a major gap...'[66]

It is evident from archive files, correspondence and the exhibition catalogue that Seitz was keen to present a curatorial 'first' which, whilst acknowledging its debt to abstract expressionism and the new American painting, would defy current fashions and mannerist tendencies. Seitz recognised the time was right for the introduction of a new concept.[67] As Seitz commented at the time of the exhibition,

> Assemblage is a new medium. It is to be expected therefore, that it should be the carrier of developing viewpoints for which orthodox techniques are less appropriate.[68]

The exhibition established historical precedents by tracing a lineage back to Surrealism and Dada. For Seitz though, the primary contemporary contextualisation was provided by Jean Dubuffet (Fig. 10). Although the American artist, Arthur Dove, had used the term 'assemblage' in 1925,[69] Dubuffet was credited with first use in 1953 with reference to his butterfly-wing reliefs.[70]

As Elderfield points out, the word 'assemblage' was largely popularised by Seitz's choice of it for the title of the show, selected as

> … its reference is, on the one hand, broader than that of the word *collage*, in including three dimensional as well as planar works, and, on the other hand, more specific than that of the word *construction*, in stressing the accumulation of found elements in such a way that they remain separately recognizable. In effect, assemblage is collage in two and three dimensions.[71]

Before the exhibition, the organisers anticipated that critical and public reaction to the show might be aggressive and extreme.[72] In a diplomatic letter to artists and dealers loaning artworks to the exhibition, Seitz highlighted that this was to be the first to survey 'assembled art', forewarning them,

> … because of the current interest in unorthodox media and the philosophical questions it raises, this is to be a topical, perhaps even controversial exhibition.[73]

Seitz may be accused of making grandiose and pompous claims for his exhibition, both before and after the event, but its audacity should not be underestimated. It presented a cornucopia of works which did not always sit well together. Indeed, it was an idiosyncratic curatorial jumble presented in a relatively conventional gallery setting.[74] Nevertheless, its rejection of traditional categories of art amounted to a considerable challenge to modernist discourses and presaged the further blurring of disciplinary boundaries under postmodernity.

In the catalogue essay, Seitz attempted to set out his criteria for the new medium, identifying two key characteristics:

1. They are predominantly *assembled* rather than painted, drawn, modeled or carved.
2. Entirely or in part, their constituent elements are preformed natural or manufactured materials, objects, or fragments not intended as art materials.[75]

Given such an open remit and the plethora of work available, one of the key problems for the exhibition organisers was deciding what to include and what to leave out. As Seitz commented in correspondence with the critic Herta Wescher,

> … because of the recent efflorescence of such work, selecting is difficult but it will largely consist of objects/collages of 'found' materials and [I] will eliminate all pure geometric decoupage and work in which collage is a substitute for paint…[76]

Consequently, on this basis Seitz decided not to include the late collages of Matisse because he argued, 'they employ collage as a technical means to achieve flat colour'.[77]

Ultimately, the choice of work reflected Seitz's artistic sensibilities to materials and, in particular, the 'poetic metaphor'. Indicating how assemblages can be read as whole or in fragments, for Seitz their 'reading' was complicated and enriched by the orchestration of objects and materials which have former histories.

> When paper is soiled or lacerated, when cloth is worn, stained, torn, when wood is split, weathered, or patterned with peeling coats of paint, when metal is bent or rusted, they gain connotations which unmarked materials lack.[78]

The final exhibition featured over 250 works of collage and assemblage by artists largely from Europe and the USA: alongside earlier work by Schwitters, Picasso and Duchamp there was work by British artists Eduardo Paolozzi and John Latham. It ranged from the purposefully 'hypercritical and anarchistic' – exemplified by Ed Kienholz with his ironic patriotic couple, *John Doe* and *Jane Doe*, made from a wooden sewing chest with fur-rimmed drawers, old mannequins, perambulator parts, rubber dolls and assorted bits of wood, plaster and metal – to the formalist constructions of the 'metal assemblagist' Bruce Beasley, who described himself as an 'unrepentant modernist'.[79] The urban character of assemblage was explored but not all artists worked with garbage or industrial waste. The show included contemporary work by artists using natural materials: for example, *Instruments at the Silence Refinery*, 1960, by the Oakland sculptor John Baxter, a beach-comber who worked with driftwood, shells and bones.[80]

Whilst some of the work had particular political contexts and narratives, Seitz chose to link assemblage much more to poetics than politics. Artists viewed as key contributors to the earlier development of the idiom exhibited multiple works: Kurt Schwitters (35 works), Joseph Cornell (14 works), Marcel Duchamp (13 works), Man Ray (7 works) and Jean Dubuffet (7 works). Few other artists showed more than a couple of works.

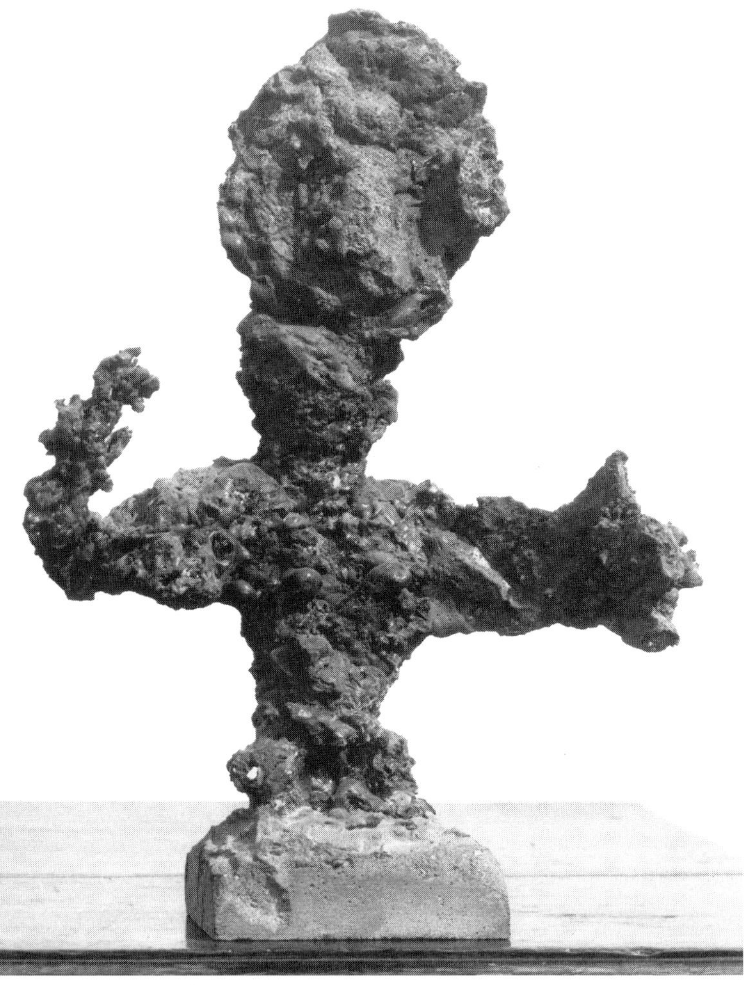

Fig. 10 Jean Dubuffet, *Le commandeur mâchefer*, April 1954. h. 36 cm. Collection privée, New York, USA. Courtesy of Fondation Dubuffet and ADAGP/DACS.

As has already been indicated, Dubuffet was viewed as responsible for taking the collage idea into new directions in the 1950s and for coining the term 'assemblage' in an art context. He pioneered the making of art from found objects and all kinds of debris with his *Petites statues de la vie précaire*, a series of figurines made in 1954, fashioned from newspaper, coal, clinker, soil, sponges, charred wood, rusty nails, volcanic lava and broken glass held together with cement and glue. (Fig. 10) The show featured three works from this series: *The Commander*, *The Duke* and *The Horseman*. The crude materials gave these humorous figures a naive but subversive character which affronted pompous notions of 'fine art'.

An important aspect of the show was the way in which it brought together a host of work by lesser-known European artists. Seitz travelled extensively, trawling for works made from junk, corresponding with critics and artists, visiting studios, galleries and dealers. He visited collectors such as Roland Penrose and made a number of trips to galleries abroad such as Galerie Rive Droite in Paris[81] and various artists' studios in Europe,[82] including Jaap Wagemaker in Amsterdam.

The works of contemporary European artists such as Arman, César, Roberto Crippa, Mimmo Rotella, Niki de Saint Phalle, Daniel Spoerri and Jean Tinguely were selected. Their work was placed alongside that of European *collagistes* and *assembleurs* from earlier generations – Schwitters, Picasso and Duchamp. Picasso's seminal contribution was acknowledged by Seitz but he was represented by just three works from 1913 to 1914 – including the important *Still Life* of 1914 with painted wood and upholstery fringe. Surprisingly, none of his post-war assemblages of objects cast into bronze were exhibited although Seitz made specific reference to his 'magnificent bronze of 1951, *Baboon and Young*'.[83]

A good deal of the selection of work by lesser-known European artists was carried out by smaller galleries or done on the recommendations of gallery owners and critics. For example, Herta Wescher suggested a number of artists working with found objects to Seitz including Lawrence Vail, Jeanne Coppel, Jean Deyrolle, Karskaya and Carlo Corsi. Wescher also urged Seitz to consider 'the more sensational objects-reliefs of Bettencourt, Kalinowsky, Arman and Baj'.[84]

The predominantly serendipitous nature of the selection process is demonstrated by the choice of work included by the British artists, Robyn Denny, John Latham, Eduardo Paolozzi and Gwyther Irwin. Latham's work had featured in *New Forms – New Media*, but a collector, Walter Goodhue, wrote to Seitz offering four of Latham's burnt book reliefs.[85] Seitz was already familiar with the work of Denny, Irwin and Paolozzi[86]– although, rather oddly perhaps in Paolozzi's case, all were represented by collage. Seitz sought advice about British assemblage artists from Gabriel White, the Director of the Arts Council who, failing to come up with any names, suggested he write to the critic Robert Melville and Dorothy Morland at the Institute of Contemporary Arts. Finally, he wrote to Ronald Alley at the Tate in the hope that he had 'his finger on the pulse of experimental art in London', commenting that he couldn't locate any other British work,

> ... so far I have not heard of any assemblers of 3d constructions from found materials...[87]

The lack of response may merely demonstrate the speculation which can result from the problems of archival research, but clearly Seitz had no information about two British artists working with junk, George Fullard and Bruce Lacey. Of course, London was on the brink of Anthony Caro's sculptural revolution – his conversion to working with abstract metal forms came in 1960 – and different artistic traditions dominated but others might have offered a useful source for the kind of work Seitz was seeking.[88]

In contrast, Seitz appears to have had few problems in either locating or acquiring work in the USA. Indeed, he was overwhelmed with offers from artists, collectors and galleries,[89] enabling him to include a substantial range of work by artists important for the idiom's early development such as Arthur Dove and Joseph Cornell, alongside the contemporary assemblages of Bruce Conner, Robert Rauschenberg, Ed Kienholz, H.C. Westermann and others. Private collectors provided a rich source of exhibits,[90] but Seitz wrote to numerous galleries, politely asking them if they could check their collections to see if they had anything relevant. Some organisations, like the Minneapolis Institute of Arts, had nothing to offer but others were clearly unsure about what this new category of 'assemblage' might be. Interestingly, the Carnegie responded with a letter apologising for the long delay, explaining that it had taken a long time to list their collage and 'assembled objects' as they had 'no such group classification'[91] but had found so much that they would institute one from then on.[92]

Whilst institutions provided lists of artworks in response to Seitz's formal requests, the response of individual artists was sometimes more idiosyncratic. In an interview with Meredith Tromble in 1988, Bruce Conner talked about Seitz's visit to San Francisco in search of assemblage work. He advised Seitz that Jess and George Herms were the most important assemblage artists in the area.[93] Conner drove him around the Bay Area but, rather than focusing on artists' studios, insisted on taking him to second-hand shops, directing him to a particular Chinese laundry on Grant Avenue. Conner explained how he wanted to show Seitz that the urban environment of San Francisco itself was like a magnificent assemblage.[94]

Seitz's inclusion of a section entitled 'the collage environment' in the show's catalogue might almost represent an expansion of Conner's idea that the city can be viewed as an assembled artwork. Here, Seitz refers to Simon Rodia's idiosyncratic towers constructed in Watts, Los Angeles. Rodia, an immigrant tile-setter, had spent over 30 years building his eccentric labyrinth of jewelled pavements and glowing grottoes from bits of tiles, pottery, glass, concrete and other household and industrial junk. Arising majestically in this destitute neighbourhood, this vernacular version of Antoni Gaudi's *Sagrada Familia* brought together Conner's exuberance for the idea of the expanded junk environment with Alloway's celebration of urbanism[95]:

> … one must agree that the proper backdrop for recent assemblage is the multifarious fabric of the modern city – its random patchwork of slickness and deterioration, cold planning and liberating confusion, resplendent beauty and noxious squalor.[96]

Whilst the exhibition was pioneering in terms of the form of artworks included, its global reach was limited as it was dominated by artists based in North America and Europe. The Cleveland Museum of Ohio was approached about Japanese work but none of their suggestions were taken up. Consequently, there was no reference in the exhibition or catalogue to the work of the Gutai group or to some of the Latin American artists working with objects, such as Lygia Clarke.[97] There were a few exceptions though. Shinkichi Tajiri's scrapyard metal sculpture, *Samurai* (1960), was included in the show. Originally from Los Angeles with a Japanese family background, Tajiri crossed a range of international boundaries in terms of work and location. Since the end of the 1940s, he had lived in Amsterdam. Aldo van Eyck described seeing Tajiri working with junk:

> You were coaxing the debris with determination, fondling the fragments… it's the story of junk – the epic splendour of what has been cast away, thwarted, bruised, spat upon, trampled underfoot. The story of what has lost purpose or never had any.… You continued what was started before, smashing the hierarchy of 'noble material' and the frozen obsolete languages allied to them…[98]

More surprising perhaps was the failure to include any assemblage work by Canadian artists.[99] This was not because of a lack of available work[100] and this was identified as a notable and controversial omission at the time. A Canadian artist, Dennis Burton, raised this point at the symposium which accompanied the exhibition. He followed this up with a long letter demanding to know why there were no Canadian artists in the show, supplying a long list of assemblage artists, such as Gordon Rayne. Burton concluded that it represented yet another example of MoMA's commitment to support American hegemony in the artworld.[101]

Certainly by the mid-1960s, Vancouver had become a major centre of experimental multimedia practices. It boasted a large interconnected community of artists, musicians, dancers, architects and poets with organisations such as The Intermedia Society dedicated to examining the socio-political role of artistic practices within communities.[102] In 1990, an exhibition held at Vancouver Art Gallery explored the affinities of four assemblage artists who emerged in the 1950s: Jess and George Herms based in California and Bill Bissell and Al Neil in Vancouver.[103] In the catalogue, Kevin Wallace outlined a 'convergence of sensibilities' between West Coast artists in USA and Vancouver, arguing that there were a host of common cultural and geographical factors.[104] Significantly, Wallace argues that, independently, they all worked with found objects and functioned outside institutional frameworks. In Wallace's view, Canadian artists were not included in *The Art of Assemblage* because, with their tendency towards an eclectic range of sources and folk culture, they were seen as 'outside the mainstream' – as 'other'.[105]

Undoubtedly, Al Neil's work would have been particularly appropriate for the MoMA exhibition. An intuitive *bricoleur*, Neil worked with banal objects and trash of all kinds – Wallace equates his work with a Whitmanesque call for a celebration 'of the beauty and libidinous interconnectedness of all things'.[106] From the 1950s onwards, Neil was an avid collector of junk which he assembled into huge constructions.[107]

> I never used driftwood but I find stuff on the beach … I'd get old chairs that were no good anymore and would start loading them with big pails of rusty wire and dolls and things cast off in the lanes in the West End. Rusty bed frames …[108]

From the 1960s onwards, Neil and his artist-partner, Carole Itter, continued to accrue junk, extending and living in a series of ramshackle structures as part of a commitment to an alternative, more ecologically attuned lifestyle.[109] In 1970, Neil commented

> … we live in a squatter's houseboat on the shore, about twenty miles outside of Vancouver. There's energy out there that's different than in the city. I'm not trying to proselytise for anything but what little strength I can muster has come from that kind of a place. My wife, for the last two or three years, has been walking out in the bush and finding various things for us to eat. One of our long range goals is to become non-consumers …[110]

Apart from creating junk sculptures and assembled environments, Neil has employed the *bricolage* principle across a range of media and disciplines, as a free improvising musician, performance artist and poet.[111] Described as 'a talismanic figure', Neil has continually experimented with a collage of sound, objects and images.[112] Unfortunately, there is an absence of recordings and there are only traces of Neil's output. As with so much of this kind of work, the fragmentary, ephemeral and multimedia nature of the work has militated against its documentation and collection and, in an artworld whose institutions and curatorial strategies depend on the acquisition and exhibition of materials and objects, this underlines the point that the museum as an institution has framed the canon. The inaccessibility, immateriality and interdisciplinary nature of work like Neil's rendered it invisible.

Finally, a particularly unique aspect of *The Art of Assemblage* was the programme of events related to the exhibition. There was an accompanying film night, showing Robert Bree's *Homage to Jean Tinguely*, *A Movie* by Bruce Conner, *Kruschev* by Robert Lebar and H. Kaplan and the atmospheric documentary, *The Watts Towers* by William B. Hale. The other key event was the exhibition's symposium, at which five key contributors – Roger Shattuck, Lawrence Alloway, Marcel Duchamp, Robert Rauschenberg and Richard Huelsenbeck – provided statements and analyses.[113] Shattuck spoke on 'juxtaposition', Alloway on popular culture, Duchamp on the readymade, Huelsenback on the 'metaphysics of assemblage'. Seitz, as 'moderator', introduced each speaker, describing Alloway as one of the first to give attention to artists that used urban waste materials. The stilted reading out of pre-prepared statements inspired audience heckling and calls for spontaneous discussion. Consequently, the audience was invited to write questions on bits of paper and drop them in a box for the panel to consider. An idiosyncratic set of questions was selected: What did the panel think of transcendence? Could anyone explain the difference between Dada and Neo-Dada? Could we have more laughter in the galleries?

Response to the show was mixed – whilst it attracted enthusiastic celebration from some quarters and was generally popular with public visitors,[114] there was also a torrent of criticism. One reviewer condemned the exhibition for presenting a 'spiritual vacuum' and 'sensationalist trash'.[115] Partisan supporters felt compelled to offer support: Philip Johnson was moved to write a personal letter to Seitz congratulating him on what he felt was 'the most exciting show at MoMA since the Alfred Barr days'.[116] Max Kozloff, writing for *The Nation*, described it as one of the most 'unnerving and compelling shows for years'.[117] Opposition was vociferous and extreme: one critic felt it was dominated by 'the cruel, the inhuman and the psychotic', and went on

> … nowhere is the power of negativity more clearly and revoltingly found than in the violent compositions of Rauschenberg and the sardonic decompositions of Kienholz … [118]

Despite the fact that it was dominated by artworks produced in North America, others viewed the exhibition as anti-patriotic: *Art News* accused the organisers of favouring 'Paris-approved chic'.[119] Paradoxically, because it failed to celebrate American post-war abstract painting and represented a demise of a peculiarly American form of modernist critique, it was seen by some as a devaluing attack on post-war US art, providing an opportunity for xenophobic commentary and a reiteration of American artworld hegemony.[120]

There was sufficient antipathy for Kaprow to write to Seitz, expressing his 'great surprise' at the 'avalanche of criticism of the forward-looking show':

> I hope that this isn't true and that gossip has gotten everything mixed up as it usually does. But if it is so, please know that the artists would be happy to stand by you with written endorsement (or whatever is necessary). Nobody can possibly quarrel with the quality of the exhibition and the historical contribution it makes.[121]

Seitz's reply was witty:

> Whatever criticism there has been … has been from quarters from which praise would have been a disaster. As for the people whose opinion I value and everyone in the museum, our togetherness could not be more complete.[122]

The exhibition's impact went beyond the art circles of New York in diverse ways. A slightly revised version travelled to San Francisco and Dallas, although not all works went for a range of serendipitous reasons. Pierre Restany invited Seitz to take the show to Paris but too many problems with fragile works prevented this.[123] More significantly, the exhibition had an immediate impact on art education as it opened up the idea that art could be made from a plentiful supply of free materials. A flurry of books aimed at children making art from junk appeared.[124] In 1972, engaging with the progressive education ethos of the time, the MoMA published a book specifically aimed at encouraging teachers to work with young people on the creation of junk assemblage. It outlined a range of projects which utilised waste from 'neighbourhood stores' and 'lumber-yards' to create environments, robots, theatre projects and kinetic artwork. The authors argued that assembling with trash 'enabled and empowered' young people, that it liberated creativity, engendered spontaneity and shifted art education away from the 'fallacy of talent':

> … the introduction of assemblage has vastly enriched the art experience by bringing to art education, new insights, a tremendous potential for stimulating creative activities, a variety of media and materials and innumerable ways of appealing to the senses … [125]

One might argue that *The Art of Assemblage* was a fairly conventionally presented exhibition which brought together a range of practices from artists in North America and Europe, constructing a genealogy which provided contemporary junk artists with a legitimating heritage. But the whole project did challenge the status quo of the artworld on a number of fronts – primarily, dissembling the domination of traditional media and forms, breaking disciplinary boundaries and providing trash with a new narrative, a cultural life of its own. It highlighted notions of collective and participatory artforms and generated pedagogical approaches to alternative forms of creativity. It looked forward to a postmodern engagement with the ephemeral, the everyday and the banal embraced by contemporary artists such as Jason Rhoades. I concur with Julia Robinson who has described Rhoades' chaotic and bizarre installations of trash as a 'voracious vernacular verification' for the way they continued the logic of 1960s' assemblage but provided it with an ongoing urgency into the twenty-first century. As she comments, it is his

> … implacable apprehension of vast contemporary networks through the object relations of his art that makes him a legitimate heir to this powerful century-long confrontation … [126]

CHAPTER THREE
Dissenters, Drifters and Poets: 'Placing' Assemblage in the San Francisco Bay Area

Introduction: The Poetics of Mundane Objects

In April 2006, I watched Lucy Puls pick over the discarded consumer goods of banal domesticity stacked up in her Berkeley studio. She talked evocatively about the raw materials of her artistic practice, handling them respectfully and with a poet's sensibility 'like an anthropologist sifting through the kitchen middens of a vanished tribe'.[1]

Puls is regarded as an artist whose subject is memory. Jeff Kelley views it as 'a transformation of forgotten objects into touchstones of remembering'.[2] Rather than romanticising the past though, her work marks the ruins of experience. Puls hoards unwanted objects, collected from thrift stores, gleaned from table-top sales and pavements (see Fig. 11). She accumulates unfashionable objects drained of currency. Out of their time, they become the fabric of communal and popular memory. Encased in resin, veiled from the viewer, they allure and seduce, exposing a contemporary fetishisation of the mundane. Puls has said that by re-working banal objects as art, they come to represent a 'new memory of something that is marginally in focus'.[3] Tanner has written of the way in which Puls compels us to think about how these objects are 'transforming consciousness'.[4] Referring to the 'mystical attraction of the unknown', she suggests that such re-worked discarded objects produce a poetic encounter, an epiphanic and revelatory moment. The poetic resonances are significant. Working with discarded junk in this particular way and in this particular place summons up more than popular memory – it engages with a whole set of histories to do with the matrices of place, identity and traditions of artistic practice.

It is pertinent to re-consider Doreen Massey's comments on the reconceptualisation of 'place' here. For Massey argues that 'there is … no authenticity of place'.[5] In her view, the search for stable identity, seamless

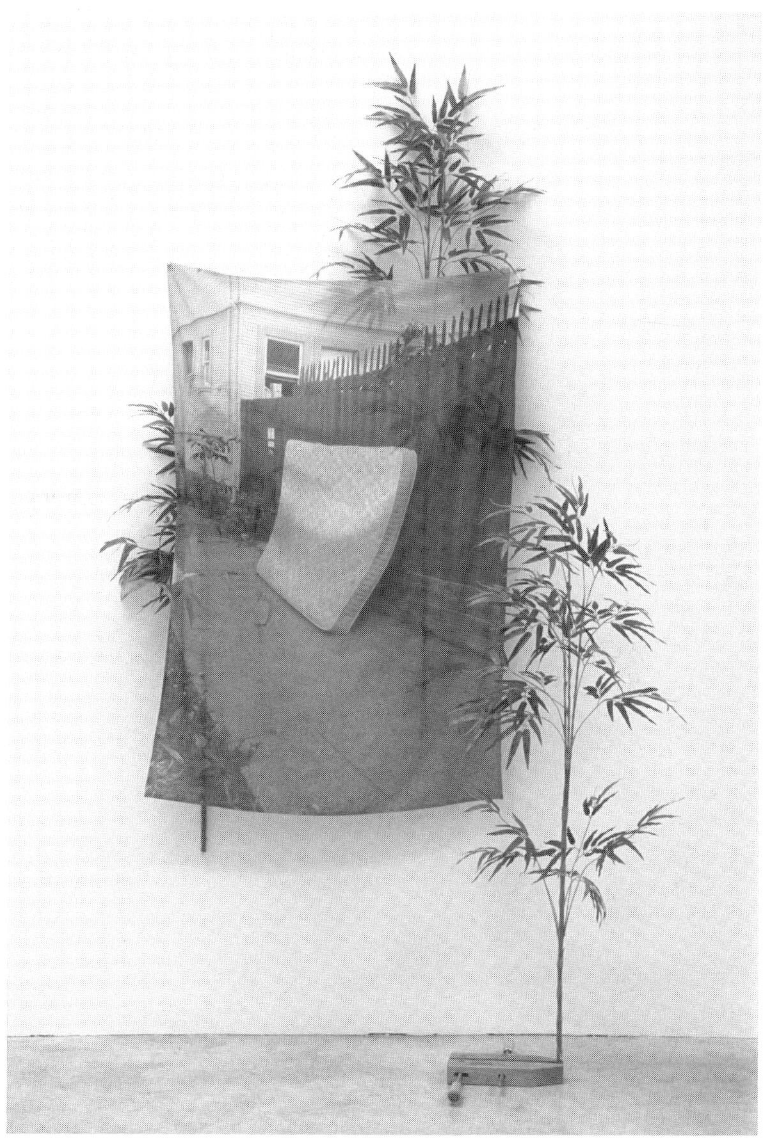

Fig. 11 Lucy Puls, *Ad Hunc Locum (Bamboo)*, 2004, 108 in × 60 in × 32 in, pigmented inkjet print on fabric, artificial plant, wood clamp, push pins. Courtesy of Stephen Wirtz Gallery and kind permission of the artist.

coherence and timelessness is fruitless and she insists that, in consideration of *particular* places, we always need to resist any seeking of a mythologised coherence of place.[6] Certainly, in the case of San Francisco, this is a difficult task – as a city on the edge of the continent, with its history of 'poet-prophets' and countercultural bohemianism, it is a conglomerate of myths, popular clichés and stereotypes. I want to be mindful, therefore, of Massey's comments when situating historical and contemporary assemblage practices within the milieu of poetic imperatives and political impulses associated with the San Francisco Bay Area.

A Bric-a-Brac Sensibility

Inevitably, Puls' work – and that of a whole range of contemporary artists based around the Bay Area – resonates with the long history of assemblage and proliferation of trash-based practices in the region.[7] Individual artists may consider their practices to have personal contexts but such practices resonate with place and past. In the 1960s, various critics and cultural commentators identified the utilisation of urban detritus and the sculptural language of assemblage as a particular characteristic of artistic practices in California and the West Coast.[8] John Coplans articulated this, for example, in an article for *Art in America* in 1964:

> Southern Californian assemblage, completely autonomous, is full of rich narrative and the closest development to true surrealist root in the American vernacular ... [9]

Coplans described Southern California as a 'natural receiver of drifters', citing John Reed as a typical 'junk assembler of pathetically absurd discards from machinery' who had wandered in and then 'disappeared from view'.[10]

After a decade of writing about Californian art for *Artforum*, Peter Plagens published his book, *The Sunshine Muse*,[11] an early exploration of the regional identity of West Coast art. Plagens was emphatic about the cultural and geographical connections – for him, place, identity and artistic production were inextricable.

> Assemblage is the first home-grown California modern art. Its materials are the cast-off, broken, charred, weathered, water-damaged, lost, forgotten, fragmentary remains of everyday life: old furniture, snapshots, newspaper headlines, dolls, dishes, glassware, beds, clothing, books, tin cans, license plates, feathers, tar, electric cord, bellows, cameras, lace, playing cards, knobs, nails and string – adhering not shiny and

whole, but piecemeal and tarnished, as melancholic memorabilia, or Draculalike social comment.[12]

Significantly, and more specifically, Plagens argued that assemblage was 'the product of a Bay Area bric-a-brac sensibility', with San Francisco as its 'natural home':

> The natural home of assemblage – its spirit more than its physical form – must be San Francisco, a wedding-cake fantasyland of tightly packed, conglomerate esthetics: ocean, hills, mansions, town houses, neoclassic granite, trolley tracks, folkisms, ethnic communities, and 'imported' culture. Its randomness is the inspiration and its gentility its target.[13]

Bruce Conner identified such a connection over a decade earlier. When William Seitz visited San Francisco in 1961 to seek out artworks for his assemblage exhibition in New York, rather than introduce him to artists, Conner took him to second-hand shops and specifically directed him to look at a laundry in Chinatown on Grant Avenue – he wanted to make the point that the city itself was like an assembled environment.[14]

Various exhibitions in the 1960s and since have highlighted and explored this connection, identifying junk assemblage with the Bay Area. A 1960 survey exhibition of Bay Area art at the San Francisco Museum of Art established the 're-association of subject matter' through 'mixed media' as a key trend. It featured the work of artists such as Jeremy Anderson, Bruce Connor, Art Grant and Roy de Forest and linked them to Dada and Surrealism.[15] Certainly by 1963, assemblage was a well-established genre: in papers related to the San Francisco Museum of Modern Art exhibition *New Directions* which surveyed recent work in the Bay Area, it was viewed as emerging in the late 1950s. The press release for a 1968 exhibition, also staged at San Francisco Museum of Modern Art Museum, referred to the 'Bay Area Neo-dada revolution' – 'a current of social comment and antiart of the mid-50s and 60s' – as one of four major influences.[16]

A range of exhibitions in the 1980s and 1990s explored and underlined the histories of what had been identified as a West Coast tradition of assemblage practice.[17] In *Lost and Found in California*, Sandra Starr claimed California as the 'birthplace' of assemblage with San Francisco and Los Angeles as key locations.[18] Starr and others traced a historical lineage of artists scavenging objects from the streets in the Bay Area.

Indeed, as early as the 1940s, Clay Spohn worked with a bizarre range of objects, culminating in the iconic *Museum of Unknown and Little Known Objects*, a quirky exhibition, more akin to a 'happening', staged at

California School of Art.[19] Albright describes Spohn's prankish humour as a comment on artistic pretentiousness, arguing that Spohn's lampooning 'set the tone for much of the funky art that was to appear in the 1950s'.[20] The array of found objects and assemblages included *Forking Events*, a collection of twisted table forks and *Mole Samplers – Mouse Seeds*, a jar filled with mouldy rice, dismantled and dispersed.

Spohn collected scrap and rubbish from bins and then displayed his objects in a museum. Refuting any suggestion that this was Dada or Surrealism, he called it 'Whimsical nature mysticism', declaring it was about the process of connecting people with objects.[21] This legendary event was, as Candida Smith comments, an early incidence of art as a process of re-assembling, revitalising, reconstituting and re-employing objects. Another early exhibition viewed as seminal by many critics was *Common Art Accumulations*, staged in 1951[22] at the Place Bar, a cafe associated with Beat culture and writers.[23]

The serious re-evaluation of the cultural production of the Beats has been a relatively recent phenomena.[24] In particular, there has been a concerted effort to situate artistic production not only within a political and social context but within a set of literary and cultural practices associated with the area. In 1990, Rebecca Solnit wrote specifically that the art of the Beat generation was still a well-kept secret.[25] She argued that West Coast assemblage was the first post-war art movement to explore popular culture. In 1995, the inter-relationship of assemblage, film and literature in the activities of East and West Coast Beats was explored extensively in an exhibition at the Whitney Museum of American Art, *Beat Culture and the New America 1950–1965*, in 1995.[26] It demonstrated the collaborative nature of the Beat movement, with assemblage – particularly on the West Coast – taking centre stage in the visual arts.

It is significant that Solnit emphasised the link between the 'outsider' status of these artists and the idiom of assemblage itself, arguing that Californian assemblage, with its use of found objects and urban detritus, challenged conventional notions of workmanship, originality and value. As Solnit puts it, at a time when paint was 'at an all-time apotheosis, assemblage artists rejected its conventions for an art which brought the dump into the gallery'.[27] Importantly, Solnit identifies assemblage and the use of junk as a metaphor for political dissent:

> … it dealt with abandonment, redefinition, juxtaposition, fragmentation and ideas of order. It proposed an order which was neither absolute nor eternal, but conditional and personal. Assemblage was an effort to come to terms with chaos – like John Cage's credo: 'not an attempt to bring order out of chaos not to suggest improvements in creation, but simply a way of waking up to the very life we are living'.[28]

Assemblage continued to dominate West Coast art into the later 1960s with 'funk art' emerging as, according to Plagens, the only direct offspring of assemblage.[29] The iconic *Funk Art* exhibition was staged at the University of Berkeley in 1967[30] and is commented on at length by James Monte in his essay 'Bagless Funk' in the catalogue for the major MoMA show, *American Sculpture of the Sixties*, of the same year.[31] Peter Selz, curator of the exhibition, included work by Conner who is often seen as the archetypal 'funk' artist – but the show embraced an eclectic range of work which was more vibrant and raunchy than dark and dirty. Writing in 1974, Plagens viewed it as prettier, more highly crafted and less soulful. For him, assemblage remained the

> most intense manifestation of the former two currents of West Coast art extant today – the 'dirties' and the 'cleans' … [32]

Outlaw Politics: Dissenting Practices?

The tendency for assemblage artists on the West Coast to self-consciously situate themselves outside the canon is a reiterated characteristic which is part of a broader discourse. California – and San Francisco and the Bay Area in particular – is articulated as a place on the geographical margins, a refuge for dissenters, drifters and scavengers. At mid-century, Starr describes the work of the first generation of assemblage artists as having 'the terrible enraged beauty of idealism betrayed'.[33] The tempering of the 'American dream' with reality produced raw, powerful work in 'an art medium that was made both for and of its time' and, for her, to be an artist was to be an outlaw from the social and economic mainstream.[34] As George Herms commented, in the paranoic atmosphere of McArthyism, being an artist meant occupying a position slightly less suspect than that of a Communist.[35]

The ecological awareness of contemporary San Francisco, with its city-wide commitment to recycling projects and environmental clean-up policies,[36] was evident at mid-century too. In a questionnaire sent out to artists in 1960, Art Grant noted his occupation as 'beach-comber' and himself as 'the worlds most foremost authority on creating, tracing and recycling discards into art'.[37]

Since the 1960s, many other West Coast artists such as Mike Kelley have displayed strong affinities with 'thrift-store aesthetics' and this has often been viewed in a political context. In 1995, the curators of the exhibition *Fabricators* suggested that there were two vital directions available to young sculptors of the day: technology (information, light/kinetics) offered one avenue whereas the other was a kind of 'thrift-store aesthetic' which drew on an amalgam of characteristic Bay Area sensibilities in which, according to them, 'beat' and 'funk' were central:

> Alvarez, Hernandez, Pokorny and Rollman, among others, are evolving a Bay Area aesthetic that recognizes the region's Funk (Robert Arneson, William T Wiley), Beat (Georg Herms, Bruce Conner) and conceptual (Terry Fox, David Ireland) ancestry, with a nod to Fluxus and Arte Povera as well…[38]

Although identified as quintessentially postmodern, Alvarez, Hernandez, Pokorny and Rollman were viewed as drawing on historical narratives of trash-based practice in the Bay Area:

> they paw through the detritus of the industrial world from recyclable materials which, when scavenged and reinvented, argue for an aesthetic of self-mocking, irony-drenched celebration of decline…[39]

The consequences and particularities of regional geography were addressed by Plagens in the 1970s when he concluded that whilst Los Angeles art acknowledged art developments in New York, the Bay Area went its own way, with its own particular countercultural history and 'outsider' rhetoric. This dissenting strategy was self-fulfilling to some degree as, even by the end of the 1970s, with just a few exceptions such as Bruce Conner,[40] the West Coast assemblage artists remained little known more generally even in the USA.[41]

In relation to discourses of dissent and artistic production, the writings of Jacques Rancière may be useful here. In *The Politics of Aesthetics*, Rancière re-examines the correlation between politics and art and discusses the notion of 'dissensus'. Addressing the notion of 'politicised art', he rejects the concept of 'committed art' as nonsensical, arguing that a person may be committed but an art object cannot.

> The core of the problem is that there are no criteria for establishing an appropriate correlation between the politics of aesthetics and the aesthetics of politics… There are only choices… There are formulas that are equally available whose meaning is often in fact decided upon by a state of conflict that is exterior to them.[42]

He goes on to write of art relating to 'acts of constructing political dissensus', dissensus being, for him, a 'disturbance of the sensible' whereby

> it creates a fissure in the sensible order by confronting the established framework of perception, thought and action with the inadmissible.[43]

Michel de Certeau's ideas on forms, systems and methods of resistance might also be related to a consideration of 'dissenting' artforms. De

Certeau writes about alternative methods of social exchange and diversionary practices and tactics – such as 'the gift', 'potlatch' and the French labour practice of 'perruque' – as undermining the free market and wage labour system. These makeshift practices are a 'making-do' of artisan-like inventiveness[44] which contributes to what Rancière might call a 'culture of dissensus' – the 'sensible order of things' is undermined and 'tricked'.[45] In this way, de Certeau asserts

> … here order is *tricked* by an art. Into the institution to be served are thus insinuated styles of social exchange, technical invention, and moral resistance, that is, an economy of the '*gift*' (generosities for which one expects a return), an esthetics of '*tricks*' (artists' operations) and an ethics of *tenacity* (countless ways of refusing to accord the established order the status of a law, a meaning, or a fatality) … […] … the politics of the 'gift' *also* becomes a diversionary tactic … [46]

For de Certeau, such diversionary tactics become acts and practices which potentially disturb the free market system.

How does West Coast assemblage engage with such discourses of dissent? Was there what Jacques Rancière terms a 'culture of dissensus' – and does the contemporary proliferation of work which utilises everyday waste and obsolescence correlate with a form of politics? Can these practices be viewed as diversionary tactics which disturb the sensible order of things?

Alongside 'dissensus', how might Bay Area trash assemblage engage with the poetic? In 1961, William Seitz wrote of assemblage as a 'Zen Buddhist' encounter. In 1974, in the catalogue for *Poets of the Cities – New York and San Francisco 1950–65*, Lana Davies referred to this in a pioneering exhibition which was one of the first serious attempts to understand the philosophy of the Beats and its relationship to poetics and art.[47] Davies identified the 'epiphany of the everyday'[48] in the assemblages of Rauschenberg. She cites John Cage's point that 'everything is a poetry of infinite possibilities' reflecting Heidegger's idea that artworks disclose the essential nature and structure of a whole world.[49] In this way, assemblage has the capacity to offer a perception of essences which are transcendent – they act as conduits to something 'other', beyond their physical materiality and properties.

This idea of finding 'epiphany in the everyday' is present in some Beat writings which have a kind of ecstatic radicalism. Allan Ginsberg's iconic poem *Howl*, for example, is concerned with the insurgent imagination – the expansion of consciousness through the creation of a quasi-religious or apocalyptic vision. Its meditative litany refers to the debased, the impoverished and the vernacular. Epiphanic approaches to the mundane and a transcendental and ecstatic apprehension of the everyday are an important poetic sensibility which carries through from Walt Whitman to the Beats. A spiritual dimension is added to this through readings on Buddhism: satori – the wholeness and lack of ego proposed by oriental philosophy – might be the seeking of other consciousness through whatever means. Albright refers to artists and poets seeking a new 'concreteness' related to Zen, which would transcend mere imagery and metaphor, citing these lines by Jack Spicer,

> I would like the moon in my poems to be a real moon, one which would suddenly be covered with a cloud that has nothing to do with the poem.[50]

So, how did poetics and politics align and intersect in Bay Area assemblage and do they continue to resonate today?

Histories and Cultures of Contrariness

> Myth and debunk dance together in the spectacle…[51]

San Francisco is a city which evokes civility and utopianism: its discourse is one of contrariness, always speaking of itself as 'other'. For Kevin Starr, the founding metaphor of San Francisco is the urban metaphor itself. He writes of its historical and geographical isolation giving rise to a peculiar self-absorption and narcissism, of a long-standing impulse for the city to be self-envisioning and self-determining. Here is an enabling city of imagination and dreams whereby the recurring rhetoric is one of utopia, a particularly persistent symbolic identity.[52] San Francisco's position on the edge of the continent is significant. Nineteenth-century writers had written of the history of isolation affecting the growth of the city, its independence, individuality and originality.

San Francisco's self-envisioning as dissenting has been reiterated extensively and cultural practices – music, poetry and art in particular – are key elements cited in this construction. Nancy Peters, for example, utilises mythic terminology, describing it as a city with a 'contrarian spirit' – 'resistant authority and control'.[53] A long history of alternative radical politics, of 'counterculture', is well documented.[54] The city has a history of working-class politics with intense labour struggles in the 1930s when it became a haven for communists, anarchists and 'Wobblies'. By 1934, building on nineteenth-century Bohemian roots, a pre-war 'underground' culture of over 700 artists had been established, later fostered by conscientious objectors' camps of writers and artists in the 1940s.[55]

In 'The Making of Counterculture', the San Francisco poet Kenneth Rexroth wrote of the city's traditions of anarcho-syndicalism and pacifism and its longstanding 'alternative' status in terms of art, literature and politics, emphasising that these developments easily predate Beat culture.[56] Rexroth, a key figure in articulating and shaping the idea of San Francisco as a 'dissenting city', arrived in 1927. He argued that poetry should have a moral and political significance; his *Thou shalt not kill*, a polemic against consumer culture, has been viewed as a precursor to Ginsberg's *Howl*. For Rexroth, coming from an anarchist tradition, the city was a teeming metropolis of labourers and artists, against the backdrop of the Sierras. Rexroth's romantic envisionings of San Francisco were partly based on his own experience, such as working on WPA mural projects, but they were also founded on his utopian goals for creating an alternative society, later espoused in 'Communalism: From its origins to the twentieth century'.[57]

Interviewed by poet David Meltzer in the 1960s, Rexroth argued that San Francisco had escaped a Puritan ethos through being settled by 'rascally and anarchistic types' and that this – and, significantly, its Asian heritage – defined the city's marginality.[58] In his poetry he always stressed the city's 'otherness'.[59] In 1957, Rexroth wrote that rather than merely boasting an underground culture like other cities, in San Francisco, 'otherness' was mainstream. As he commented,

It is dominant, almost all there is.[60]

So the context of contrariness and political radicalism was established well before the New Bohemians – the 'poet-hipsters'[61] – converged on San Francisco in the mid-1950s to become part of the 'fictive history' of the Beats.[62] James Brook has written of this dreamy visionary city having a 'poetic impulse' – characterised by a boom-bust mentality, from the Gold Rush and catastrophic earthquakes to the 'dotcom' boom. This provided hospitality to poets and propelled the body impolitic towards riots and spontaneous demonstration.[63] Much of this romanticising and mythologizing narrative is anecdotal and apocryphal and, as Michael Davidson commented in his study of the San Francisco Poetry Renaissance,[64] we need to be conscious of 'how a certain literary subject was inventing itself through representations of freedom, emancipation and participation'.[65] Undoubtedly, there is a need to question the authorial voice in these 'contrary histories' as the writers were often complicit in the events. Kerouac's fictional alter-egos embodied the independence he could never obtain himself and, as Davidson indicates, the same applies to 'Kenneth Rexroth's vision of the engaged proletarian artist and Robert Duncan's projection of a heavenly city of art'.[66]

Davidson contends that Beat rhetoric is often cast in terms of transcendence but he argues that the necessity behind this was social.[67] The Beats were a disparate heterodox group of individuals with no common formal critique or political programme. Generally, they eschewed official institutionalised forms of protest, rejected party affiliations and stressed individual over group actions. Despite individualist aspects of the Beats though, Davidson argues that, collectively, they offer one of the most public instances of a countercultural tendency. Even if they became 'fictive history' in the 1990s, they were certainly viewed at the time, and since, as 'dissenting' poets.[68] They may have lacked a 'programme' but sexual politics and the politics of obscenity were overt. Clearly, as Peter Selz indicates in his recent study, *Art of Engagement*,[69] a number of artists and poets – for example, Robert Duncan, Jack Spicer and Jess – were exploring gay identity through their work. Duncan's remarkable essay, 'The homosexual in society' published in 1944, is a case in point.[70]

Furthermore, in the mid-1950s, there were connections and collaborations between artists, poets and writers who shared a critical language and social values. Regular collaborators included assemblage artists Jay De Feo, Wally Berman, Joan Brown, Wally Hendrick and Bruce Conner. A community of artists and poets shared readings and multimedia events at places such as Lawrence Ferlinghetti's bookshop City Lights which opened in 1953. Arriving in San Francisco in 1954, Ginsberg famously performed his incantatory *Howl* the following year at the Six Gallery.[71]

Briefly then, in the mid-1950s, there was a kind of coalescence of art, poetics and politics. At the time, William Seitz certainly viewed the Beats as politically effective symbolically. In recent assessments, both Richard Candida Smith and Peter Selz have argued that, although the artists and poets of the 1950s around the Beats contributed little to a critique of poverty or to the civil rights movement directly, the ideas expressed through their art and poetry played a vital role in fostering dialogue on issues related to sexuality and gender construction, capital punishment, ecology and the Vietnam war. Collectively, their work signified an oppositionality and created a symbolic mythic – if not actual – alternative community. In Rancière's terms, it 'disturbed the sensible order' and contributed to a 'culture of dissensus'.

In the 1960s, San Francisco established itself as *the* countercultural capital of post-war USA. Haight Ashbury in particular, a district in decline, became a site for oppositional communities such as The Diggers[72] – a group which emerged in 1966 from the San Francisco Mime Troupe. They were instigated by the mythic figure Emmett Grogan[73] who insisted on his own anonymity as a diversionary tactic. The Diggers had a hotchpotch philosophy of social anarchism and direct action; they employed guerrilla theatre, arguing for a 'university of the streets' and working to erase the boundary between art and life. Strategies included bartering and the daily distribution of free food – if anyone gave them money, they burnt it. The Free Food Theatre evolved into the Frame of Reference, 'a free store, brimming over with liberated goods to be shared with whoever needed them'.[74]

> The Diggers are hip to property – everything is free – do your own thing – human beings are the means of exchange – food, machines, clothing, materials, shelter and props are simply there … when materials are free, imagination becomes currency for spirit …[75]

The detritus of the city provided raw materials for a series of happenings, as Grogan recounts one particular Haight event:

> … two hundred car mirrors were removed from wrecks in the junk-yard … Now posters were silently distributed and 3–4000 people chanted the streets belong to the people …[76]

On garbage, Grogan condemned the communally organised 'clean-ups' as pathetic as he argued that the real trash was ignored.

> People are USING it, picking it up FREE on the streets, living on it, they no longer respond to the seduction of the state, there's no way to get a HOLD on them.[77]

Often mistakenly viewed as a footnote to hippie history,[78] they offered no moral direction or social revolutionary imperatives. For the Diggers, street-scavenging epitomised a Californian self-made community which took joy in making something from nothing; it also reflected collective re-sistance to a commodity exchange culture based on money. The idea that the free exchange of materials, goods and services would create alterna-tive power bases independent of state systems and would lead to a series of uprisings was optimistic to say the least. However, such confrontational practices were diversionary; they were against the sensible order of things in every way and contributed further to the entrenchment of an encultur-ated dissensus.[79]

The Diggers were just one brief episode in the countercultural histo-ries of San Francisco. Some of the earliest anti-war and anti-draft demon-strations were in Berkeley; from around 1966, there were struggles for civil and gay rights and the developments of the African-American and Asian-American rights movements: identity politics and the immigrant experi-ence have been at the heart of a number of struggles in which San Francisco has played a major role.

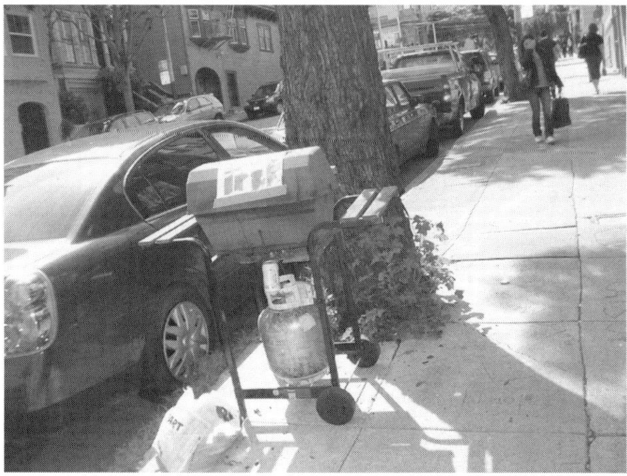

Fig. 12 Discarded object left on pavement for free exchange in Haight Ashbury, San Francisco, April 2006. Photograph by the author.

But were these contexts of 'contrariness' and 'cultures of dissensus' reflected more specifically in assemblage practices? How did the idiom of junk assemblage engage with narratives of dissent?

Assemblage in the 1950s and 1960s

In the late 1980s, Sandra Starr equated Californian assemblage with Dada – not for the use of trash, but because she identified their shared sense of disgust with the world at large. For Starr, with a backdrop of the Korean War and the Cold War, Californian assemblage raged against Rockwell's nostalgic American dream, racial segregation, sexual repression, hypocrisy, platitude, euphemism, conformism and censorship.[80]

Looking back in the 1980s, Gordon Wagner, who had been making art out of detritus since the 1940s,[81] talked extensively about the character of assemblage on the West Coast and its jumble of influences. Wagner started making small beach-combed assemblages in 1948 when he lived beneath the pier amongst the beach community at Hermosa Beach. For Wagner, the dump was the only place to understand civilisation – especially in California where whole towns grew up quickly, then were abandoned with everything in them, offering a treasure trove of objects.[82] Foraging on the beach and streets, he talked about the production of what he termed 'poetic assemblage' and 'protest assemblage', referring to works made from the debris of the Watts riots by Noah Purifoy and others.[83] Wagner explained that 'poetic assemblages' were like amulets or fetishes as they provoked feelings, whereas 'protest assemblage' might involve burning or trapping objects and was about agony, disaster, greed, lust and hunger. For him, there were also erotic, humorous and spiritually themed objects.[84]

Wagner also emphasised that the 'funkiness and kitsch' of Mexican culture appealed to many artists in the 1960s. He spent six months in Patzcua collecting junk and visiting cemeteries, describing the whole place as a junk environment of 'campy stuff':

> … taxicabs with pushing-on brakes, animal heads lighting up in the back … and dicecube gearsticks … mythical spectacle … of symbology, objects and assemblage.… The whole place was like an assemblage, Mexico. It was like walking through a giant assemblage …[85]

Wagner – like Conner later – produced a series of works inspired by Mexican culture. Candida Smith probes Wagner's motivations, asking if all this represented a romanticisation of non-Western cultures or a critique of American life. Wagner viewed them as a kind of contemporary fetish, a search for roots rather than social critique.[86]

The erotic content – 'love objects' – identified by Wagner was another key feature of Bay Area art. A reviewer of an exhibition at San Francisco Museum of Modern Art in 1969 commented that four key artists – Jeremy Anderson, Fred Martin, William Wiley and Robert Hudson – had

> … dynamically influenced the Bay Area's current crop of artists, most noticeably in recent developments flavoured by the dada-surreal, symbolist mythic projections and the protest forms of kitsch and funk …[87]

In particular, Plagens saw Anderson as a 'bridge' because his work, with its bulbous vulgar forms, connected the surrealist strains of the late 1940s with 1960s Pop and Funk.[88]

Art Grant, whose assemblages featured in *A Look at Recent Bay Area Art*, an exhibition of Bay Area Art in 1960 which included Jeremy Anderson and Bruce Conner, brought an ecological approach to using junk for art. Involved in lots of educational projects, Grant used mixed media and found objects to create pieces such as *Homage to a Dirty Agitator* and *A Rock and Roll Wiggly Jiggly Twirly Toy*,[89] and his *Instant Zoo*, a menagerie of objets trouvés.[90] Consumer waste was a major concern for him:

> The average American throws away seven and a half pounds of trash or garbage or junk or scrap everyday. Now if you multiply seven and a half times three hundred and sixty five days of the year times, say, the three million people who live in the San Francisco Bay area – you are going to get a heck of a lot of junk.[91]

A number of assemblage artists had close associations: Bruce Conner, Joan Brown, Carlos Villa and Georg Herms were based in San Francisco and collaborated on various projects with writers and poets.[92] The artist Jess was the partner of poet Robert Duncan; Wallace Berman was a close associate of Michael McLure and David Meltzer. John Coplans regarded Berman as a key figure:

> The California assemblage movement stems from one artist, Wallace Berman... Berman is a major link to the existential and surreal poets, dramatists and writers, and helped establish assemblage as a poetic art with strong moral overtones in California. The genuine and very real spiritual overtones in his work are mixed with an incredibly raw existential wit, expressed with great simplicity and directness.[93]

Herms' objects had erotic and spiritual overtones but, unlike Berman, they were not to do with the cabala but were to do with 'love', his adopted signature.[94] Described by Wagner as a 'true bohemian', Berman was a producer of 'poetic assemblage' who acquired mythic status as an underground cult figure. In 1957, he was living in an assembled environment on Hermosa Beach, a small seaside town outside Los Angeles. The year after, he moved to a ramshackle shack in Larkspur where he harvested and accumulated objects from the beach.[95] In the 1960s, various critics described him as a 'poet-alchemist', interested in the 'cosmic rightness of things' and as a romantic artist, 'anarchistic and absolutely apolitical'.[96] For Plagens, he was 'the first *real* hippy artist':

> where Conner's work is a fluoroscope of bestiality and futility, Herms's assemblages offer hope – expressed in his ubiquitous motto, 'Art is Love is God' – affected but sincere Cornellian expressions of cosmic influence and astrological kindness, as in the *Zodiac* boxes.[97]

In an act which might be viewed as 'diversionary' and 'against the sensible order of things', he installed an array of assemblages in his *Secret Exhibition* on a strip of land where houses had been razed to the ground. Described as the 'ultimate recycler',[98] he left them to be taken, destroyed or to decay.

One of the most important Bay Area assemblage artists, Bruce Conner, has continued to maintain his 'outsider status' through a range of political contexts.[99] He practised a politics of anonymity and used his work to explore notions of personal and social identity: echoing Grogan's tactics, he refused to sign work for a period in the 1960s[100] and created a set of buttons when he ran for supervisor of San Francisco city in 1967, inscribed 'I am Bruce Conner' and 'I am not Bruce Conner'.[101]

Conner described himself as radical rather than political and always rejected being categorised as an 'engaged artist'.[102] At the inaugural show at the opening of the Batman Gallery, the press release declared a ban on 'all imitators and cocktail painters', describing Conner's work as an

> intense grappling with the harmony of pure beauty and the break-through to a fiery consciousness of human injustice and a deep anarchic humour. The show is monumental and extremely shocking. A new lyricism in art.[103]

Violation of the individual and acts of social violence were common themes. Conner was fascinated with the debris of society, household garbage and unwanted objects gathered from thrift stores.[104] He embraced the 'trash-heap' completely: in an exhibition in 1964, he listed one of his works as *Temptation of St Barbey Google (trash)*, with 'trash' specified as the medium.[105] In contrast with Rauschenberg, a 'painterly collagiste', Conner had little interest in cubist collage, viewing his work as more 'to do with theatre'.[106] Conner's appropriation of objects was theatrical: it presented revolting imagery, unutterable horrors, brutality and melancholic despair. Repugnant objects and 'formless' materials resemble charred flesh and allude to violent forms of death. Philip Leider highlighted this in 1962, writing on Conner's *Oven*, a squat box with a small aperture at the front,

> Clinging to this mouth of the oven are a scattering of human, or human-appearing, hairs, tightly curled, tough, immediately pubic in association. The simultaneous evocation of the crematories and the erotic charges the atmosphere with depthless evil – and guilt. But the piece, hideous in the extreme, speaks a language universal to this generation, contains a logic we understand only too well. The point is not simply an ugly pun, turning on the slang word 'oven' for the female genitalia. It refers to an even more murky connecting between the sexual and the maniacal, the never-ending dark dialogue of sexual sickness and the social sickness.[107]

Some of Conner's assemblages had specific political narratives: for example, *The Child*, of 1959, presents a grotesque child effigy, modelled in wax and entwined with nylon. This referred directly to the execution of Caryl Chessman, who claimed he had been forced to sign a confession under police brutality after being arrested for rape and robbery in Los Angeles. Widespread protest ensued and the sculpture reflects his strong opposition to the death penalty. Conner's *Black Dhalia* 1960, which also directly related to a murder case,[108] has been viewed as misogynistic.

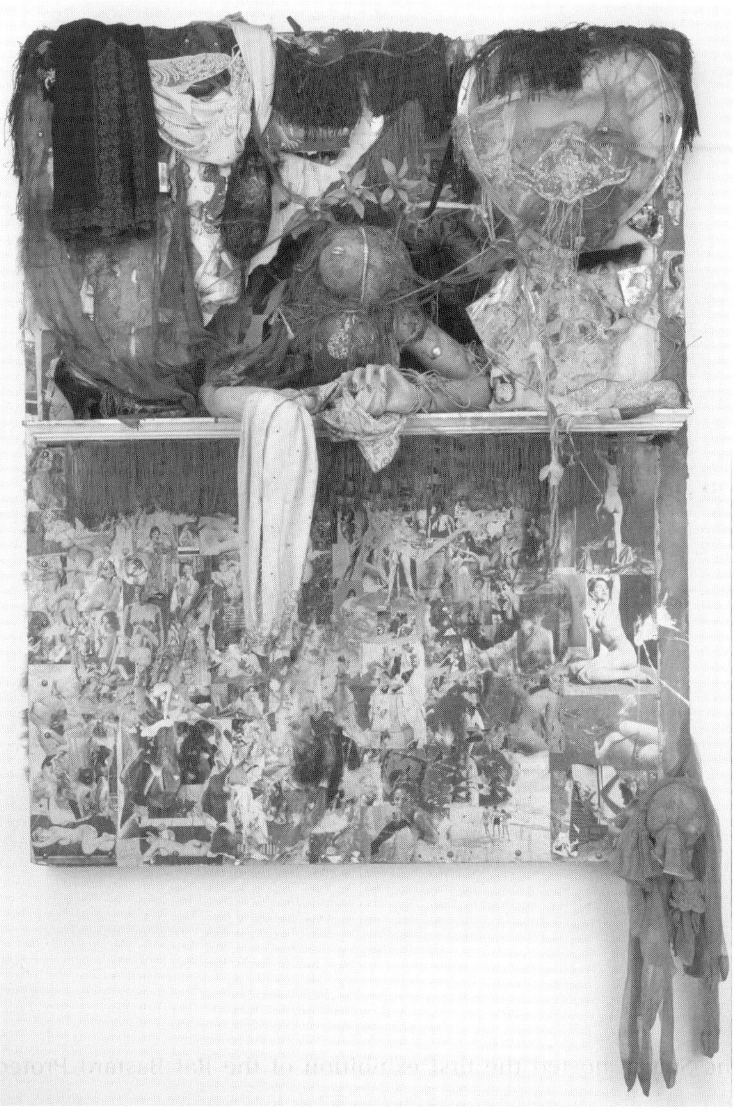

Fig. 13 Bruce Conner, *Looking Glass,* 1964, mixed media, 153.67 cm × 121.92 cm × 36.83 cm, San Francisco Museum of Modern Art. Gift of the Modern Art Council © Estate of Bruce Conner and with kind permission of the Conner Family Trust.

However, like the work of Berman, they should be seen as engaging criti-cally with sexual politics and the politics of obscenity and pornography.

His pendulous assemblages of torn soiled nylon and formless objects also have gothic surrealist qualities. Rebecca Solnit links the air of vio-lence, rot and decay in Conner's objects directly to the slow annihilation of the Victorian houses in the Western Addition, a black neighbourhood whose 'decline-and-fall romanticism' fascinated many artists in San Francisco.[109] Additionally, like Wagner, Conner was particularly interested in the Californian encounter with Mexican culture and with the diverse roots of what he called the 'natural folk art' of contemporary America.[110]

The activities of these Bay Area assemblage artists, working with the detritus of society, contributed to an alternative culture of dissensus. Ad-ditionally, they shared a conscious resistance to the commodification of art and its developing markets through involvement in artist-run galleries. Peter Selz believes that these were a key factor in engendering forms of artistic expression which were not locked into art as a commercial enter-prise. Indeed, he argues, they thoroughly rejected the 'market-driven or-thodoxy of New York City'.[111]

Spatsa Gallery, set up by Dmitri Grachis on Filbert Street, was typical of a series of small artist-run anti-commercial galleries.[112] Originally a small garage, the first show featured four artists: Joan Brown, Bruce Conner, Wally Hedrick and Peter Forakis. Hedrick was one of the first artists to use his practice to oppose the Vietnam War. The Spatsa belonged to a lineage of galleries around Fillmore Street; the King Ubu Gallery had been started up in 1952 by the poet Robert Duncan and his male partner and artist, Jess. Others were Metart Gallery (1949–50), the Six Gallery (1954–8) and later the Dilexi and Batman which were less experimental and more commer-cial.[113] Before King Ubu Gallery opened, Brown, De Feo and Hedrick all showed their work in coffee houses on North Beach and at City Lights and The Place. The co-operative Six Gallery was set up by Jack Spicer and Wally Hedrick as a space for poetry readings and art, achieving a wave of pub-licity through Kerouac's fictionalised references to Ginsberg's reading of *Howl* in *The Dharma Bums*.

The Spatsa hosted the first exhibition of the Rat Bastard Protective Association, a group set up by Conner for

> people who were making things with the detritus of society, who themselves were ostracised or alienated from full involvement with society.[114]

The Society, named after the San Francisco refuse collectors, included poet Michael McLure and artists Jay De Feo, Joan Brown, Wally Hedrick, Alvin Light, Manuel Neri and Carlos Villa. For Natsoulos, it represented an ironic comment on their own marginal foraging existences that, in turn, were commentaries on the affluent post-war world.[115] Its acronym – RBP – was a witty reference to the Pre-Raphaelite Brotherhood and, mimicking the rituals of an exclusive club, individuals paid membership fees and artworks were authenticated with a rubber 'stamp of approval'.[116] Conner showed his piece *Superhuman Devotion* at Spatsa and, in a further act of discarding, threw it in the sea from the Staten Island ferry. In another event, they hoisted a coffin along Grant Avenue as Conner recounted,

> One time the Rat Bastards and Dave Hazelwood and the poets decided to organize a parade through North Beach with banners and standards. It was totally unannounced and all of a sudden there were about two hundred people walking down Grant Avenue and across Broadway…[117]

Society members extended the 'rat' metaphor into environmental installations. Conner made a series of rat pieces and covered a ceiling with fur, using scavenged materials. Although there was no particular RBP style: as Whitney Chadwick noted, there was

> an ambience of decay, visual richness and multiple cultural associations endemic to funk art.[118]

An exploration of ethnicity was a central aspect of Carlos Villa's manipulations of pulp, gauze, feathers, bones and hair. For Villa, certainly since the 1970s, the assertion of ethnic difference, and chicano culture in particular, has been the focus of his practice.[119] Fellow RBP member Joan Brown, later known for her obsessive paintings of cats, created *Fur Rat* in 1962, an oversized, more funky than scary, rodent studded with nails (Fig. 15).[120]

Conner's work explored the metaphorical rot at the heart of post-war culture – militarism and commodification of women and sex. Rebecca Solnit has written of Conner's work revealing the beauty of an atomic explosion and the pathos of pornography with a sense of horror. His macabre still lives, of scavenged trinkets and shards of mirror glass, have an ambience of gothic decay – but she places them in a lineage of folk art rather than Dada.[121]

By the mid-1960s a genealogy of Californian assemblage artists and junk sculptors was firmly established but, initially at least, theirs was a set of art practices which identified itself, and was identified by others, as outside the mainstream – this was *contrary* practice. The problems of evaluating the political nature of a range of diverse practices and artists are many. Later memoirs reveal the inner crisis and conflict which quickly surfaced as these artists were drawn into the marketplace. Joan Brown remained highly critical of the artistic 'I' which had replaced the 'we'. David Meltzer

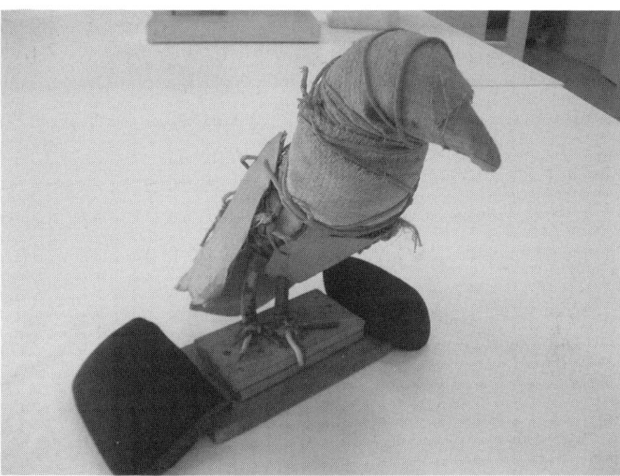

Fig. 14 Joan Brown, *Untitled (Bird)* 1957–60, cardboard, fabric, string, wood, and electric wire. The sculpture is seen here undergoing treatment in the conservation lab at San Francisco Museum of Modern Art in 2006. Photograph by the author, reproduced with permission of San Francisco Museum of Modern Art and Gallery Paule Anglim.

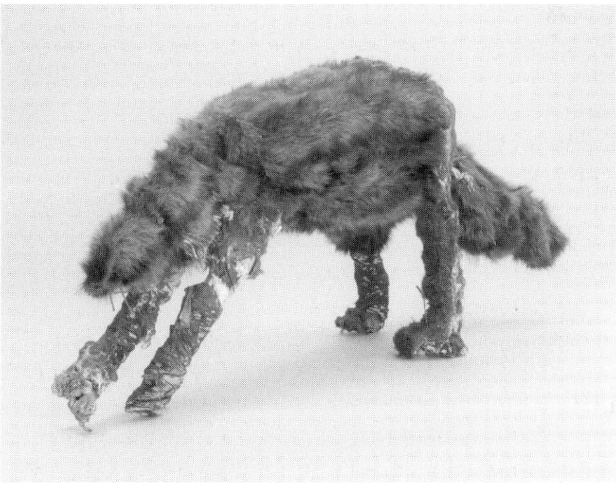

Fig. 15 Joan Brown, *Fur Rat, 1962*. Wood, chicken wire, plaster, raccoon fur 52.1 cm × 137.2 cm. Kind permission of University of California, Berkeley Art Museum and Pacific Film Archive and Gallery Paule Anglim.

felt that in the 1950s, artists and poets had joined together to form a community which shared transcendent goals. In the 1970s, he was fiercely critical of the market-mentality which trivialised those experiences, arguing that the original project which artists and poets had embarked upon in the 1950s had gone awry.[122]

Claims of lost authenticity by individual participants need to be viewed with scepticism: retrospective and nostalgic accounts are part of the process of subjective mythmaking and romanticising. However, the 'visual politics' of California, as Peter Selz and Susan Landauer have suggested, is embedded and enculturated.[123] Richard Candida Smith argues in *Utopia and Dissent* that poets and artists did operate and engage in a politic context. They redefined the boundaries between public and private and, by insisting upon public expression of experiences that had previously been seen as entirely personal, this was political in itself. As Smith comments, the utopian and the foolish intermingle so closely that it was, and remains, easy to dismiss their activities as irrelevant. However, I would ally with his view that artists and poets did have symbolic importance in the developing contention and conflicts and that acts of personal transgression challenged structures of public order.[124]

Contemporary Culture of Dissensus and Empire of Scrounge

Historical cultural narratives inform the present in odd ways. Kathryn Spence and Lucy Puls, referred to at the outset of this chapter, are two contemporary artists who work in the Bay Area with obsolete materials. They do not 'represent' San Francisco artists in any way: Spence was born in Germany but chooses to live and work in San Francisco because of the particular culture of the city; Puls has lived in the Bay Area since the early 1980s.[125] Nevertheless, their individual practices resonate with the political and poetic impulses of the city – with its 'culture of dissensus' – in oblique ways and forms (see Figs. 11 and 16).

Spence's range of furry, feathered and fabric-bundled animals and birds are deceptive. They evoke playful responses but have serious themes. Besides obsolete objects and thrift store finds, her practice utilises waste, slime and mud but not in an exploration of 'the abject'. They do explore 'formlessness' but their source of interest is taxonomy and methodologies of classification. Spence creates ambiguous objects which subvert classification. Poignantly though, the series of pigeons she made from street mud echo Joan Brown's feral *Pigeon*, a pathetic bundle of string and paper which she made in the 1950s (Fig. 14). Spence's abandoned objects also express a pathos with social problems endemic to the area surrounding her studio in the Mission District where illegal immigrants queue up

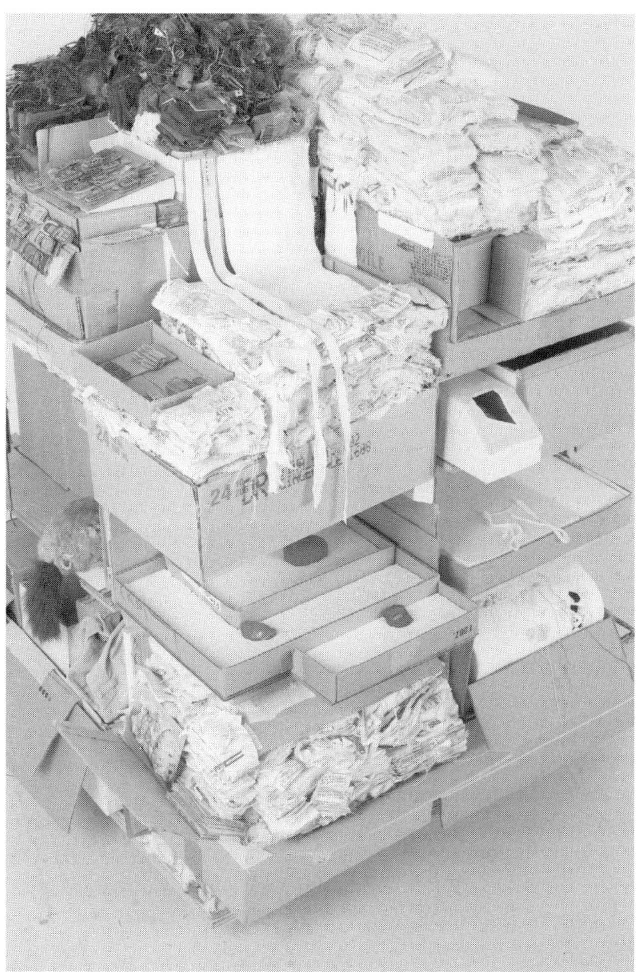

Fig. 16 Kathryn Spence, *Untitled* (detail), 2005–6. Cardboard, plywood, thread, ink, bobby pins, pillow feathers, towel scraps, clothing remnants, paper, safety pins, bed sheets, 'How to Wash' labels, 'Do Not Remove' labels, upholstery and mattress tags, photographs, magazines, paper towels, cell phone advertisements, toy squirrel, styrofoam, string, cotton batting. 56 × 46 × 49 inches. Courtesy of Stephen Wirtz Gallery and kind permission of the artist.

everyday for work.[126] Studio space is difficult to find but, in an echo of the Digger mentality, she and other artists consciously use a bartering system, exchanging artwork and services rather than paying rent in a small but significant De Certeau-esque 'diversionary tactic' which serves to undermine the money-based system of commodity exchange.

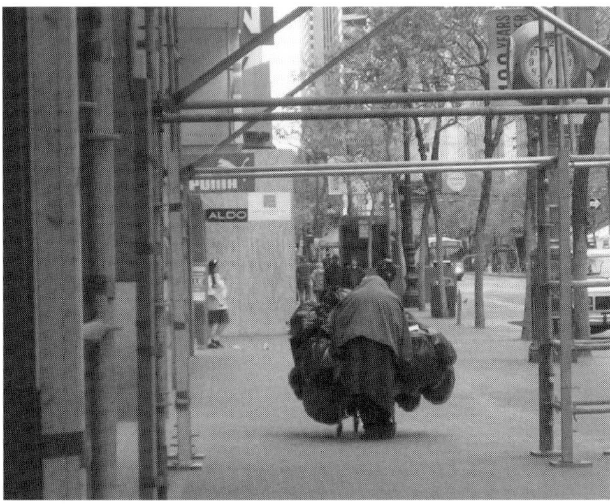

Fig. 17 A homeless person pushing bundled possessions through the streets of San Francisco, April 2006. Photograph by the author.

Spence creates her 'homeless animals' as part of a strategy to work with materials and forms which echo the destitute on the streets.[127] The ambiguous bundles in the studio are analogous with the homeless population bound in plastic and cardboard, trudging with their shopping trolleys of salvaged garbage through the streets of Berkeley (Fig. 17).[128]

Finally, I want to return to Puls' work in the light of the histories and narratives of dissent discussed. Besides thrift stores and garage sales, she uses things which people leave out on the pavement with instructions for passersby to take them. In a series of photoworks, she records the estranged objects *in situ*. Puls also locates things for her assemblages through extensive use of the online community at *craigs list*[129]: there, she targets objects which people want to give away. Both in the neighbourhood and online, these 'gifts-in-waiting' offer new forms of rogue economic practice and offer a different form of participatory politics.

Nicolas Bourriaud has identified and theorised a sharing culture and an increasing shift towards participatory modes of practice – exemplified by the forms of exchange found on *craigs list*. He has outlined the possibility of a relational art concerned with human interaction and its social contexts rather than the assertion of independent, private symbolic space associated with modernism, and argues that the 1990s has witnessed a growing trend for DIY communities attempting to circumvent capitalist economic contexts and undermine official systems.[130] Although theirs are individual acts of artistic endeavour, Spence and Puls engage with a discourse of collaboration and their work can be positioned within these modes of 'relational' practice.

San Francisco is a place which has witnessed a complicated and inter-linked cultural and economic history bound up with narratives of counterculture and dissent. I return to Doreen Massey, who warns against

> a view of space as bounded, as in various ways a site of an authenticity, as singular, fixed and unproblematic in its identity[131]

As she argues, we must always think of identities of place as 'unfixed, contested and multiple' with their particularities constructed not by boundaries but by a mix of links and interconnectedness to that beyond. Places viewed this way, she asserts, are 'open and porous' – always in a state of becoming.[132] The art critic and environmental activist, Rebecca Solnit, has, extensively and eloquently, examined the cultural histories and the intersection of art and politics of San Francisco. In *Hollow City*, she deplores the displacement of its radical past by dotcommers and property speculators and argues for a re-valuing of 'a kind of urban free space in which ideas circulate'. As she says,

> The life of the imagination is now more critical than ever.[133]

Despite its transformation, San Francisco remains contradictory and conflictual. It is, following Massey's line of argument, in a state of becoming – but at the core, its contrariness endures. Perhaps this means that rather than a re-engagement with politics in a narrow sense, cultural practices are embedded in the political in a much more diffuse but fundamental way. Participative rather than polemical, the work of Spence and Puls enables us, in divergent ways, to reflect on both the historical and contemporary cultures of dissensus and the poetic impulses of San Francisco.

CHAPTER FOUR
The 'Comedy of Waste': A Load of British Rubbish

Introduction: Counterworlds and Mirth

Junk Culture is city art. Its source is obsolescence, the throwaway materials of cities, as it collects in drawers, cupboards, attics, dustbins, gutters, waste lots and city dumps … Junk culture rests, not on esoteric fetishes, but on *the comedy of waste*… [1]

The joke is made, comedy is found – in persons above all, and only by extension in objects, situations and the like.[2]

My old man's a dustman,
He wears a dustman's hat
He wears cor-blimey trousers
And he lives in a council flat …[3]

The comic, at its most intense, as in folly, presents a counterworld, an upside-down World ….[4]

For centuries, art has employed humour as a political tool, from the satirical caricature heads of Honoré Daumier to the subversive practices of Dada photomontage and cabaret. Indeed, more recently, comic forms have become such common ploys that they might be considered to be part of the battery of postmodern clichés. As Judith Olch Richards points out in her introduction to the exhibition catalogue *Situation Comedy: Humour in Recent Art*, artists have injected a wide range of forms of humour – including irony and slapstick – to break down barriers of taste, question authority and encourage laughter in the museum environment – a place where, even now, it is often unheard.[5] Contemporary practice, such as that of Bob and Roberta Smith and David Robbins, frequently draws its humour from being irreverent and satirical about the high seriousness of art culture itself. Other artists explore the awkwardness of selfhood, bad taste and vulgarity through wordplay, foolery and a whole range of comedic gestures, acts and practices – Paul McCarthy, John Bock and Jason

Rhoades being prime examples of artists who have routinely used carnivalesque slapstick, silliness and crude jibes to make 'seriously' funny artwork.[6]

As Molon and Rooks indicate, art which incorporates humour facilitates a recognition that

> …the self-acknowledgment of our inner tramps, fools, and blunderers is both a disarming and liberating exercise.[7]

A growing body of literature on women, art and humour has generated new configurations of gendered ways of being and complex subjectivities.[8] Postmodernity's erosion of patriarchal 'authority' – through feminist apprehensions of the 'death of the author' discourse, Barthes's *jouissance*, Kristeva on the 'libidinal economy' and Cixous's 'Medusa'[9] – both facilitated and unleashed, as Jo Anna Isaak has indicated, a plethora of feminist art practices which demonstrated the 'revolutionary power of women's laughter'.[10] Through the 1980s, she writes of the eruption of 'a riot of women artists exploring the potential of laughter, hysteria, the grotesque and the carnivalesque'.[11]

> They donned the masks of the masquerade, or they went too far and took them all off. They enlisted the hysterics gesture of resistance, or they became grotesques. They put on gorilla masks and marched on the museums … […]…Using the subversive strategy of humor, they have radically reformulated contemporary art and called into question art history's long-held verities concerning creativity, genius, mastery and originality. Their critiques of art history and theoretical reflections on gender, sexuality, politics, and representations have shattered central assumptions about art and its relation to society.[12]

For Isaak, women artists invoked laughter as a metaphor for transformation, a catalyst for cultural change whereby laughter is a performative act of subordination and subversion. Of course, beyond the question of gendered subjectivities, subversive forms of humour offer strategies of resistance in a range of contexts and circumstances for individuals, social groups and communities.[13] The comic can be a form of rebellion: the workplace, for example, contains all sorts of contestive humour. Indeed, when the comic reaches a certain degree of intensity, it contains the potential to threaten the social order, to become dangerously insurgent.

> Dangerous, precisely, to the maintenance of ordinary everyday reality or, if you will, to the business of living. Both phenomena produce ecstasies – literally, experiences of standing *outside* ordinary reality. Such ecstasies are tolerable, indeed useful both psychologically and

sociologically, if they are temporary and carefully controlled. The danger is that they might escape the efforts at control and thus undermine the social order.[14]

Often, humour provides a coping strategy, enabling us to deal with trauma, to confront the unconfrontable. Indeed, at times, pain and humour are not far apart. As Slavoj Žižek comments,

> The comic effect proper occurs when, after the act of unveiling, one confronts the ridicule and the nullity of the unveiled content – in contrast to encountering behind the veil the terrifying Thing too traumatic for our gaze.[15]

Equally though, the comedic deals with ordinary mundane existence. Rather like Barthes's *punctum*, the intense comedic moment has the capacity to puncture the quotidian and provide a *satori*, a flash of sudden meaning, transcending the everyday and reaching into what Berger terms a 'counterworld – an upside-down World'.[16] The comic concentrates on the unfamiliar within the familiar, reminding us of the strangeness of things to which we have become inured. It highlights how we accustom ourselves to alien matters and circumstances – dirt, effluence, waste and death – through processing them in various ways, transforming it into something we can deal with. Comedy can defuse, enlighten and heal – apart from making us laugh.

In a short but seminal article on 'Junk Culture' in 1961, the American critic and writer Lawrence Alloway made a passing comment on the 'comedy of waste'.[17] This curiously insightful comment provides the impetus for an exploration of a particular set of practices in which British artists have utilised trash. Reverberating with those earlier masters of the literary comic – Alfred Jarry and Samuel Beckett[18] – Alloway's comment underlines the ludicrous nature of waste. The 'comedy of waste' occurs in the oscillation between its drawing our attention to its commonality and familiarity and, simultaneously, to its strangeness.

> The extraordinary thing about humour is that it returns us to common sense by distancing us from it, humour familiarises us with a common world through its miniature strategies of defamiliarisation. If humour recalls us to *sensus communis*, then it does this by momentarily pulling us out of common sense, where jokes function as moments of what we might call *dissensus communis*, uncommon sense.[19]

Critchley's commentary on *sensus communis* and *dissensus communis* is pertinent here as I think this is precisely what Alloway alludes to with his phrase, the 'comedy of waste'. Significantly, Alloway expanded on it in a subsequent discussion of the work of Eduardo Paolozzi (discussed later in this chapter). Furthermore, Alloway's reference to comedy has a particular relevance to a discussion of the use of junk in the context of British art as there appears to be an identifiable correlation here: British assemblage and its use of rubbish and humour enjoyed an odd symbiosis at mid-century.

Domestic refuse appeared to provoke hilarity. 'Rubbish' was at the heart of a series of popular British television 'sitcoms' in the 1960s and 1970s including *Steptoe and Son*[20] and *The Dustbinmen.*[21] The humour of Lonnie Donnegan's rendition of *My Old Man's a Dustman*[22] was founded on the subject of the song – singing about someone who collects rubbish was seen as funny. The employment of 'rubbish' as a material in art was also viewed with a certain degree of wry derision in a British context. Of course, religiosity does not necessarily preclude laughter – consider, for example, the role of laughter in Mahayana Buddhism – but there is evidence that assemblage with rubbish was not treated as 'serious' art and that, in some cases, visual-object puns offended a dour protestant streak operating within the British artworld at the time.

Humour has taken different forms at different times and some are demonstrably more socially acceptable in an art context than others. Silliness is enduringly problematic and frowned upon though – perhaps because it becomes involuntary as corporeal hilarity sets in. Paroxysms of mirth can lead to hysteria, a dangerously contagious phenomenon.[23] Is such disapproval founded on the defencelessness of the body when laughing uncontrollably? Is this why the adoption and performance of clowning activities as an artistic strategy – such as that of the contemporary British artist Mark McGowan[24] – raise such acerbic criticism? Or are there other issues to do with critical readings of particular forms of humour being unknowingly 'othered' through an unconscious link to social class and an unarticulated hierarchy of comedic gestures?

And is there a peculiarly British aspect to the production and reception of humour here – or does such a question presuppose the 'trap' of essentialising a non-differentiated British character? Writing on humour, Simon Critchley argues that ethnicity and ethos cannot be sidestepped, and he directly confronts and explores their relationship. Addressing *ethos* and *ethnos,* he asserts that humour has strong connections to place, arguing that it not only returns us to physicality and animality, but

> ... it also returns us to *locality,* to a specific and circumscribed *ethos.* It takes us back to the place we are from, whether that is the concreteness of a neighbourhood or the abstraction of a nation state ... [...] ....
> A sense of humour is often what connects us most strongly to a specific

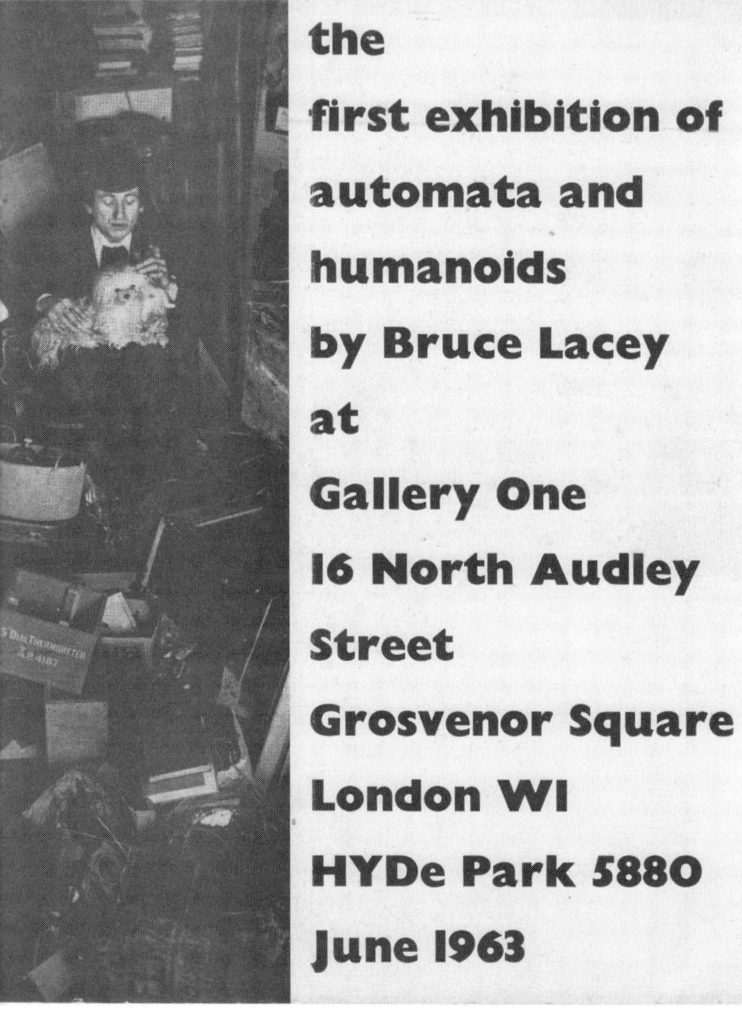

Fig. 18 Bruce Lacey, *Gallery One Exhibition Catalogue*, 1963. Photograph Tony Evans. Courtesy of the artist.

place and leads us to predicate characteristics of that place, assigning certain dispositions and customs to its inhabitants.[25]

This chapter starts from the perspective, then, that the comedic as critique is, indeed, a significant aspect of a good deal of British work which incorporates trash, carrying through, as we will see, from the 1960s to contemporary artistic practice, from 'Professor' Bruce Lacey's *An Evening of*

British Rubbish in the 1960s to Tim Noble and Sue Webster's *British Rubbish* in the 1990s.

On Comedy

The comic transcends the reality of the ordinary, everyday existence.[26]

Humour is to be found universally and in all cultures, and it is a significant force within contemporary mass culture. As Michael Billig contends, an 'understanding of humour is necessary for understanding serious social life'.[27] Moreover, an understanding of the theorising of humour and the comic is an essential pre-requisite for considering its use and reception as a strategy within art practices employing trash.

In addressing the fundamental question – why do we laugh? – Marcel Gutwirth has looked extensively at theories of the comic and identifies three distinct avenues of enquiry: functionalist (whereby the comic 'keeps the peace' by bonding humans together), psychological (focusing on the emotional benefits of humour) and intellectualist (centred around perceptions of incongruity).[28] In his attempt to synthesise these different approaches, he argues that humour is often bound up with both language and culture.[29] Surveying the vast domain of 'the comic', Gutwirth concludes that no single definition is possible, although, for him, 'folly' offers the widest possible category as a whole gamut of personas and guises is available to the fool

> …near-deified in the trickster figure of native American myth; taking the boards as Pierrot or Harlequin; infiltrating epic and romance as Reynard, Eulenspiegel, Panurge, or Simplicissimus; surviving marginally as a circus clown, centrally as a stand-up comic – the Fool is as versatile as he is immortally ubiquitous, popping up now as *Ubu Roi*, now as Sad Sack, Mortimer Snerd or Donald Duck.[30]

But what are the boundaries of this nebulous entity we call humour? Under what conditions is laughter impermissible? How and when does humour become offensive?[31] Ridicule is a form of humour which can easily cause offence and divide sections of the community. Billig notes that the 'darker, less easily admired practice of ridicule' constitutes what he refers to as the 'social core of humour' rather than that which brings people together in 'moments of pure, creative enjoyment'.[32] Alongside 'positive' humour which might encourage group solidarity, he also explores 'negative' genres which divide, separate and exclude.[33] Humour can bond or it can disparage and degrade. Certainly, the politics and social psychology of humour is problematic and complex: a joke which was conceived as rebellious might be received as reactionary, sometimes concurrently by different individuals. Meaning is often determined by difference rather than consensus. Like art, humour is open to a multiplicity of readings depending on hermeneutics and the subjectivities of its audiences.

Looking at the history of the development of humour theory, Billig indicates that a social hierarchy of humour has operated. For example buffoonery and crude vulgarity were – and continue to be – associated with the working and labouring classes. He points out that early superiority theories show that 'humour was bound up with an ideology of order, taste and superiority'.[34] In contrast, 'gentlemanly' laughter was associated with the development of incongruity theory, which looked at laughter's cognitive processes rather than its emotional dynamics.[35] Subsequently, 'relief' theories, originating with Herbert Spencer and Alexander Bain in the nineteenth century, were founded on laughter's capacity to relieve psychological pressure and procure physiological benefits.[36]

Henri Bergson and Sigmund Freud, with their respective studies of laughter and jokes at the turn of the twentieth century,[37] remain key influential figures in the articulation and formulation of modern ideas about humour. These studies, for the first time according to Billig, placed laughter under scrutiny and suspicion.[38] Bergson offered the first social critique of different forms of comedy and how they provoke laughter, highlighting the tension between ideas that humour serves a disciplinary function and those that suggest it functions in the service of elasticity. Interestingly, Bergson gave priority to the visual over the verbal, giving preference to 'bodily humour' in the form of 'slapstick' – a form which had been denigrated in early centuries for its association with the crudities of carnival and the 'lower orders'. Importantly, Bergson was not championing the vulgar. A key component of his argument revolved around laughter's cruelty and that the pleasure of laughter depends on a lack of sympathy or, as he put it, a 'temporary anaesthesia of the heart'.[39]

Freud's work on jokes grew out of his theory of the unconscious and dream-work. Founded on the idea that the human condition is marked by self-deception, Freud believed that jokes are inherently social but express the unconscious desires and secret intentions of individuals. For Freud, jokes – like dreams – make manifest the hidden and latent content of the unconscious.[40] In his seminal study, he examines verbal humour, distinguishing 'innocent' from 'tendentious' – primarily lustful or hostile – jokes. In Billig's view, this is the most important aspect of Freud's analysis: in the joking moment, the repressed desire is released but it is hidden as a joke.[41] Freud's identification of the 'tendentious' purpose of jokes provides the basis for a *critical* approach to humour: it avoids the dangerous supposition that all humour is necessarily to be applauded for being wittily clever.[42]

Particularly important for this study of trash and art – with its strong focus on 'the found' – is Freud's distinguishing between the comic, the humour and the joke. Identifying the comic with the *objet trouvé*, as 'something found', he noted:

> The joke is made, comedy is found – in persons above all, and only by extension in objects, situations and the like.[43]

Freud's particular association of the comic with the found object, then, seems particularly apposite.

Overall, of course, no single theory can hope to explain the complexity of humour.[44] Indeed, Billig is intrigued by humour's inconsistent and contradictory nature and he identifies three specific paradoxes: first, its universality and particularity; secondly, its social and anti-social aspects (essentially its capacity to simultaneously unite and exclude); and thirdly, its mysterious resistance to analysis in conjunction with the fact that it is also understandable and analysable.[45] As we will see, Billig's insights are pertinent as paradox is a fundamental element in a good deal of art assembled from trash and found objects.

Finally, before turning to specific art practices, it is important to briefly highlight particular forms of comedy and humour which have direct and indirect connections to some of the work. For example one classic form rooted in literary narratives of excess and affect is scatological humour with its focus on what Gutwirth terms 'the body excremental',[46]

> …the comedy of the body's shameless all encompassing physicality, of its huge appetites and correspondingly vast outpourings at the nether conduits, has a name: it is Rabelaisian.[47]

Here, the allusion is to Gargantua and Pantagruel[48] and the orgy of unbounded outrageous sexual and physiological behaviours which obliquely inform a range of twentieth-century and contemporary art practices that adopt 'obscenity' as a critical strategy.[49]

The absurd – described by Berger as 'an outlandish, a grotesque representation of reality'[50] – is another literary mode which overlaps with an anarchic comic approach. Alfred Jarry's *Ubu Roi*, with his ridiculous demented dialogues and outbursts of expletives, is commonly viewed as a precursory figure for the Theatre of the Absurd.[51] In Jarry's pataphysics, says Berger, we see

> … the construction of a counter-world by means of a counterlanguage and counterlogic[52]

and, more pertinently, in relation to the artifice, affective and imaginary world of art

> … where they do overlap, they reveal the most profound aspect of the comic – namely, a magical transformation of reality.[53]

The phenomenon of 'play' offers another 'counterworld' related to the surreal and imaginary world constructed by both artist and comedian. Comedy plays with the verbal and the visual, facilitating an emigration – an interlude – from the reality of the everyday.[54] Satire, whether it is conceptualised as a form of militant irony or a verbal or visual mocking of moral or political standpoints, is bound by social and temporal contexts. As a form of humour it is tied to its own time and culture – but, like the world of play, it too offers a transient counterworld, a fugitive interlude which distracts us from the everyday and challenges conventions and norms.

Beyond all this silliness, buffoonery and witty social critique, the verbal and visual world of the risible accommodates mockery, lampooning, parody and puns across a social and political spectrum. Laughter may be claimed to have revolutionary power, but it can also consolidate reaction. On the other hand, it might merely draw our attention to the strangeness of everyday stuff – offering us a glimpse into a counterworld of *dissensus communis.*

Assemblage in Britain in the 1960s

> Paolozzi's use of the body as a frame for samples from the comedy of waste is dictated by his sense of the multiplicity of things, a sense of ways in which man is embedded in the plenitude of the world.[55]

Lawrence Alloway's association of 'junk culture' with the 'comedy of waste' in his 1961 article for *Architectural Design* was more than a generic comment about artists working with urban detritus as, a year earlier, he had expanded on the phrase at some length in an essay for *Cimaise* about a series of sculptures made by Eduardo Paolozzi. Along with George Fullard (Fig. 19) and Bruce Lacey (Figs. 18 and 20), Paolozzi was one of a triumvirate of British artists working extensively with junk and assemblage techniques from the mid-1950s and into the 1960s. It is no coincidence that these three artists were considered by the critic Jasia Reichardt, later assistant director of the Institute of Contemporary Arts (ICA) in London, as *the* most significant sculptors of the 1960s.[56]

Undoubtedly, the work of Paolozzi, Fullard and Lacey was part of the contemporaneous surge of interest in collage and assemblage, the 'collage explosion' as Alloway called it,[57] in the USA and Europe. The 're-discovery' of the earlier collage techniques of Kurt Schwitters and the readymades of Marcel Duchamp contributed to this. In 1958, the Lord's Gallery in London staged the first major British public showing of the work of Schwitters. Remarkably, no public gallery owned or had exhibited Schwitters's work previously, and even the major retrospective that had toured Europe in 1956 had bypassed Britain.[58] Notably, Alan Bowness commented that the combination of 'playful humour and serious intent' in Schwitters's work had been an obstacle to its wider appeal. For Schwitters, of course, one material was no more valuable or appropriate than another:

> I don't see why one shouldn't use in a picture, just as one uses colours made by the paint merchants, things like old tram and train tickets, scraps of driftwood, cloakroom tickets, ends of string, bicycle wheel spokes – in a word all the old rubbish which you find in dustbins or on a refuse dump.[59]

This view, and the anti-aesthetic approach it implied, was fundamental to the idiom of assemblage as it developed at the end of the 1950s. However, it is important to emphasise that Paolozzi, Fullard and Lacey – working with what Alloway called 'samples from the comedy of waste' and the 'plenitude of the world'[60] – were working on the periphery in terms of British sculptural practice.

Essentially, the turn of the decade was a point of transition for British sculpture. Following the critical success of the British sculptors who showed in the 1952 Venice Biennale,[61] the early and mid-1960s were dominated by the new direction – acclaimed by critics as a 'revolution in British sculpture'[62] – taken by Anthony Caro. In an interview with Alloway after a visit to the USA in Autumn 1959, Caro explained how he had abandoned his lumpy figures modelled in clay and had started to construct sculpture from welded metal.[63] Profoundly influenced by the sculpture of David Smith, American abstract colour-field painting and Clement Greenberg's modernist ideals, Caro's new work was abstract, lean and, subsequently, drenched in unmodulated colour. His work – and that of his 'New Generation' followers at St Martins[64] – had none of the soiled, lewd 'down-Beat' manner of the sculpture being made by American artists such as Bruce Conner, Jim Dine or Ed Kienholz. In giving primacy to the work of Caro, Greenberg provided the theoretical justification and authentification for a British sculptural practice that focused on abstraction – it represented a privileging of self-referential work which could be viewed as autonomous from the social material world. Indeed, Greenberg's ideas provided the foundation for the setting up of a series of aesthetic dichotomies and were primarily responsible for self-congratulatory 'monolithic' accounts of British sculpture, which stifled the exploration of unconventional connections and experimental practices – or at the very least, marginalised them. Such a singularising perspective obliterated receptivity to difference. In 1981, Lynne Cooke expressed such a view:

> The euphoric appraisals of British sculpture in the late 50s can be seen retrospectively, to be insular and narrow: not only do such accounts ignore contemporary developments in America as well as outside the European mainstream, but they gloss over internal divisions and nascent idioms.[65]

The considerable attention devoted to a relatively small group of sculptors of the 1950s and to Caro's sculptural 'revolution' in the first half of the 1960s ensured that other developments – such as assemblage – have been viewed as peripheral. When, in 1959, George Fullard was piecing together his first assemblage, *Striding Woman and Child*, from old door frames, chair-legs and offcuts of timber, there were few other sculptors working in this idiom in Britain. Nevertheless, there were other British artists experimenting with collage techniques and developing three-dimensional work, constructing environments, events and performances from found materials and junk throughout the later 1950s and into the 1960s. Working loosely with the language of assemblage, they displayed a subversive irreverence for Caro's 'revolution' with which they had little in common.

Eduardo Paolozzi's 'Topical Relics'

> Paolozzi's encrusted homo faber, plastically simple, texturally elaborate, hieratic as a mummy but as wild as a drugstore, has what Erich Auerback, writing about Rabelais in Mimesis, called a 'lyrico-everyday polyphony'.[66]

As discussed earlier, Paolozzi was one of the few British artists who contributed to the *Art of Assemblage* exhibition in New York in 1961 – although it included his collaged work rather than the bronze sculptures cast from assembled objects featured in Alloway's 'comedy of waste' essay. Fundamentally, all Paolozzi's activities stemmed from a rejection of elitist notions of 'high' and 'low' art and an embracing of the idea that no material, language, objects or, indeed, technology should be considered 'unacceptable' for making art.

These ideas were part of the ethos of the Independent Group (IG), formed in 1952 at the Institute of Contemporary Art in London, with

Richard Hamilton and Lawrence Alloway as founder members. Hamilton, Paolozzi, Alloway and others in the IG shared an intent on formulating what they referred to as 'an Expendable Aesthetic' during the short life of the group from around 1952 to 1955.[67] An iconic and contributing event was Paolozzi's *Bunk!*, in which the artist 'presented' a collage of adverts, scraps from sci-fi mags and comic strips, bringing together text and images in ironic juxtaposition to create multi-layered visual narratives. Similarly, he incorporated a vast range of *kitsch* material into his scrapbooks which were just one part of an extensive collection of ephemera, toys and junk which Paolozzi had been accumulating since the 1940s.[68] Paolozzi's collections, and the activities of the IG with its fascination with the mass media, vernacular culture and everyday objects, reflected a shift towards an anthropological approach to art – a model which Alloway particularly favoured.[69] As Robin Spencer indicates, events like *Bunk!* enabled the IG to 'counter the hegemony of certain forms of modern art in England and the critical language then in use to support it'.[70] For Spencer, Paolozzi's work restored metaphor, allegory and writing as an integral part of the visual process and – most importantly, in this context – represented 'a resistance to a reductive form of art divorced from the experience of life'.[71]

Besides using collage techniques in graphic work, collecting junk and compiling 'scrapbooks', Paolozzi also made 'cut-ups' of poetry, and similar to Bruce Conner, he created a series of short films made up of quotations and snatched images. The notes Paolozzi made about his 1962 film, *The History of Nothing*, are a collage of random ideas and words put together to create a kind of surreal comic strip

> … space monkey Grinning Pathos Distorted lunatic cat Whiff of anti-war Bottom of rocket Hybrid mutant boiler head attached to winged clowns mask Hybrid in interior Close up Readymade Technics room …[72]

However, in his 'comedy of waste' essay, Alloway focuses on Paolozzi's series of bronze sculptures – including *AG5* (1959), *Greek Hero* (1957), *Figure* (1958) and *St Sebastian III* (1958–9) – which were made by pressing into wax a variety of obsolescent and expendable objects – plastic toys, locks, cutlery, radio and clock parts, and bits of old machinery – and then casting the whole assemblage. The monolithic primitivistic figures with their encrusted surfaces reflected Paolozzi's fascination with surrealism and *art brut*, but they also resembled alien monsters from the world of sci-fi and pulp fiction which might lumber into action at any moment. As Alloway remarks, CoBrA's bestiary is in there, but Paolozzi's creatures inhabit the contemporary urban environment. Rather than expressionistic and anxious, his metamorphoses of rubbish are playful 'topical relics' which transport us to a comic-gothic counterworld of B movies.

> His figures are battered and opened, but their state is not a code for suffering or anguish. The Frankenstein monster, for example, whose silhouette and lumbering stance (caused by the Baron's rugged surgery) haunts Paolozzi's sculpture. There is pathos in the strong hampered figure of Karloff, and in Paolozzi's interpretation of this modern folk image.[73]

George Fullard and His 'Menacing Baby Saints'

From the end of the 1950s, like Paolozzi, George Fullard also worked with discarded toys, bits of furniture and found materials, sometimes embedding them in clay and later – as with *Mounted Infant* (1963) – casting the assembled objects in bronze or – as with *War Game* (1962) (Fig. 19) – in cement.[74] The kind of unity which Paolozzi achieved by casting conglomerations of objects into bronze – a technique perfected by Picasso – was Fullard's expressed intention for many of his early wooden figures. Although Picasso's sculpture was rarely exhibited in Britain, both artists would have been aware of the artist's earlier and contemporaneous assemblage techniques and, specifically, of the series of works cast from found objects that he made in the mid-1950s.[75] Picasso's irreverence for the nobility of particular materials, his enduring playfulness and his ability to turn household objects, such as kitchen utensils and children's toys, into extraordinary images impressed many artists, including Fullard.

In 1953, *Studio* featured a photograph of Picasso's *Ape with Young* (1952), which was on show in Paris attracting large crowds. In his regular 'Paris Commentary', Alex Watts enthused about this sculpture, with its monkey body cast from a *pot-au-feu* and head cast from two toy cars, describing it as the *pièce de résistance* of the exhibition, a work that was at once startling but '…bestial, powerful and primitive'.[76]

Fullard certainly visited the retrospective exhibition of Picasso's work held at the Tate Gallery in 1960. Although no sculpture was included, it showed various early works of *papier collé* and also the important *Still Life* of 1914 which incorporated painted wood and an upholstery fringe.[77] Prior to that, it is possible that both Fullard and Paolozzi visited the Picasso exhibition at Marlborough Fine Art in 1955, which showed ten bronzes cast from assembled objects, including *Pregnant Woman* (1950), *Goat's Skull and Bottle* (1951–2) and *Ape with Young* (1952).[78]

Fullard was sensitive to the transformatory potential of discarded domestic objects. As he frequently remarked, he aimed to replicate the kind

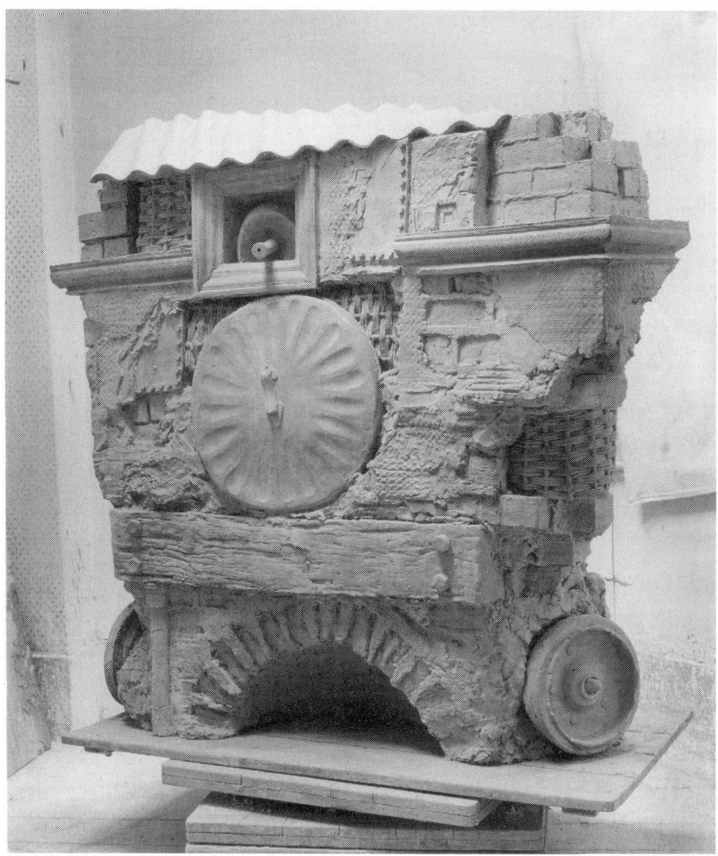

Fig. 19 George Fullard, *War Game*, 1962, ciment fondu 148 cm × 146 cm × 71 cm. Photograph courtesy of George Fullard estate.

of effortless and intuitive inventiveness which children display when playing with things they find. Indeed, for Fullard, art was a ludic activity.

> Just as the child, without effort, slips through imagination out of life to make a pepper-pot, or the heaving deck of a ship-wreck of a placid pavement, so the artist works towards the miracle of making visible that which apparently could not exist.[79]

International critics identified Fullard's work with 'Neo-Dada', and his early wooden pieces had a lot in common with the work of other European artists, particularly Vic Gentils, who constructed objects from wooden mouldings, ornate picture frames and piano parts. One review of Fullard's solo exhibition at Gallery One in 1961, for example, described the artist as 'un jeune sculpteur, utilisant des matières de rebut, objets trouvés dans la bonne vieille tradition dadaiste'.[80]

Gallery One was an important venue as the proprietor, Victor Musgrave, brought to London the work of a series of contemporary European avant-garde artists, many of whom worked with junk and the assemblage idiom – such as Vic Gentils, Daniel Spoerri and Ben Vautier. Indeed, Musgrave was the first to exhibit work by Jean Dubuffet and Yves Klein in London. Artists such as Fullard and Lacey had precisely the kind of idiosyncratic artistic sensibility and techniques sought by Musgrave.[81]

Fullard included seven of his bric-a-brac assemblages in the Gallery One show. Jasia Reichardt was entranced with their contradictory lyricism.

> To the artist there is a contradiction between the figure and a chunk of wood, between a systematic approach and an emotional end. From this disparity Fullard builds powerful and extraordinary images, sad and intense, musical and utterly human.[82]

For William Seitz, the language of assemblage was akin to that of poetry where the juxtaposition of metaphor, alliteration, simile, onomatopoeia and oxymoron produces work open to a range of interpretations (see Chapter 2). It was these poetic aspects of assemblage that Fullard exploited in his own work. By bringing together incongruous objects and giving his sculptures playful titles with serious messages, he created a series of three-dimensional oxymorons – particularly with his paradoxical assemblages about war. At the turn of the decade, Fullard had plundered a treasure trove of debris from bomb sites and derelict houses around his Chelsea studio, to produce a series of whimsical figures with jaunty details. However, the series of assemblages made between 1961 and 1964, which specifically explore the theme of war and infant games, have a different character: paradox and incongruity are key elements here. They are playful and idiosyncratic, but, unlike the earlier figures, they have a macabre sense of the absurd.[83]

Fullard admired the writings of Samuel Beckett: in particular, the dark humour and sense of absurdity appealed. Beckett exploits the fact that when we laugh, our defences are down and then comes the realisation that it's not really funny and there is, as Critchley writes, an 'undertow of doubt':

> … when the laughter dies away, we sense, with a sadness – a *Tristram-tristesse* – that is always the dark heart of humour, what an oddity the human being is in the universe.[84]

Beckett's writings encapsulate, as Critchley remarks, the 'black sun of depression' at the centre of the comic universe. Fullard's ramshackle war assemblages do something similar. They revel in precisely what the surrealist André Breton called 'l'humour noir',[85] which, for him, was the opposite of joviality, wit or sarcasm: instead, 'black humour' was

> ... a partly ironic, often absurd turn of the spirit that constitutes the 'mortal enemy of sentimentality' and beyond that a 'superior revolt of the mind' ...[86]

The Patriot (1959–60), *War Ghost* (1961), *Mounted Infant* (1963), *The Infant St George* (1962–3) and *Death or Glory* (1963–4) were all gloriously ironic sculptural puns which subject chivalric symbols of Englishness and patriotism to ridicule and satire. However, their 'black humour' is underpinned by an intensely personal connection to the horrors of the battlefield.[87] The ghoulish *War Ghost,* a makeshift barricade and military scarecrow for warding off the enemy, has had the back of its head blown away. *Death or Glory* plays on the chivalric associations of Fullard's own regimental motto: the irreverent sculpted image, in which one can pick out the 'death's head' of the regimental badge, is both tribute and parody.[88]

Reichardt described *The Infant St George,* with its oversize head and tiny golf-club feet, as Fullard's 'menacing baby saint'. In her view, his 'babies' had the 'domineering quality of miniature Napoleons'.[89] Undoubtedly, Fullard's toybox 'junk war'[90] battalion presents a complex and contradictory set of messages – he exploits discredited clichés and uses parody and irony to convey the insanity of war. The antithesis of Caro's anonymous abstraction, Fullard's vision was extremely personal and he rarely collaborated with other artists, but it was by no means eccentrically individual. It reflected a set of international practices which, in Britain at any rate, did not get the kind of critical support and exposure available to artists working in assemblage in Europe and the USA.

Sick, Scatological and 'Therapeutic Lunacy'

Whilst Fullard never had any particular connections with other artists, his work certainly had sympathy with that of Bruce Lacey and a strand within British art that had direct links to both American-style Beat culture and to European *Nouveau Réalisme.* Adrian Henri – Liverpool poet, painter and assembler[91] – emphasised these connections in one of the few published contemporaneous surveys of developments in Britain. His book, *Environments and Happenings,* published in 1974, situated British events and activities firmly in an international context.[92]

Besides documenting marginalised practices in the 1950s and 1960s, Henri made his own contribution to British assemblage. Obsessed with Jarry's Ubu character and profoundly influenced by surrealism, American jazz, blues and Beat poetry but also aware of the activities of the Independent Group, Henri's assemblages and collages have an essentially English quality which links them to the work of the 'Kitchen Sink' painters of the mid-1950s.[93] From 1960, Henri incorporated real pieces of advertisements and *objets trouvés* of popular culture in his work, reflecting the artist's personal experiences of working on a fairground in Rhyl in the 1950s. The mundanity of British-style consumerism appealed to him, a style that had more to do with chip butties, best bitter and 'pram wheels rather than chrome hubcaps'.[94] Henri used urban detritus from the 1960s through to his 'debris' series in the 1970s, adamant that it was always possible to find beauty in any bit of urban wasteland 'if you look at it the right way'.[95]

Nevertheless, Henri's ethos was more than merely a whimsical taste for English vernacular: it was rooted in a strong sense of social class and political injustice. In a lecture given at Bradford in 1967, he talked about the kinds of radical 'do-it-yourself' protest activities and the 'small revolution' going on across the UK, Europe and the USA, specifically citing the New York 'Black Mask' rebels and the Amsterdam 'Provos' with their White Bicycle Plan. Henri particularly noted the inventive use of junk by the Los Angeles 'Provos': they collected urban detritus from the squalid streets of Watts and, in a supreme act of generosity, 'gave it away' to the rich of Santa Monica and Beverly Hills.

> … a broken greasy gas-store left on a smoothly manicured lawn pointing up the social injustice of The Great Society better than any manifesto …[96]

In *Environments and Happenings*, Henri wrote of the activities of a loosely connected group of artists which included Bruce Lacey, Jeff Nuttall and John Latham. They were involved in producing assemblages and 'environments' created from junk in obscure venues such as the basement of Better Books, a bookshop on Charing Cross Road in London.[97] Along with the Scottish Situationist poet, Alexander Trocchi, these artists were involved in various events and activities heavily influenced by the writings of the American Beats and 'happenings' in the USA. Indeed, Nuttall, a poet, jazz musician and assembler, corresponded with William Burroughs, and subsequently produced his own 'cut-ups'.[98] In his book, *Bomb Culture*, written between 1967 and 1968, Nuttall described the *sTigma* environment they built in 1965 in the basement of Better Books. The violent image evokes a scene from a Burroughs's novel, but it also recalls the dark erotic assemblages of Bruce Conner and the unsettling macabre tableaux of Ed Kienholz:

> The entrance to *sTigma* was through three-valve-doorways lined with old copies of the *Economist*. The last you could just squeeze through,

but not back, no return. The corridor this led you to was lined with hideous bloody heads, photos of war atrocities, Victorian pornographic cards, tangles of stained underwear, sanitary towels, French letters, anatomical diagrams; the passage narrowed into complete darkness – tin, glass, wet bread, plastic, sponge rubber, then a zig-zag corridor of polythene through which you could glimpse your goal, a group of figures. They were gathered around a dentist's chair which had itself been turned into a figure, with sponge-rubber breasts and a shaven head. On the seat of the chair was a cunt made of a bed pan lined with hair and cod's roe. Detergent bubbles spluttered from between the slabs of roe, which remained spluttering for weeks … [99]

In particular, Lacey, who had assembled the putrefying dentist-chair figure for *sTigma*, epitomised the anarchic spirit which William Seitz had associated with assemblage. Lacey's continuing and lifelong obsession with accumulating junk emerged in the robotic sculptures he made, exhibited and used in performance on stage and in films from the mid-1950s (Fig. 20).[100] Significantly, Lacey had met and assisted Jean Tinguely at his 'Meta-matics' event at the ICA in 1959 – at the time, Tinguely invited him to become a permanent assistant. However, Lacey declined and teamed up with the Grey Brothers to form The Alberts and staged, amongst other events, *An Evening of British Rubbish*, a curious mix of vaudeville, jazz and kinetic assemblage at the Comedy Theatre in 1963.[101] Looking back, Nuttall wrote of them as 'conscious eccentrics – very Milliganesque (goony)'.[102]

Lacey's bizarre dummies with their false limbs, wires, tubes and cogs were fascinating and repellant.[103] A reviewer for *Burlington Magazine* expressed disgust and horror when a series of Lacey's assemblages, including *Old Money Bags, The Womaniser*[104] and *Mr. Show-Biz*, were exhibited in 1964. They combined the nastiness of Conner's 'Funk' with a strong dose of 'black humour' – they were the sculptural equivalent of the 'sick' humour of the American cult comic, Lenny Bruce.[105] As with Bruce, Lacey's stuttering machines had a serious edge – as Nuttall recognised,

Lacey made his magnificent hominoids, sick, urinating, stuttering machines constructed of the debris of the century, always with pointed socialist/pacifist overtones but with a profound sense of anger, disgust and gaiety that goes far beyond any simple political standpoint … [106]

Lacey's work, viewed as lightweight and frivolous at the time, was grossly misunderstood and undervalued as art. In his robotic assemblages of the 1960s, Lacey dealt with social themes and anecdotal tragedies – the

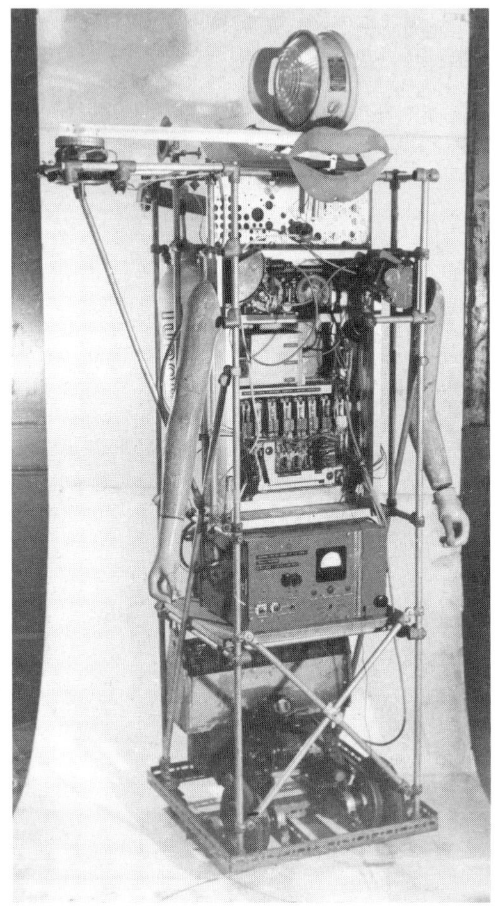

Fig. 20 Bruce Lacey, *R.O.S.A. B.O.S.O.M.* 1965; acronym for radio-operated actress, battery or standby operated mains. Photograph Robin Hughes. Courtesy of the artist.

horrors of war and the inhumane treatment of the elderly – but they were frequently viewed as offensive because of the irreverent jokes he made in his treatment of taboo subjects. Yet playing 'silly buggers' – through buffoonery and the employment of nasty materials and repulsive imagery purposefully selected to evoke accusations of obscenity and disgust – was a conscious part of Lacey's attack on the art school establishment and the complacency of wider society, perceived as morally hypocritical and heading towards nuclear disaster. As Alex Seago indicates, Lacey's approach was one part of a whole raft of activities, performances and art practices

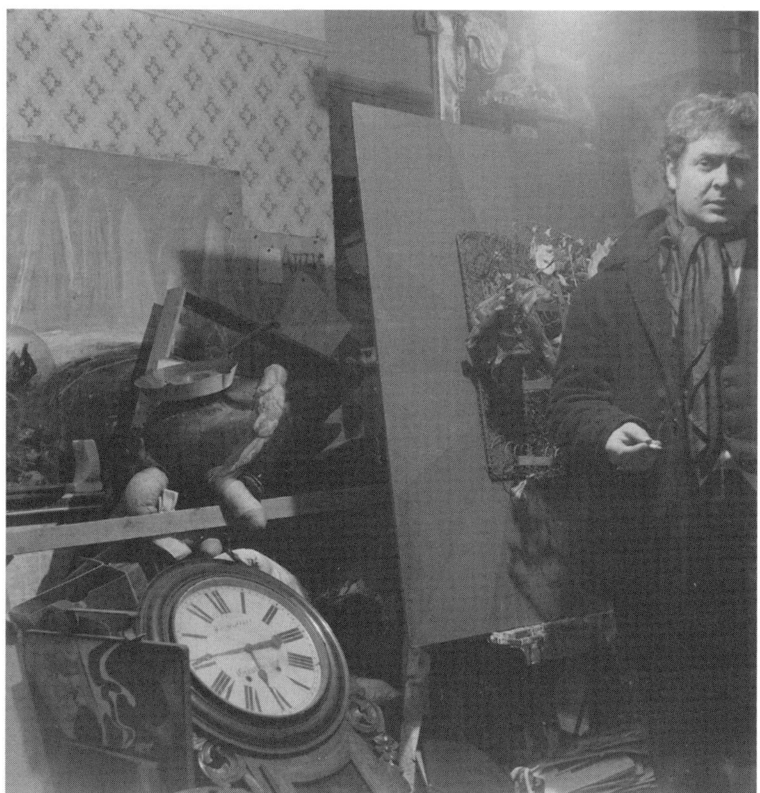

Fig. 21 *Jeff Nuttall and bric-a-brac*, London, 1960s. Photograph Dave Trace and with the kind permission of Dave Trace estate.

in Britain which, presaging a postmodern sensibility, were about 'burning the box of beautiful things'.[107]

For Nuttall, Lacey's 'stuttering machines' echoed the 'real burst blister of sick humour – William Burroughs' slaughterhouse carnival *The Naked Lunch*'.[108] Indeed, throughout his prolific and diverse activities – as a writer, poet, artist and performer – Nuttall employed the politics of obscenity and scatological humour as a kind of 'therapeutic lunacy', something he viewed as a necessity in a society that was 'sick' (Fig. 21).[109] Nuttall's own creative output – from the mimeographed cut-up journal *My Own Mag* (co-edited with William Burroughs) and his protuberant boxed assemblages of the 1960s to the extensive body of writings and poetry he published through to the 1980s – had a Rabelaisian character. His poetry, prose and performances all used collage techniques with raw imagery and a ribald sense of the vernacular.

Nuttall's writings, performances and art practices sit uncomfortably within feminist and postfeminist contexts, but the works demand a more problematising and complex analysis than has previously been provided. Bodily humour was an essential feature, but rather than simplistically dismissing them as misogynistic, for me, they represent what Jo Anna Isaak – paradoxically, in a feminist context – terms, 'the jouissance of the polymorphous orgasmic body'.[110]

> The flop, the brewer's droop, the leftover umbilical, the worm, the squashed snail, the boneless disaster. The Oo-Lah-Lah, the Fol-De-Riddle-I-Do, the Lawks-a-mussy-me, medals showing, fast flash, sausage on a clown's string. The warm doll. The prick, the nudger, the weapon, the tool, the chopper, the willy, the John Thomas, doggle, doodie, Hampton, pisser, old man, beef ration. 'I say, pianist, do you know your cock's 'angin' out?' 'You whistle it mate, I'll pick it up.'[111]

Nuttall's primary intent was to achieve intense *affect*, incorporating erotic and poetic aspects of corporeality, but at the same time, he thoroughly explored the comedy of the body through the scatological, that precise place which, as Critchley puts it, lies between the metaphysical and the physical,

> …in the gap between our souls and our arseholes …[112]

Industrial Dereliction, Getting Wasted and More *British Rubbish*

Of course, a plethora of British artists – far too many to mention here – have continued to work with the 'comedy of waste' since the 1960s. The beauty and banality of trash was portrayed particularly deftly by Keith Arnatt – a conceptual trickster known for his tautological and philosophical twisters in the late 1960s and early 1970s – in a later series of photographic studies of abandoned landscapes, marked by detritus and human absence.[113] His studies of black polythene bags bursting with rubbish, dumped in dead-end lanes and litter-covered grass verges, have a lonesome romantic quality, but they also resonate with the politics of industrial dereliction and urban decay of their time.

Whilst the early 1980s witnessed a series of 'ends' – history, art history, theory and art itself – paradoxically, there were 'returns' too, including the much-documented 'return of the object' with the emergence of a

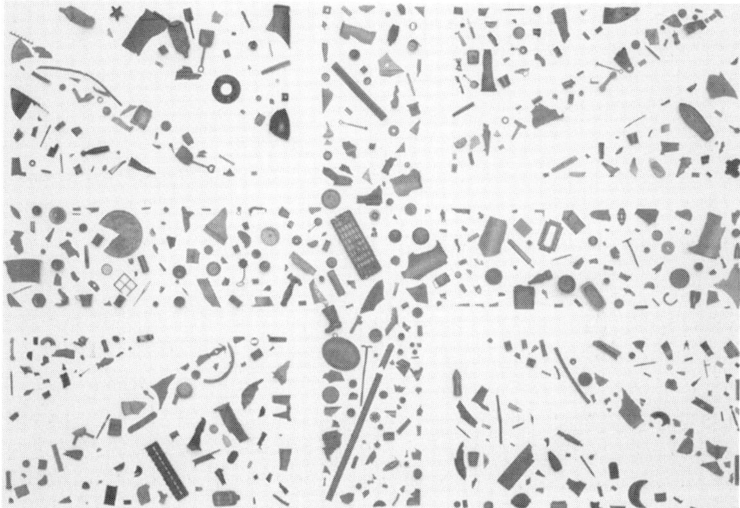

Fig. 22 Tony Cragg, *Union Jack, Postcard Flag* 1981, plastic. Reproduced with kind permission of the artist and Leeds Museums and Galleries.

young generation of artists and 'New British Sculpture'.[114] In particular, Richard Wentworth, Bill Woodrow (Fig. 23) and Tony Cragg (Fig. 22) made extensive use of bought and found objects in their sculpture, reflecting a resurgent contemporaneous interest in 'recycling' and the readymade with a witty element which was often cuttingly satirical. Wentworth has extensively explored incongruous chance pairings of materials and found or manufactured objects through photography and sculpture. His eye for the quirky and the unexpected is conceptual and idiosyncratic rather than aesthetic, but this results in pieces which are sometimes poetic, sometimes comically curious. In the 1980s, Woodrow was known for a series of sculptural 'puns' in which a new object emerged from an intricate process of deconstructing discarded household objects and urban scrap such as in *Twin-Tub with Guitar* (1981) and *Twin Tub with Beaver* (1981) (Fig. 23). He has continued to place banal objects at the centre of his work, usually with a wry sense of humour. Cragg, on the other hand, made subtle political satire out of the re-arrangement of found materials. Although Cragg's early works with plastic debris demonstrated a formal aesthetic, a series of floor and wall murals made in 1981 – a year dominated by the Thatcherite jingoism of the Falklands War – clearly engaged with contemporary political events and oppositional perspectives. *Union Jack* (Fig. 22), *Policeman* and *Britain Seen from the North,* made from fragments of plastic trash,

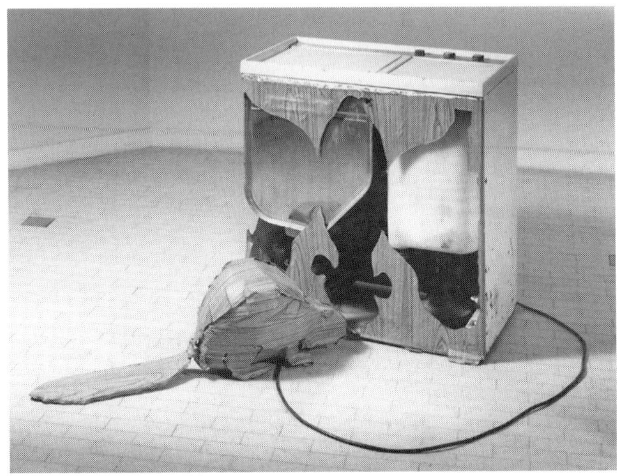

Fig. 23 Bill Woodrow, *Twin-Tub with Beaver* 1981, mixed media. Reproduced with kind permission of the artist and Leeds Museums and Galleries.

viewed against the Toxteth riots and general civil unrest about mass un-employment, industrial decline and cuts in public services, operate as a wittily understated social critique.

Indeed, in the last 20 years, practices based around the use and reuse of trash have proliferated, with the 'strange alchemy' of Cornelia Parker,[115] Hew Locke and Brian Griffiths being just a few of the artists producing work in Britain which redresses and repositions the found object in diverse ways and settings. In particular, Locke brings a complex understanding of invented and hybrid cultures to his assemblages of eclectic objects con-structed from toys, souvenirs, jewellery and consumer waste. Using his own experience of being brought up in Scotland and Guyana, works such as *The Kingdom of the Blind* (2008) invite an interrogation of notions of identity as they oscillate around questions of individuality, ethnicity, cul-ture and nationality.

Humour is just one of the performative strategies adopted by the British artist, Sarah Lucas, who explored gender stereotypes from 'trash culture' throughout the 1990s. In a collection of studies of gendered practices which focuses on 'difference' and 'excess', David Hopkins explores the 'bad girl' image and 'burlesque' treatment of working-class tropes in Lucas' self-portraits and photographic work.[116] Lucas's parodic performances and narcissistic scenarios – such as *Get Off Your Horse and Drink Your Milk* (1994) – and her installations and assemblages of objects – such as *Au Naturel* (1994) – represent a carnivalesque re-appropriation and inversion of gender stereotypes. Wittily – though with some degree of exploitation – they play with the vulgarities of language and the expectations of 'excessive' gendered behaviours as they relate to social class and what has been derogatively termed 'white trash'. There is a self-conscious indulgence about Lucas's treatment of these themes, which is firmly of its time, reflecting the relentlessly self-conscious 'transgressive' character of much of the work of the Young British Artists (YBAs).

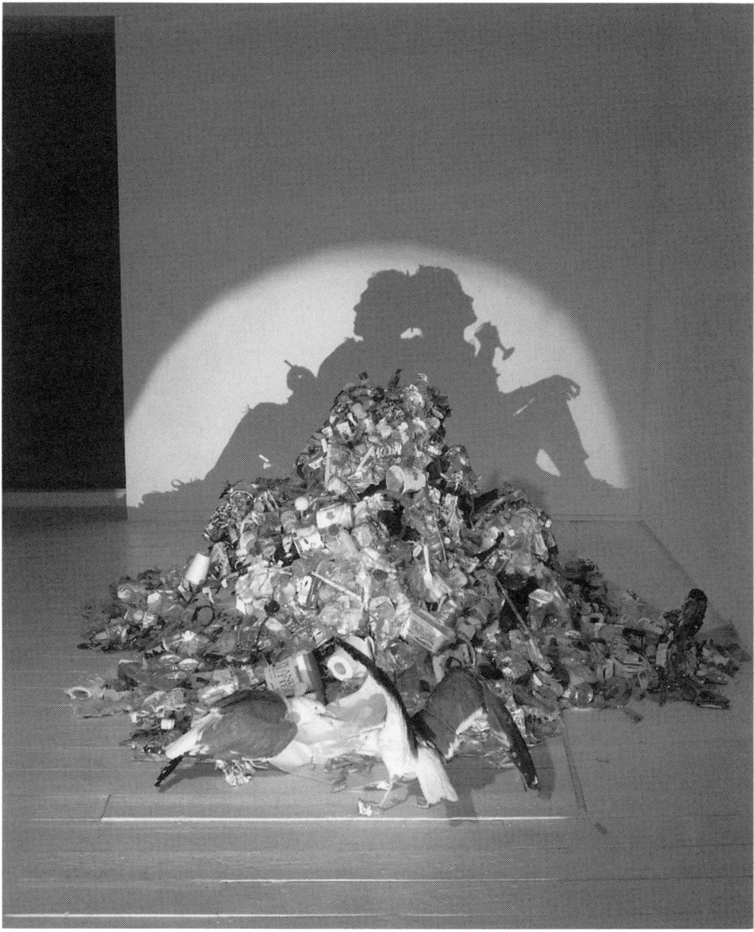

Fig. 24 Tim Noble and Sue Webster, *Dirty White Trash (with Gulls)*, 1998. Six months, worth of artists' trash, two taxidermy seagulls, light projector. Images courtesy of the artists.

Perhaps though, Tim Noble and Sue Webster, the two precocious artists known especially for their back-lit 'shadow' installations made from piles of rubbish, stuffed animals and birds, are the British *enfants terribles* of YBA 'trash practice' and, therefore, leading contemporary contenders for the 'comedy of waste' (Fig. 24). Frequently described as 'pranksters', since 1986 they have worked in partnership on self-consciously transgressive artworks exploring themes to do with youth culture, sex and consumption in a range of media from iconic light sculptures to life-size wax models.[117] In an unconscious echo of The Alberts's event in the 1960s, Noble and Webster presented an exhibition entitled *British Rubbish* in 1996 at the Independent Art Space in London. Through the 1990s, the duo characteristically employed parody and irony in their deceptively crafted installations of rubbish layered with meaning and cultural references. In a recent survey, Deitch traced their anti-art roots and situated their confrontational approach firmly within an alternative vernacular 'pop' tradition, typical of the generation of YBAs, with whom they exhibited in *Apocalypse* at the Royal Academy in 2000.[118] Although they quickly became a clichéd joke, their signature trash shadow installations – *Dirty White Trash (with Gulls)* (1998), *Wasted Youth* (2000), *The Undesirables* (2000) and *Real Life Is Rubbish* (2002) – were self-conscious punk-inspired provocations which capitalised on the hype and success of the YBAs, and yet initially at least, they also had a resonance with a contemporary wave of social derision for youth in general and an increasingly obsequious obsession with a British 'underclass' in particular.

The Joyous Consciousness of Our Finitude

> As the joyous consciousness of our finitude, the capacity to be amused at what holds us in check bespeaks an awesome resilience. It endows human nature with the means to turn the corner, perpetually, on the disasters sown in its path by its own freedom from instinctual programmation.[119]

For his 80th birthday party in Norwich, Bruce Lacey decided to conduct and participate in a remarkable piece of performance art. Having recently undergone a life-saving heart bypass operation, he created a hilarious event in which he acted out the surgeon's procedures on an exact replica of his own body, complete with 'death mask'. The audience – including the actual surgeon – gasped as he extracted a bloodied (pig's) heart from the chest on the operating table. Lacey's performance, for me, was one which expressed the ultimate comic refusal – to laugh in the face of death – it was the epitome of the 'comedy of waste'.

Billig's rumination on humour ends with a reference to Herbert Marcuse's book, *Eros and Civilisation*, commenting that history is a dialectic between love and aggression. He adds that it is also a dialectic of humour and seriousness, laughter and unlaughter. As Lacey's performance demonstrated,

> …each needs the other for its existence, even as they struggle for momentary supremacy' …[120]

CHAPTER FIVE

Accumulations, Panoplies and *Le Quotidien*: French Practice and the Transfiguration of Everyday Mess

Walking in Paris and *Plat Du Jour*

> Stories about places are makeshift things. They are composed with the world's debris …[…]… Things *extra* and *other* (details and excesses coming from elsewhere) insert themselves into the accepted framework, the imposed order. One thus has the very relationship between spatial practices and the constructed order. The surface of this order is everywhere punched and torn open by ellipses, drifts, and leaks of meaning: it is a sieve-order.[1]

It is early morning on 15 August 2007, a national holiday in France, and I am making my way across Paris to meet Elizabeth Gower, an Australian artist who works with rubbish, as she is in residence at the Cité Internationale des Arts in the Rue de l'Hotel de Ville (Fig. 25). I walk from my apartment in the Rue de Sèvres, meandering through the eerily quiet streets of the *rive gauche* to the Marais. My footsteps create pathways, enunciating the lived urban space around me. Michel de Certeau's ruminations on the walker making 'pedestrian speech acts' – crossing, drifting, improvising with shortcuts and detours, actualising and disturbing the 'constructed order' of the city – have a particular resonance.[2] The stilled city, reverberating with processions of chanters and the ringing of celebratory church bells, is work-free – well, almost. Bright green cleaning vans swish around the pristine pavements of the Pantheon, removing all traces of accumulated dust and debris from street corners. The order is disturbed by the familiar blocks of wood, wrapped with old carpet and tied with string, which efficiently direct rivulets of water downhill into drains. Strewn haphazardly on the cobbles, these bundles lay at each bend of the steep roads, like discarded multiples of Christo's wrapped objects.

Crossing the bridge across to the Louvre, I pause and sit.

Fig. 25 Elizabeth Gower, *Cuttings (from Paris)*, 2007. During her residency (awarded by the Art Gallery of New South Wales) at the Cité Internationale des Arts, Gower worked with printed papers found at the Cité or gleaned from the streets of the nearby Marais. The works reference wallpapers from the Musée Carnavalet and Versailles as well as memories of Parisienne hotels and suburban Australian houses. Photograph courtesy of the artist.

Each moment, a modality of presence, offers an absolute for thinking and living.[3]

In my Lefebvrian 'moment', subjectivity interjects and the disorder of existence disturbs authorship as I contemplate my own 'mess': in the last few weeks of hospital tests, my mind and body have had a precarious journey to achieve even de Certeau's 'sieve-order'. The external world re-enters. Sparkling clean green bin-bags rustle; American tourists chatter in the distance. The harsh stone of the entrance to the Louvre assaults the eyes; along the Seine, the *plage* employees are washing pavements, cleaning steps, hosing walkways. On Pont Neuf, a lone shabby figure leans against the wall; methodically reaching into a crumpled paper-bag he carefully lines up his edible pickings, classifying and categorising the food he has found after systematically searching the waste-bins. Other *chiffoniers* emerge from the shadows of the river bank; idling by with the flickering downward stare of the daily scavenger, they occasionally stoop to pick up an object or torn wrapper. Then, clutching their *plats du jour* – leftovers gleaned from this imposed, but 'leaky', urban order – they retrace their steps back to makeshift cardboard homes, huddled amidst the concrete pillars of the Cité Internationale des Arts.

Philosophies of the Quotidian

Undoubtedly, as Lynn Gumpert commented in the late 1990s, the concept of *le quotidien* has held a special place in twentieth-century French philosophy and culture; indeed, everyday lived experience has been subjected to extensive critique and obsessive sociological scrutiny since the 1960s.[4] This fascination provided the foundation and impetus for the exhibition *The Art of the Everyday: The Quotidian in Postwar French Culture*, which Gumpert researched and curated for the Grey Art Gallery at New York University in 1997. The show focused on a disparate group of eight young contemporary artists, living and working in France, whose photographic practices explored various aspects of daily life. Identifying and relating their work to histories, traditions and chroniclers of *le quotidien* – through the demi-monde of Baudelaire and the *flâneur* and the lenses of Eugène Atget, Henri Cartier-Bresson and André Kertèsz – it included the work of Claude Closky and Philippe Mairesse with their employment of found images and discarded amateur snapshots, Valérie Jouve's photographs of the marginalised inhabitants of the *banlieues* and Frédéric Coupet, whose performances as a politician from the fictitious *Mouvement Quotidien* directly addressed the transformatory potential of Lefebvre's everyday 'moment'. Later in this chapter, I will return to artistic explorations of the everyday, specifically through an examination of work by the Nouveaux Réalistes which directly employed detritus and found materials and their fascination with the stuff of daily existence. First, briefly, I want to map out some of the key thinking which has excavated the transformatory possibilities and politics of the everyday.

As cited earlier, Michel de Certeau's opaque but imaginative book *The Practices of Everyday Life* is a seminal text. Tellingly, its author dedicated it to the unremarkable, the commonplace and the ordinary:

> To a common hero, an ubiquitous character, walking in countless thousands on the streets … […]… The increasingly sociological and anthropological perspective of inquiry privileges the anonymous and the everyday in which the zoom lenses cut out metonymic details – parts taken for the whole.[5]

Of course, de Certeau's poetic and philosophical exploration of the everyday practices that characterise contemporary life responds to and invokes the writings of Henri Lefebvre, Raoul Vaneigem and others. These writings have provided a focus for considerable analysis, and a number of recent Anglophone studies have reinvigorated and reclaimed the concept of the everyday as a key context for debates on politics, cultural theory and cultural production.[6] These studies explore the philosophical, literary and political traditions through the ideas of a range of writers including Marx, Freud, Lukács, Heidegger, Bataille, Leiris, Queneau, Benjamin, Gramsci and Perec, with the writings of Lefebvre, Barthes and de Certeau at the core.

Certainly, Lefebvre's explorations of the everyday are central. As Shields points out, for Lefebvre, the everyday is an undifferentiated space of the mundane interrupted by a primordial form of time, the 'moment'.[7] That said, Lefebvre's cultural sociology of everyday life was concerned with much more than revelatory instances: his theorising on 'moments' was partly a response to a linear historicity of progress found in Marx.[8] Indeed, his was a serious inquiry into the social spaces of the everyday and their political complexities.[9] His *Critique of Everyday Life* developed and emerged over almost 40 years, distinguishing itself by rejecting the idea that daily life was merely trivial and routine and identifying it as a source of renewal, revolutionary potential and human enrichment. Lefebvre drew on the surrealist concept of *le quotidien* as banal, but then,

> In true Nietzschean fashion, Lefebvre attempts to realign the common French 'daily life' (*la vie quotidienne*) with the critical concept of an alienated life summed up in the term *le quotidien*.[10]

In his reappraisal of theories and practices of the everyday, Michael Sheringham identifies two distinct phases of analysis, arguing that, by the turn of the 1980s, a body of ideas and a set of discourses on *le quotidien* – associated with Lefebvre, Barthes, de Certeau, Perec and others – was available to articulate and inspire new insights and that these have been explored and investigated via a considerable range of media since then.

Sheringham cites recent interest in 'experiential realities' and the intersection of the referential and the fictional alongside 'the realignment of the ethnographic gaze to focus on the near at hand rather than the exotic' as factors contributing to current preoccupations with the everyday.[11]

Although Barthes makes only cursory reference to Lefebvre, his *Mythologies*, written between 1953 and 1955, draws heavily on Lefebvre and extends his *Critique* by applying serious analysis to everyday practices.[12] The ideas of Charles Baudelaire (on the transitory and the fugitive), Georg Simmel (on fashion and the metropolis) and Walter Benjamin (on urban material culture) are implicit in Barthes' slim volume. Reflecting on 'some myths of daily life', he addresses the incidental and the anecdotal – such as soap powder, steak, chips and toys – using them to raise ideological issues and open up questions of social and political power.[13] As here on 'ornamental cookery':

> Cookery in *Elle* is ... an 'idea' cookery. But here, inventiveness, confined to a fairy-land reality, must be applied only to *garnishings*, for the genteel tendency of the magazine precludes it from touching on the real problems concerning food (the real problem is not to have the idea of sticking cherries into a partridge, it is to have the partridge, that is to say, to pay for it).[14]

In *Philosophizing the Everyday: Revolutionary Praxis and the Fate of Cultural Theory* (2006), John Roberts returns us to the term's political contexts, charting its earlier histories and articulating what he perceives as the gradual erosion of its revolutionary roots at the end of the twentieth century. He argues against convivial notions of the everyday, asserting that it must be neither narrowly identified with the popular nor associated just with consumerism. Roberts engages with the work of the usual associated key thinkers including Lukács, Arvatov, Benjamin, Lefebvre, Gramsci, Barthes, Vaneigem and de Certeau, but he argues strongly for an understanding of the concept as 'revolutionary praxis'. As Alex Law indicates,

> Roberts registers the contradictions of everyday life as unending struggle against suffocating conformism. Cultural politics can only be re-energised by restoring the philosophy of praxis to the everyday, to re-load culture with a transformatory, democratic and, above all, political charge.[15]

The idea of the everyday being 'politically charged' echoes Raoul Vaneigem's passionate and poetic contribution *The Revolution of Everyday Life*, published in 1967. Vaneigem, a key figure in the Situationist International from 1961 to 1970, called for urgent attention to be paid to the 'insignificant':

People who talk about revolution and class struggle without referring explicitly to everyday life, without understanding what is subversive about love and what is positive in the refusal of constraints, such people have corpses in their mouths.[16]

The *quotidien* has, then, been configured and re-configured, and, if anything, the ubiquity of the concept of 'the everyday' threatens to render it meaningless. Certainly, there is an extensive and growing body of literature addressing its significance and relevance for contemporary cultures which are dominated by discourses and rhetorics of democracy and social inclusion.

In 2003, Jean-Luc Nancy returned to Maurice Blanchot's attempts to grapple with a central problem of the everyday. In doing so, he identified an important paradox. If *insignificance* is one of its defining qualities, this presupposes that the *quotidien* moment is resistant to 'the canons of the significant' and, therefore, invariably it attracts little attention. There is an eternal problem here, as the Lefebvrian moment of crystallisation – the one in which we might find an 'absolute for thinking and living' – might be missed. On the other hand, as Sheringham indicates,

…this very difficulty suggests something precious and compelling in the quotidien, when it succeeds in resisting the sway of the spectacular and the eventful: a dissidence that might pertain specifically to a dimension of experience whose value we relinquish at our peril.[17]

New Realism and *Le Quotidien*

… the passionate adventure of the real … The introduction of a sociological continuation of the essential phase of communication. Sociology comes to the assistance of consciousness and of chance, whether this be at the level of choice or of the tearing up of posters, of the allure of an object, of the household rubbish or the scraps of the dining-room, of the unleashing of mechanical susceptibility, of the diffusion of sensibility beyond the limits of its perception.[18]

Nouveau Réalisme, the movement founded in Paris on 27 October 1960, based on the manifesto written by the French critic and theorist Pierre Restany,[19] involved a diverse range of artists, most of them from Nice, working in a variety of media. Original members included Arman, François Dufrêne, Raymond Hains, Jean Tinguely, Martial Raysse, Jacques de la Villeglé and Daniel Spoerri, with Yves Klein as charismatic leader: later, the group attracted César, Christo, Niki de Saint-Phalle, Gérard Deschamps and Mimmo Rotella. Many of these artists were represented in *The Art of Assemblage* exhibition in 1961.[20] Here, I will largely focus on three of these artists – Arman, Gérard Deschamps and Martial Raysse. With the extensive use of 'real objects', both urban detritus and manufactured artefacts, their work lends itself, in different ways, to a consideration of how they might be related to notions of *le quotidien*.

Nouveau Réalisme has been commonly viewed as a reaction against the prevailing aesthetic of gestural abstraction which dominated American painting through Abstract Expressionism and European forms associated with Tachism and Art Informel.[21] Though such emphatic distinctions are not particularly helpful as events such as Tinguely's 'Cyclomatic evening' at the Institute of Contemporary Arts in London (1959) and his self-destructing *Hommage à New York* (1960) and works such as Saint-Phalle's *Tirs* both parodied and reflected the processes of Action Painting. Indeed, one might argue they were parasitic on Abstract Expressionism.

Invariably, Nouveau Réalisme is frequently also read as a form of European Pop and as a critical response to 'invasive' US-style mass production and consumerism, and this is a perfectly valid context. As Michéle Cone indicates, the 'consumer' phase of the modernization of France broadly coincided with de Gaulle's years in power (1958–69): by 1968, the 'Americanization' of France was well established, with over half of all French households owning a washing machine. Cone argues that the Nouveau Réaliste artists 'rehabilitated the byproducts, the indigestible leftovers of the *société de consommation*, toward aesthetic ends'.[22] In 2000, Marco Livingstone commented on the use of new and used objects by these artists 'often in the dizzying profusion or with an aggressive and numbing repetition suggestive of assembly-line methods of manufacture'.[23] Here, Duchamp's 'readymade' was being recast in the era of the 'Waste Makers'.[24]

> The wastefulness of western overproduction, linked to the commercial considerations inherent to the built-in obsolescence of manufacture under the capitalist system, lie behind much of the sculpture produced by Arman and his fellow sculptors during the 1960s.[25]

It is important to stress, however, that their relationship to both Americanism and consumerism is dubious and complex, with specific works offering both celebration and critique at the same time. Indeed, Arman spent a great deal of time in the USA, becoming an American citizen in 1973. Jill Carrick has taken a much more ambivalent view of Nouveau Réalisme, suggesting that it occupied a paradoxical position, caught between the seriality, optimism and commercial icons of 1960s modernity and a rampant nostalgia and mourning for the past. For her, works by the Nouveaux Réalistes enact a dialogue with themes of consumption and commodification, but their positionality is much less clear:

Carrick explored the complexities of these issues in a short essay for the major Paris exhibition *Nouveau Réalisme* held in 2007.[26] Elsewhere, she has identified spectacle, seduction and abjection as key characteristics. Her analysis of Saint-Phalle's notorious and spectacular *Tirs* focused on the artist's deployment of strategies associated with feminism, fetishism and masquerade to enact a powerful critique of gender inequalities and social violence.[27]

Here, however, I want to identify aspects of Nouveau Réalisme which shared and declared a preoccupation with both the *facticity* of everyday life – sometimes through a profusion of objects, sometimes through the systematic ordering of quotidian stuff – and the *affective* qualities of such practices. I want to proffer a reading of these works, which goes beyond narratives of their enactment of consumerist critique and reaches towards two possibilities: their restoration of a philosophy of praxis through the 'political charge' of the everyday and also the potential for their encompassing of everyday things – even *ersatz* objects – to provide Lefebvrian 'moments' of crystallisation. Here, I am mindful of de Certeau's project as one which Nigel Thrift aligns with 'non-representational' approaches to cultural and social practices, with its emphasis on

> … the diachronic succession of now-moments of practice … moments which are to some extent their own affirmation since they are an 'innumerable collection of singularities'[28]

The 'now-moment' offers new ways of rethinking the unreadable and 'articulating otherness' – it has strong resonances with transcendental notions of epiphany and key concepts within Eastern philosophies.[29] With the recent acknowledgment of a growing 'post-secular spirituality',[30] I want to raise the *affective* potential of such work to be acts of 'ensoulment'.[31]

> Everyday life includes possibilities for withdrawing from, defending against, its own aliveness to the world, possibilities of, as it were, not really being there, of dying to the other's presence. The energies that constitute our aliveness to the world are, in other words subject to multiple modifications and transformations.[32]

Everyday *Poubelles*

> The systematic and limitless process of consumption arises from the disappointed demand for totality that underlies the project of life …. Consumption is irrepressible, in the last reckoning, because it is founded on *lack*.[33]

Restany, the impresario and indefatigable promoter of Nouveau Réalisme, was also central to the theorisation, creation, narration and retrospective mythologizing of the movement. In the first manifesto of April 1960, he focused on the need to engage 'sociologically' through artistic practice. With all the enthusiasm of a critic keen to associate himself with a 'maelstrom' of avant-garde activity, he argued for 'the passionate adventure of the real' and the idea of 'reintegrating with reality'. He identified points of convergence and divergence with the American neo-avant-garde, emphasising that, among the Europeans, 'the basis for realistic appropriation was far more extreme from the start'.[34] Eventually, by 1963, Restany's insistent attempts to unify a disparate group of artistic practices forced Arman to talk about the need for a process of 'derestanysation'. Nevertheless, Restany's extensive association of their approach with 'la réalité sociologique toute entière ...', no matter how nebulous that may have been, did establish a kind of socio-political context for their work.[35]

A concern for the proliferation of manufactured goods – Baudrillard's 'pullulation of objects'[36] – their place in contemporary culture and their impact on the environment was a major preoccupation informing the various series which Arman produced from the 1960s to the 1990s: from *les allures, les accumulations* and *les poubelles* to *les colères, les coupes* and *les combustions* (Fig. 26). As Marco Livingstone indicates, the title of one of his works, *Plan of Obsolescence* (1964), consisting of rows of sliced toy cars lined up as if on an assembly line, makes this explicit. Arman – artist, archaeologist and anthropologist – collected and collated objects, sometimes dissecting them, sometimes destroying them, sorting and ordering manufactured fragments. As he said,

> I didn't discover the principle of accumulation: it discovered me. . . . As a witness of my society, I have always been very much involved in the pseudobiological cycle of production, consumption and destruction. And for a long time, I have been anguished by the fact that one or more conspicuous material results from the flooding of our world with junk and rejected odd objects.[37]

Arman's *accumulations* – the extensive series of works in which he collected multiple objects and presented boxed collections including cameras, dolls, coffee pots, gas masks, cycle headlights and bottle tops – resonate with Baudrillard's assertion that 'the will to live itself is discernible in an ever-receding materiality'.[38] The artist's accumulations undoubtedly make explicit comment on the wastefulness of mass production and the consumerism of the 1960s. However, his use of urban

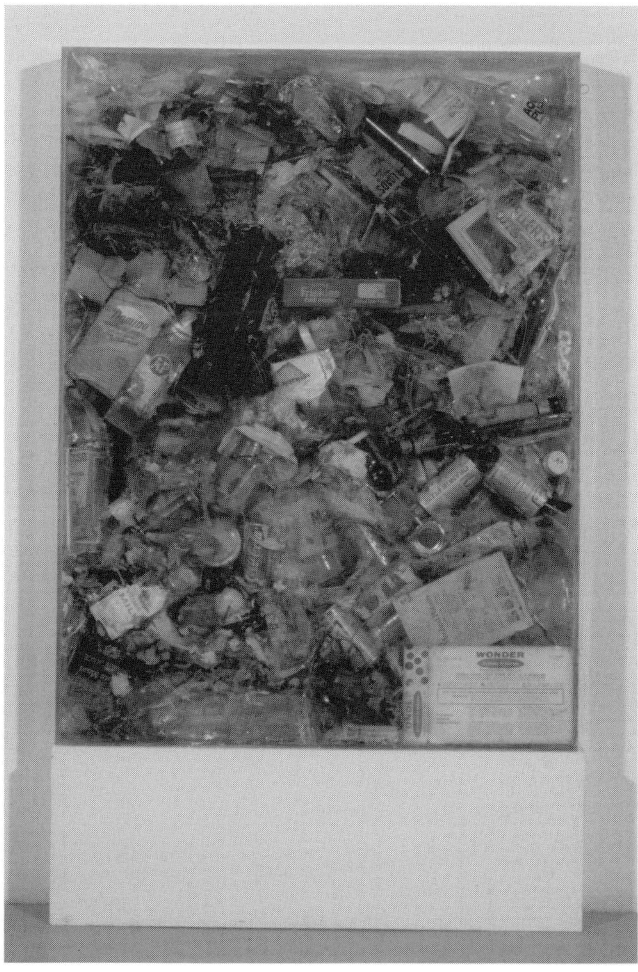

Fig. 26 Arman, *Poubelle de Warhol*, 1969. Collection du Musée d'Art Moderne et d'Art Contemporain, Nice. Courtesy ADAGP/DACS.

detritus suggests, as Jeffrey Robinson commented in 1989, that he 'doesn't necessarily work with objects as much as he does with the ideas that are manifested with objects'.[39] The urge to acquire a totality of things, as Baudrillard noted, not only reminds us of our existence in the world, but also highlights the futility of such a task and, ultimately, forces us to reflect on our mortality.

Equally, the everyday task of organising and putting out the daily garbage – *les poubelles* – might also remind us of our finite time on earth.

Of course, Arman worked extensively with *les poubelles*, encasing ordinary household trash in boxes and vitrines and setting particular named collections in resin (Fig. 26). For example, these presentations of daily debris – screwed-up handwritten letters, cigarette packets, torn magazines, scraps of fabric and packaging – become momentary portraits, freeze-framing the 'ever-receding materiality' of existence. They testify to the wastefulness of everyday life but evoke an individual lived moment too. Moreover, they attempt to capture, control and order the *mess* of everyday life.

Le Plein, the event in which, in 1960, Arman stuffed Iris Clert's Paris Gallery full of rubbish, encapsulated these dialectics perfectly. In a riposte to *Le Vide* (the void), in which Yves Klein had invited viewers to experience an empty gallery, Arman created *Le Plein* (the fullness) by gathering detritus from streets and refuse bins and packing it into the gallery space such that the exhibition could be viewed only through the storefront window. Invitations to the exhibition were sent in small sardine cans, marked 'Arman – Full-Up – Iris Clert' on the front.[40] *Le Plein* created a quotidian spectacle out of insignificant leftovers: it enacted the process of entropy and de-materialisation as 'event' rather than as art object.

Arman's activities articulate a critique of capitalist waste of course, but they can be read through the prism of diverse discourses of the everyday. Significantly, they communicate an interest in Eastern philosophy which Arman shared with Yves Klein. At the time, Klein's *Le Vide* was greeted by many critics as an empty meaningless charade, a theatrical joke. For Klein, however, it represented a spiritual, sensual experience which highlighted the idea that the individual is just a tiny, integral part of 'this great body that is humanity, the entire earth, the universe, or God'.

> Art does not depend on vision, but on the sensibility that affects us, on affectivity, therefore, and that much more than on all that touches our five senses.[41]

This *affectivity* is, for me, reflected in Arman's immersion in the ordinary stuff of everyday life. His preoccupation with mess and order and his collection and rearrangement of the insignificant remnants of daily routine have a distinct affinity with Zen approaches both to the notion of 'practice' and to the transformatory potential of stuff as 'nothing special'.[42]

Panoplies and Patchworks of the Mundane

In 2003, Gérard Deschamps was still being described as 'le plus précoce' and 'aujourd'hui le plus secret', following his 'rediscovery' as one of the less familiar Nouveaux Réalistes after the exhibition *Les Années 60s*, held

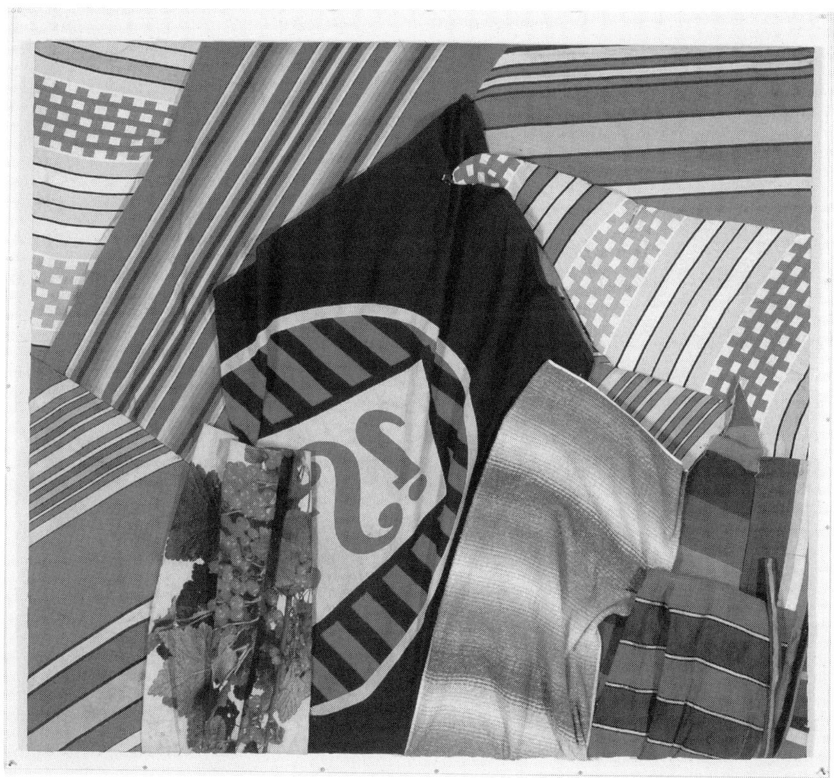

Fig. 27 Gérard Deschamps, *Is Bayadére*, 1963. Collection du Musée d'Art Moderne et d'Art Contemporain, Nice. Courtesy ADAGP/DACS.

in Nice in 1997.[43] Soon after Restany met Deschamps in 1954, he started to work with tissues, plastic bags, rags and chiffon, bringing a *tachiste* spirit to the 'reality' of mundane materials. The folded and pleated fabrics in his reliefs, collages, *tableaux* and *plissages* were later followed by a series of 'patchworks' of tissue and cloth. Sometimes, as in *Plastique au Deux Marguerites* (1961), his tableaux combined garish plastic tablecloths with kitchen utensils. Largely though, Deschamps presented a relentless *panoply* – a term adopted by the artist[44] – of swathes of fabric, scarves, tablecloths, curtains and clothes which are hung, draped, knotted, pleated, rolled and wrapped (Fig. 27).

Through the 1960s, Deschamps accumulated and worked with women's underwear, collaging, bundling and wrapping *lingerie* into bulky assembled forms, creating signature works such as *Les Chiffons de la Châtre* (1960). As Restany noted,

> … les dessous féminins, gaines, soutiens-gorge, corsets et faux seins, qu'il entasse accumulations quasi obsessionelles, insistantes par leur présence plastique …[45]

Not surprisingly, at the time, the artist's use of soiled torn underwear, often resembling shrivelled flesh, was viewed as immoral and obscene. Deschamps was accused of being a lewd fetishist and his work was frequently banned from exhibition. Such prurient dismissal missed a series of potential narratives which had more to do with a sensitivity to human vulnerability through the experience of war than anything else. Indeed, in 1960, when Deschamps returned from Algeria after two years in the army, his work revealed the obsessive traces and trappings of military service – uniforms, insignia, tarpaulins. On return, in a market in Puces, the artist came across a pile of army *bâches,* large canvas sheets with fluorescent patches just like the ones used to demarcate improvised military airfields.[46] The pinkish-orange patina of the thin fabric bore an uncanny resemblance to human skin.[47] Michel Giroud notes that Deschamps's interests, displayed in the series of 'tarpaulins of signs' he made in 1961, were in the fabrics of everyday life and industry.[48] More specifically, for Bernard Blistère, Deschamps's work, with its lexicon of military references, dealt with the aftermath of his experiences in North Africa.[49] His use of flimsy fabrics might also signify the precarious state of France, immersed in Algeria's struggle for independence, as much as his own psychological trauma.

Through his later work, as Blistère has argued, Deschamps has continued to explore the 'politics of the body' alongside the salvation of the commonplace.

> Every piece is the salvation of ordinary objects, everyday things. The rags, the underwear, the various tarps are the often exhausted survivors of a society of crap clothing and manufactured goods, ever more ordinary and standardised.[50]

And so, oddly enough, even with the bizarre *pneumostructures* exhibited in 2005 – the series of inflatable burlesque *zanimaux* such as *Choo Choo!* (2004) – Deschamps has retained a connection to the everyday. Now employing polystyrene, phenoplast and other plastics, his subject has become the banality of mass-produced culture, and the 'no-run colours of the modern fabrics' of his early work is now replaced by the 'ersatz materials of our contemporary world'.[51]

Daily Hygiene

The first World Detergent Congress (Paris, September 1954) had the effect of authorizing the world to yield to *Omo* euphoria .... These products have been in the last few years the objects of such massive advertising that they now belong to a region of French daily life which the various types of psycho-analysis would do well to pay attention to if they wish to keep up to date.[52]

As Barthes's cultural analysis indicated, the late 1950s saw the development of detergents which not only removed dirt and grime but also made the user feel as though they were liberating the object from 'its circumstantial imperfection' and engaging in a moral battle against evil.[53] Singularly, from around 1957 to 1960 or so, the Nouveau Réaliste artist Martial Raysse worked constantly with consumer objects and detritus of daily hygiene, creating assemblages from a battery of household cleaning paraphernalia (Fig. 28). In 1960, Raysse helped Arman gather urban trash to fill Iris Clert's gallery in Paris for *Le Plein*, and the following year, Arman and Raysse showed together at Galerie Schwarz in Milan. The exhibition catalogue cover shows the two artists surrounded by piles of rubbish. However, as Alain Jouffroy indicates, calling Raysse a 'trash artist' would be misleading as later he worked with collage, photography and film, and was more of a 'poet-painter', creating strange dreamlike imagery and tableaux.[54]

In many ways, in the few years in which he was assembling sculptures such as *Arbre* (1959–60) (Fig. 28) and *Supermarché Magie Multicolore* (1960) from pharmaceutical bottles, detergent packaging and waste plastic, of all the Nouveaux Réalistes, Raysse was the closest to Anglo-American Pop artists, sharing a preponderant fascination with advertising imagery and motifs from mass media. Here, however, was an artist celebrating plastic – the material which, for Barthes, was *the* stuff of the twentieth century – in all its vibrant *ersatz* glory. Using artificial flowers, flashing lights and the objects of everyday sanitation rituals, Raysse was determined to embrace the ordinariness of a *synthetic* modernity. He elaborated on his *Hygiène de la Vision*, a shop-window type of installation of tacky goods he created for the Paris Biennale in 1961, by calling for artists to bring '*les matériaux de la rue*' into the galleries.[55]

One of the most interesting aspects of Raysse's vision of everyday modernity though is that his work was saturated in a Mediterranean sensibility. His deployment of detritus was the antithesis of Gothic. As he said,

Je voulais exalter le monde moderne, l'optimisme et le soleil.[56]

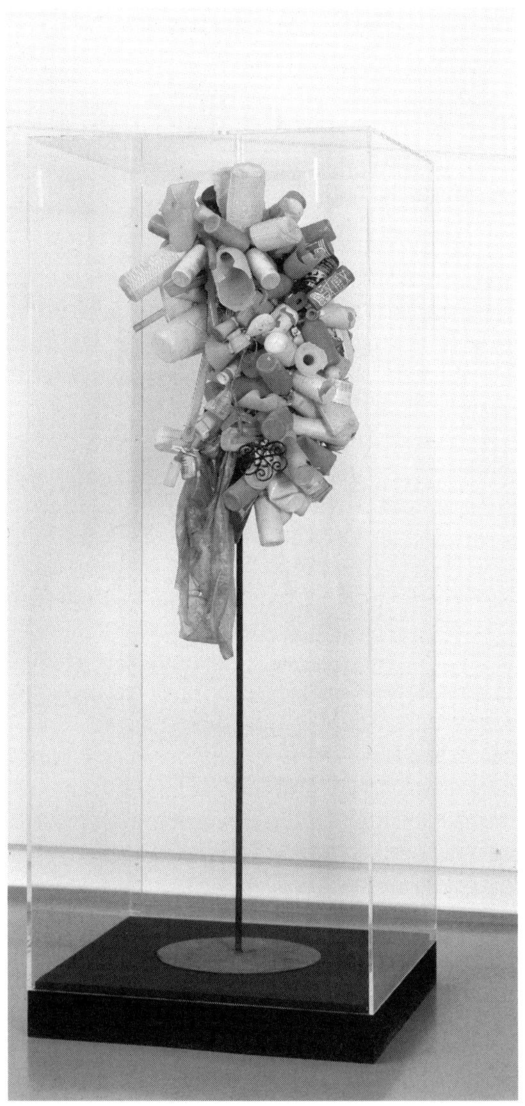

Fig. 28 Martial Raysse, *Arbre*, 1960. Collection du Musée d'Art Moderne et d'Art Contemporain, Nice. Courtesy ADAGP/DACS.

Instead, his assemblages and installations, with their employment of rainbow-coloured plastic and neon strips echoing the primary hues of blow-up beach balls and the inflatable sunbeds of the Mediterranean, encapsulated the sun-drenched Niçoise Côte d'Azur. Indeed, Raysse was a central figure in the 'Ecole de Nice', a term first articulated by Claude Rivière.[57] In 1960, Rivière wrote that Klein, Arman and Raysse had the idea that *un nouvel axe artistique* was emerging, which would connect Nice with Los Angeles and Tokyo.[58] Of course, these were just part of the entourage of artists, including the infamous self-promoting Fluxus impresario Ben Vautier, who met and worked around Nice in the early 1960s.[59] Another Nicoise artist, also obsessed with *le soleil* (and with Nice itself) was Claude Gilli, who created a whole series of *kitsch* assemblages – such as his 'ex-voto' and 'souvenir' series of boxed popular relics – between around 1961 and 1964. These 'devotional' icons made from found objects, photographs and plastic souvenirs resembled religious shrines. In 1962, in a symbolic ritual act of *hommage*, Gilli burnt all his work on the beach.[60] Interestingly, *la plage* was a pivotal feature of daily life for these artists. As Arman once asked,

> Existe-t-il un dénominateur commun, un ton, une qualité, propres aux artistes niçois ou à certain d'entre eux … Le pan bagnat à midi sur la plage, plaisanta l'artiste …[61]

Raysse's celebratory vision of the sun, sea and the joy of life was encapsulated by his 'beach' installation – *Dylaby* – created in an innovative exhibition, *Dynamisch Labyrinth*, at Stedelijk in Amsterdam in 1962. Echoing the much earlier exhibition, *This Is Tomorrow*, staged at the Whitechapel Art Gallery in London in 1956 and also 'environments' such as Claes Oldenburg's *Store*, six artists including Robert Rauschenberg, Daniel Spoerri and Niki de Saint Phalle, each created a separate installation in their own room. The whole project was the experimental curatorial vision of Stedelijk's designer-director Sandberg, and it was meant to create a visceral multi-sensory experience for the viewer who was invited to become disorientated as they moved through the rooms, touching exhibits. The artists mainly worked with urban debris, which was returned to rubbish bins after the show. In his 'beach', Raysse recreated the summery playful atmosphere of lazy days with models of bathers, rubber rings, swimming pools and plastic toys, juke-boxes and parasols.[62]

Raysse used everyday stuff from a new, antiseptic modern world to create his assemblages which were often enclosed in transparent plastic boxes like a selection of marketing samples. His apprehension of the everyday, however, extended beyond the field of commodified objects and addressed daily rituals. With works such as *Dylaby*, Raysse not only echoed Kaprow's notion of 'blurring the boundaries' between art and everyday life, but also highlighted the idea of art being no more 'special' than any other form of 'practice'.

Back to the Minutiae of Daily Life ...

As stated at the outset, since the 1950s and 1960s, the intersection of artistic practices and the everyday has been a constant theme in French culture. Inspired by the Situationists and the disruptions of 1968, a group of artists, which included Christian Boltanski, Jean Le Gac, Annette Messager, Gina Pane and Sarkis, made a whole series of public and street interventions between 1968 and 1972 which, as Cone commented, highlighted a numbing cliché of everyday life – 'metro, boulot, dodo (commute, work, sleep)':

> Fighting the threat of anonymity, they explored the boundaries between creative acts and banal, everyday acts. Instead of a simulacrum of experience, they offered evidence of their own actions; instead of the media 'spectacular', they offered the minutiae of daily life ...[63]

So, returning to the present, as I walk away from Elizabeth Gower's temporary studio at the Cité Internationale des Arts in the Rue de l'Hotel de Ville, having appreciated the pristine and methodical way in which she works with the mess from the Paris streets, I re-enter the material minutiae of daily life. I step back into the rich historic environment around Notre Dame to find people emerging to have convivial lunch *en famille*. Restaurants are opening up, young lovers are strolling in pairs, throngs of people are moving together, enunciating the space á la de Certeau. I join the crowd, but as it swoops under the old stone arches of a Marais street, it falters at some kind of barrier. People file onto the road, circumventing the inert obstacle which is as wide as the pavement and stacks up to the roof of the walkway: it is a huge toppling assortment of stuffed plastic bags, hessian sacks and cardboard boxes tied around the middle with string and rope. The wrapped bundle totters precariously on a set of old supermarket trolley wheels. The lop-sided package stirs. A woman, swathed in coats, huddles asleep at the front, holding onto the collection of street gleanings that is her 'home'. Everyone goes about their daily business around her, ignoring her inertia and her distress.

Coincidentally, at the Centre Georges Pompidou, the retrospective exhibition of Annette Messager's extensive *œuvre* is attracting huge crowds. Messager expresses ' a deliberate affinity with everyday life and relies on a need to pinpoint, capture and transpose'.[64] The artist gathers, collates and presents her inventories of stuff in such a way that there always seems to be the potential for further accumulation. Her repertoire of assemblages, hangings and installations of assorted stuffed animals and plastic bags have a curious resonance with the moving bundle which, like everyone else, I walked by.

Across at the Palais de Tokyo, amidst the airy exhibition spaces dedicated to contemporary art, there is an aesthetic of curated shabbiness, and the manicured mess extends into the underground tunnels of the Metro where flyposters are pinned in a carefully marked area. As I walk back across to the *rive gauche*, above the doors of one of the University of Paris VIII buildings, there is a pointed reminder of one of the most significant everyday practices of urban poetics of the Nouveaux Réalistes, *affichisme*. A triptych mural of ripped posters reminds me that this city is a palimpsest of *le quotidien*. I halt and contemplate this singular special moment and its transformatory potential.

CHAPTER SIX
Cross-Cultural Encounters and Collisions: The Annandale Imitation Realists and Australian Modernism

At different times the work has been called Fine Art, and Anti-Art, and irresponsible Nihilism, and Junk Culture, and mere Junk, and Modern Totemism, and modern reliquary, and satirical goonery, and inspired or uninspired doodling, and Sheer Corn, and Dada, and Neo-Dada and Lah-de-dah and what-you-will. It has also been said to comprise a new Art Movement. God Forbid.[1]

Some of the central tenets of Imitation Realism sprang from these activities: improvisation, collaboration and assemblage using commonplace items, and the notion – then radical – that art was for everyone.[2]

In 1962, Mike Brown, Colin Lanceley and Ross Crothall spent a week dragging urban detritus from the streets of Annandale – 'a decidedly unfashionable area for Sydney artists'[3] – to construct a ramshackle environment. This extensive assemblage of 'toys, crushed cans, cigarettes, wire, bottle-tops, cheap jewellery, old scales, chains, pages from women's magazines and sheer rough carpentry'[4] was variably referred to as funny, irreverent, erotic, silly, clumsy and transgressive. The three artists – the Annandale Imitation Realists (AIR) – collaborated on an exuberant, chaotic installation of junk objects. Primarily, they shared a keen desire to develop an artistic practice of dissent. As Crothall declared, 'we have discarded orthodox formulas'.[5]

Visitors to the first AIR exhibition in Melbourne (Fig. 29) were confronted with a set of bizarre and comic characters such as *Mug Lair, The Young Aesthetic Cow* (1961–2), constructed from egg boxes, cardboard and metal; *Captain Orpheus* (1962), a fragile figure constructed hastily from bits of plastic, cork and wood; and the collaborative piece *Sailing to Byzantium* (1961) (Fig. 31), with its Polynesian motifs and borrowings: audience and critics were bewildered. Describing it, derisively, as a 'cosmic lunar park', one reviewer warned that it may leave some viewers

…speechless with shock …. They will recognise only an artform from the garbage tip – art built from bottle-tops, pink paint, fenceposts, jam labels, misspelt slogans. Puerile, juvenile, destructive art.[6]

Beneath a comic veneer, the first AIR exhibition represented a serious confrontation with aesthetic orthodoxies and modernist conventions. The surrealist painter James Gleeson summed this up, commenting that the second AIR show at the Rudy Komon Gallery in Sydney (Fig. 30) was 'extremely rich in entertainment value – lively, irreverent, mocking and ribald …', but also

> Growing up in an age of chaotic values, these young artists have used their highly developed sense of the ridiculous as a weapon of criticism …but their underlying purpose is serious …for all is apparent fantasy and excess, much of it is a deadly true mirror, reflecting the follies of our age …[7]

Reviews revealed the introverted nature of Australian art criticism as, at the time, few contextualised AIR's activities within an international body of parallel work. Exceptionally, Robert Hughes argued that it articulated a common theme of anti-consumerism and saw it as being 'in some kind of continuum' with Neo-Dada and Pop:

> All these movements stem from a love–hate relationship with the materials, especially the waste materials of our age. A society symbolises itself as much by what it throws away as what it keeps; so that the junkster artist assiduously gathers the rubbish and confronts us with it again, assembled in a new form but relying on the pariah-like associations of its original materials.[8]

Importantly, one of the most balanced and informed reviews came from Daniel Thomas,[9] who situated AIR within a history of Australian Dada and viewed their work in line with current international trends such as Neo-Dada and *affiches lacérés*. Thomas noted that, since *The Art of Assemblage* exhibition in New York in 1961, the majority of acquisitions at the Museum of Modern Art had not been abstract expressionist paintings, but had been assemblages. For Thomas, the AIR work was clumsy and 'overloaded', but it was 'tremendous fun'. More significantly, it explored the poetry of contemporary everyday life.

> Byzantium today for us is Surfers' Paradise or any Woolworths …[10]

Despite their two group exhibitions being described by Gary Catalaneo in 1976 as 'the most important held by any group of young Australian artists',[11] until recently, AIR has hardly been mentioned in wider accounts. Partly, this is symptomatic of a persistent Eurocentrism and, despite all attempts to counter this, the Western domination of art history.[12] Indeed,

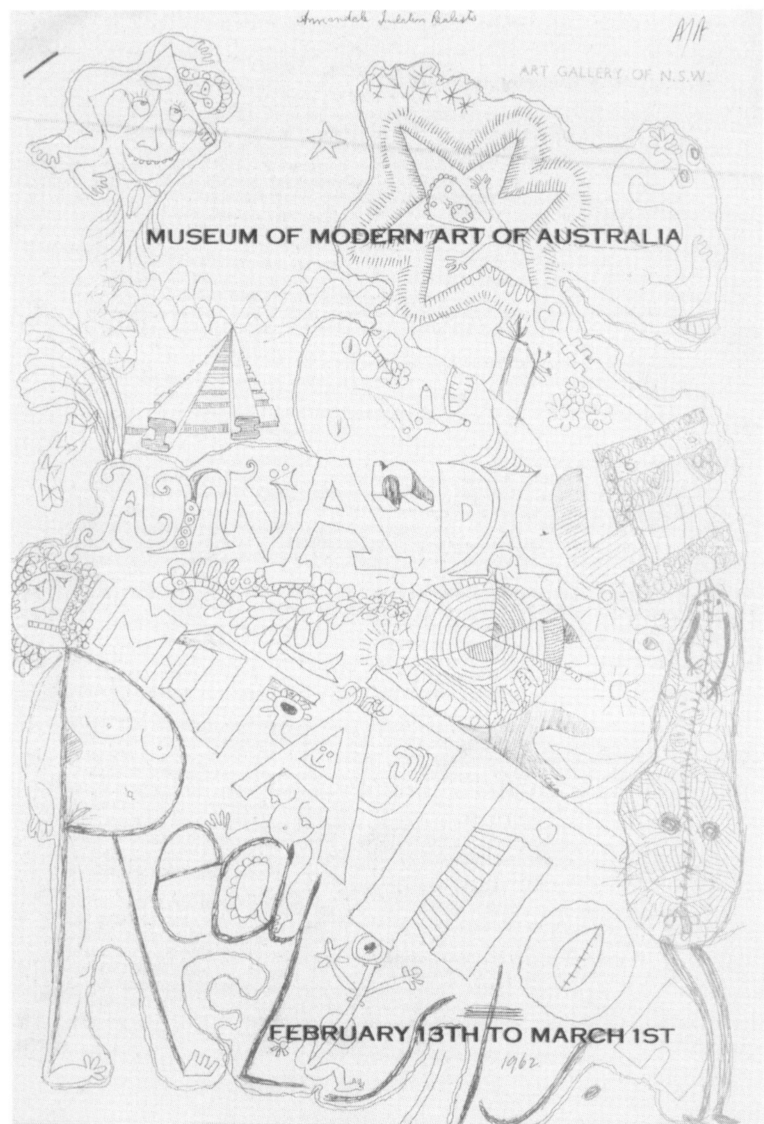

Fig. 29 Annandale Imitation Realist exhibition catalogue, Museum of Modern Art, Melbourne, 1962. Collection: Art Gallery of New South Wales Library and Archive. Photo kind permission of Art Gallery of New South Wales.

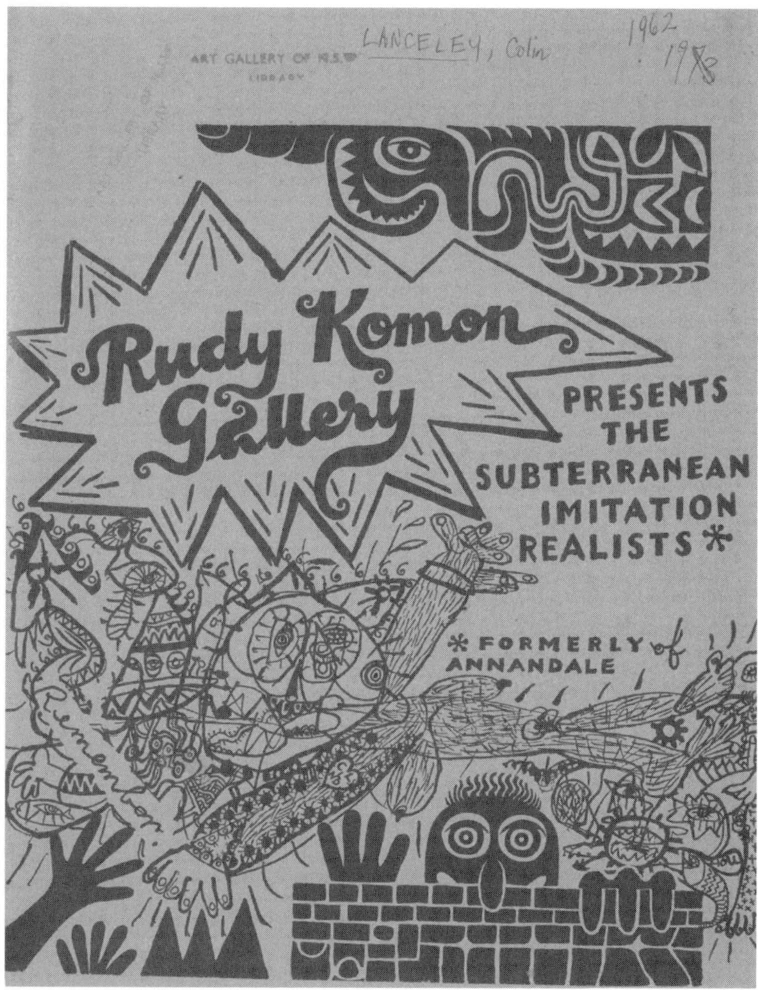

Fig. 30 Annandale Imitation Realist exhibition catalogue, Rudy Komon Gallery, Sydney, 1962. Collection: Art Gallery of New South Wales Library and Archive. Photo kind permission of Art Gallery of New South Wales.

AIR does have obvious analogies with 1960s West Coast assemblage and with Pop.[13] In 1963, Elwyn Lynn explored AIR's Pop connections, identifying shared elements of narrative and satire within British Pop Art, proclaiming both as 'sheer burlesque and sex ran poetic riot'.[14] Lynn admitted that, although there were parallels, there were particular distinctions. The AIR collaboration defied reductive evaluations.

> …their cornucopias of *kitsch* or elementary folk-art assemblages did express emotional states like an ironic disgust with life's ephemera or a mesmerized bewilderment at the glut of mass-produced rubbish…[15]

At a formal level, there are parallels with European and US-based assemblage, but efforts to ally AIR with Pop or with Funk have fallen into the trap of locating it within the Western canon as a way of valorising it.

Indeed, it is not such parallels that are interesting but the differences – and these relate to the specific circumstances and situation of AIR – in terms of what it represented and signified then, since and now. What I want to explore here are the specific complexities of the particular histories and circumstances of AIR – and its legacies. Two particular issues come to the fore: first, its role, contribution and position in relation to Australian modernism. Since the 1970s, the interrogation of Australia's relationship with everywhere else has been an all-absorbing obsession. Secondly, and most significantly, it can be viewed as part of the continuing Australian narrative of cultural encounters or, as Blair French has termed it, 'unreconciled cross-cultural collision'.[16]

> In Australia, as in other colonial nations, modernism's legacy is found in its complicated encounters with indigenous culture. Based in contradictory acts of hostility and identification, of acknowledgment and exploitation, Australian modernism's relationship with Indigenous culture has, for example, bequeathed us a particular expectation that form bears specific meaning, even in its most elemental or abstract manifestation…If in the present day we accept that contemporary art is burdened (albeit willingly) by the assumption that it must bear meaning, then we must recognise that such an assumption here in Australia is inseparable from an unreconciled cross-cultural collision…[17]

AIR facilitates a reading of the employment of trash through the lens of postcolonial discourse. The reconciliation of 'cross-cultural collisions' is a fraught question. The notion of 'reconciliation' – a term which is central to every aspect of social, cultural and public policy in Australia – is laden with value and meaning, given the histories of indigenous peoples. The way in which AIR artists related to and drew on indigenous art was much more complex than Western art's relationship to its colonial distanced 'other'. Furthermore, the relationship of indigenous culture to that of incomers is one which has been at the heart of Australian culture for some time.

As Andrews Sayers comments, since the beginning of the nineteenth century, Australian visual arts have been preoccupied with the relationship of Australia to the rest of the world.[18] He argues that, for the most part, Australia has been concerned with 'the tyranny of distance' from European and American centres of cultures, in both a physical and an intellectual sense. In the 1970s though, he argues, there was a critical rethinking of this long-standing notion of Australian culture and a major shift towards a concern with the Australian/Anglo-Celtic relationship with its own dislocated/indigenous culture.

AIR does reflect something of that shift and might be regarded as a nascent site of that developing discourse as it reveals a dialogue of cross-cultural encounter which was unusual in the 1960s. Rather than allying it to forms of appropriation of the 'primitive' associated with earlier modernism in Western Europe, AIR reflects a much more complex – if 'unreconciled' – relationship which continues to play out within contemporary Australian culture. But was AIR a cross-cultural encounter, or was it a collision? Lanceley, Brown and Crothall have been described as 'urban primitives' who created 'ethno-kitsch'. But was their work operating in the 'third space' of hybridity,[19] and did they initiate a space for new dialogues and conversations about ethnicity and aesthetics?

'Janus-Headed' Modernism: Looking Inwards, Looking Outwards

Given Crothall's comments that AIR positioned itself in opposition to what they perceived as the stultifying orthodoxies and conservatism of the current art scene,[20] it is essential not only to examine the terrain of Australian modernism and its roots, but also to situate AIR in relation to their Australian, indigenous and international contemporaries. The history of Australian modernism has a peculiarly dialectic narrative – vacillating between looking inwards and looking outwards.

Rex Butler has written about the historical quest for 'Australian art' as something of a misnomer.[21] Nevertheless, this has been a major preoccupation for artists, critics and historians from Bernard Smith's *Place, Taste and Tradition*, first published in 1945, through to the various writings of Robert Hughes, who persistently returned to the vexed notion of 'Australian art'.[22] In the 1960s, Hughes argued that one of the specific characteristics which shaped Australian art was a resistance to international art styles, but he also identified a paradox. Whilst he argued vehemently against an enforced insularity, in *The Art of Australia* he also countered the chauvinistic assumption that the task of the artist is to define the collective imagination of the country.[23]

The comment by Hughes and others, about the problematic notion of the self-envisioning of Australia as 'isolated', has been overtaken. One of the most significant shifts in the last 20 years has been an acknowledgement that Australia is outside Europe, both culturally and geographically, and there is much evidence of this in its re-orientation towards the Asian-Pacific cultures. The simple East–West model of geopolitical division fails to acknowledge this.[24]

A good deal of the writing about Australian art in the twentieth century has been embroiled in the question of Australian identity and its relationship to overseas sources and influences. Its provincialism and 'overriding conservatism'[25] was certainly a dominant mid-century narrative. The novelist Patrick White commented extensively on Australia's 'lack of an intellectual tradition'. In a bleak diatribe, White depicted the parochial, stifling atmosphere of Australia in the 1960s:

> Australians are an uncivilised race, trapped in a hopeless, horrible, suburbia … in Europe with its theatres, museums, parks – one can escape from suburbia in their cosmopolitan cities …[26]

White's views were echoed by Hughes, who, in a short essay on 'The Intellectual in Australia' published in 1968, maligned the lack of intelligent radicals. Hughes, with his usual acerbic wit, wrote that the 'womb-like ambience of political stability' was built on the keystone of racial intolerance of 'White Australia', commenting,

> … there is no tradition of intellect in Australia. There are only intelligent men.[27]

This clichéd sense of alienation has been explored at length. Interestingly, Stephen Alomes has identified 'intellectual frustration' and alienation as a generic colonial theme.

> Like other colonials around the world, Australian intellectuals felt the frustration of being inferiors far from the centre with which they sought to identify.[28]

Similarly, looking both inwards and outwards was an omnipresent dynamic within the visual arts at mid-century too.

> Australian Art, like that of other young countries today, is janus-headed. One face turns inward to observe and record those aspects of life and landscape that seems significant to the contemporary eye, while the other is directed outwards in contemplation of that complex surge of international Art that has its source in Paris, London and New York.[29]

This comment by the artist James Gleeson appeared in his introduction to the exhibition *Contemporary Australian Painting*, which he curated and toured to the Pacific in 1956. This 'looking out' – towards Europe initially and then from around the mid-twentieth century to the USA – was symbolised, for Jennifer Phipps, by the transporting of Gleeson's exhibition to

California aboard the *Orcades*, the Orient Lines' most modern ship.[30] In terms of connecting to London, the Art Gallery of New South Wales had an established link to Britain through its advisor Bryan Robertson, then director of Whitechapel Art Gallery – a reciprocal relationship of expanding dialogue between the two countries.[31]

Of course, geographically speaking, Australia is 'isolated' only in relation to the idea that there is a centre elsewhere. Australia's envisioning of itself as 'outside' is important though as the narrative of the singular, folk-hero is a common feature which reflects this. Sydney Nolan, with his Ned Kelly works, was commonly regarded as an untutored naif – 'the billycan poet amongst the taxicabs'.[32] In 1961, Hughes decried the idea of the artist as 'bush-ranging hero' as a fiction with artists all too ready to don the mask of the naive visionary.[33] That aside, for him, much of Australian abstract painting was vacuous, consisting of poor copies of Western modernism and abstract expressionism with Sydney-based art an over-inflated, bland 'charm school' producing painters of 'bad pastoral sentimentality'.[34]

The AIR represented a Dadaistic reaction against all these models. Although there was no earlier history of Dada, there was a flowering of Neo-Dada with Barry Humphries playing a provocative role. As a young student in 1952, he organised 'The First Pan-Australian Dada Exhibition', and for the next six years, he and a few artist friends, including Brack and Pugh, exhibited collages and assemblages in Melbourne, contributing to the city's alternative cultural ethos. In 1953, he was welding junk, making works such as his *Forkscape* and *Cakescape*.[35] Before the 1960s, there were very few others working in an assemblage idiom – except, of course, one of the most prominent Australian sculptors, Robert Klippel. Margaret Plant describes his early wood constructions, done in collaboration with Gleeson in the 1940s, as unique in terms of Australian assemblage. Later, Klippel created intricate and delicate metal pieces. For Plant, Klippel was a 'mixed mentor' as she felt that his work was 'remote in spirit from Dada or Surrealist disruptions'.[36]

Finally, in terms of establishing contexts for AIR, the artworld's historical incorporation and interest in indigenous culture – its own 'looking inwards' – is a key aspect. Current shifts taking place in Australia are not just about a re-engagement with indigenous populations but also with diasporic groups.[37] Transculturation is not exclusively a late-twentieth-century phenomenon: it has a complex history. In 1997, Howard Morphy and David Elliott indicated some of that complexity, pointing out that previous exhibitions had tended to divide work into two categories: Aboriginal art and work produced in a Western art historical tradition. In their view, this perpetuated the idea of separation, masked the history of dispossession and ignored shared positive cultural exchanges.[38] They attempted to counter the separate categorisation of work as 'Aboriginal' and highlighted evidence of a hybridising and exchange of cultures going back to the early twentieth century.

The exploitative and destructive relationship between incoming white colonisers and the indigenous population is well documented. Australia continues to revisit its histories in various attempts to come to terms with colonial acts, land appropriation and the process of reconciliation – and all this has been reflected in cultural production. Aboriginal culture has been exploited and romanticised as 'other' and, latterly, embraced and incorporated. In the 1960s, Hughes was particularly critical of artists like Drysdale who approached Aboriginal culture sympathetically but patronisingly and with sentimentality, whereby Aboriginal culture was portrayed as a 'refuge of innocence' and Arcadia.[39]

The early twentieth century reflected a fascination with 'native genius' and particularly with incidences of Aboriginal adoption of European practices, techniques and traditions. These were often at the cost of forsaking indigenous cultural practices as can be seen, for example, with the establishment of communities like the Hermannsburg watercolourists in the 1870s and church missions in the Arnhem land and coastal areas.[40] Margaret Preston wrote extensively in the 1920s and 1930s on the role of 'place' in Australian art and on Aboriginal motifs and their recurrence and influence in the decorative arts.[41] By the 1940s, metropolitan Australia was increasingly interested in Aboriginal artforms. In 1941, the David Jones department store in Sydney hosted an exhibition, organised by Frederick McCarthy, a close association of Margaret Preston, which primarily explored the interrelationship of Australian and Aboriginal art.[42]

Although until the advent of desert-painting in the 1970s, most interest and familiarity with Aboriginal art was largely confined to bark paintings, it is important that, around 1960 and just before the AIR exhibition, there is evidence of an increasing understanding of Aboriginal artefacts. A crucial issue here was, rather than towards an *ethnographic* appreciation, this shift was towards an *aesthetic* appreciation. Indeed, the late 1950s saw a series of important acquisitions of major pieces of Aboriginal art. In 1959, for example, the Art Gallery of New South Wales bought a collection of bark paintings from Yirrkala, and the spectacular grave posts from Melville and Bathurst Islands were installed under the guidance of Tony Tuckson.[43] Important exhibitions included *Australian Aboriginal Art* in 1960–1, a show of 115 objects of mostly bark paintings and sculpture from Arnhem land with, subsequently, a book with the same title (published in 1964) with six essays, including one by Tuckson.[44] Hence, whilst they were certainly not the first artists to have an interest in indigenous art,[45] it is important to emphasise that AIR emerged at a time of transition when an expanded sense of what Australian art might have been and might become was emerging.

The Annandales: Myths and Realities

The three main artists – Mike Brown, Ross Crothall and Colin Lanceley – met at a coffee house in the Darlinghurst area of Sydney.[46] They were all students at the nearby East Sydney Technical College and shared a general disaffection with their studies there.[47] In accounts of AIR there is a good deal of mythologising – much of it generated by the artists themselves and revisited in the 1990s by Lanceley and Brown.[48] Lanceley, keen to attach their efforts to a surrealist lineage, suggests that their 'coffee-shop games' had parallels with surrealist automatism.[49]

Early critical accounts, such as Margaret Plant's, contributed indirectly, linking AIR to earlier artistic partnerships and lineages:

> … the three together became gentle anarchists, plotting escape routes from art-school conditioning, directing their irreverence as much toward the Sydney Establishment as to process and materials … [50]

The mythologising of AIR as artists on the periphery is perpetuated here by Richard Haese – but he also indicates a more complex interpretation of their chosen name. The group adopted the name AIR as an ironic comment on the 'imitative' abstract art which they abhorred. They did not produce 'realist' work but used the ordinary stuff of everyday life. As Haese comments,

> Roped together as an oxymoron, Imitation Realism embodied a deliberate paradox and was intended, Dada fashion, as a repudiation of normal logic and conventional expectation.[51]

Besides sharing an aversion to a ubiquitous painting style which they viewed as trivial and over-glamorised,[52] they also shared living space. In late 1960, Crothall moved into 28 Rose Street, Annandale, joined quickly by Brown and Lanceley a few months later. The first artwork adopted as an AIR piece was an installation of 1500 Craven A cigarettes created by Crothall.[53] After that, the three artists began to gather, paint and assemble junk sculptures from whatever was to hand. Using egg boxes, buttons, cheap rhinestones and offcuts of wood from the nearby furniture factory, they encrusted and bejewelled objects and reliefs, producing a kind of contemporary baroque.

The choice of Annandale, a suburb west of Sydney City Centre, was important. As Haese points out, its shambolic disorderliness suited them:

> rising above the waterfront between Glebe and Leichardt, its somewhat run-down Victorian architectural base was overlaid with the disorderliness of light industrial activity and the polyglot results of postwar immigration ... [54]

Significantly, its multicultural character also appealed:

> Ross Crothall was the first to recognize the attractions of the hybridized character of Annandale, which Brown would later describe as 'cultural stew' ... [55]

In mid-1961, Lanceley invited the painter John Olsen around to see what they were up to, and Olsen's enthusiasm eventually led to the organisation of the AIR show. After various efforts to secure a gallery in Sydney fell through, the first exhibition was finally staged at John Reed's Museum of Modern Art in Melbourne from 13 February to 1 March 1962 (Fig. 29).[56] At this event, 212 works were crammed together for what was, in effect, an environmental installation of junk objects and artworks. Bizarrely, the show was opened by the Duke and Duchess of Bedford, who even bought one

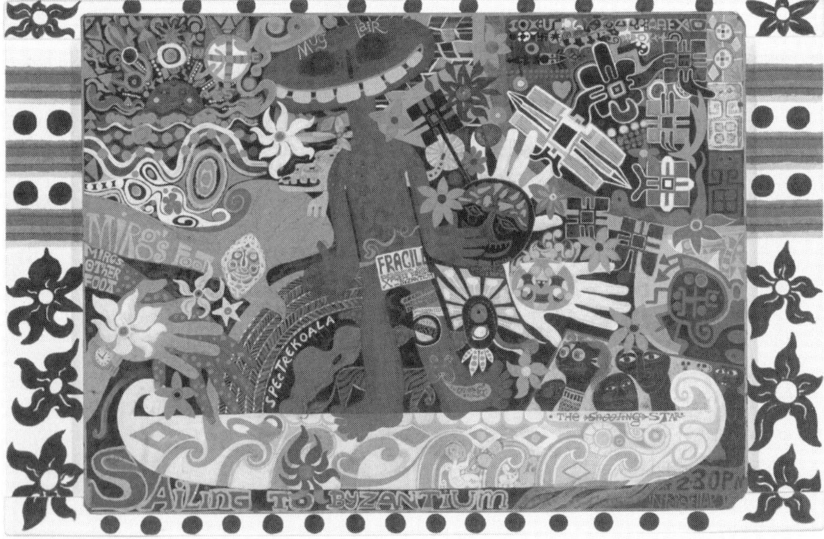

Fig. 31 Mike Brown, Ross Crothall, *Sailing to Byzantium*, 1961. Enamel, pencil and oil crayon on composition board, 91.5 cm × 122.1 cm, National Gallery of Australia, Canberra. Purchased 1981 © Estate of Mike Brown.

of the AIR artworks on show.[57] The catalogue was equally eccentric, featuring jottings and hand-drawn checklists with works assigned to 'Pancho Brown', 'Countdown Lanceley' and 'Day Crothall'.[58]

In April 1962, the second AIR show was presented – now as the 'Subterranean Imitation Realists' – at the Rudy Komon Gallery in Sydney (Fig. 30).[59] In the early 1960s, the Komon Gallery was one of just a few galleries showing and dealing in contemporary Australian art. It had quickly gained a reputation as a cosmopolitan place which provided space for 'outsider' art. At the Komon, the AIR exhibition private view card, printed on dusky pink paper, invited viewers to look at their 'one-way three-way exhibition sideways upstairs at the Rudy Komon Gallery next door but one to two doors down from 124 Jersey Road Woollhara'.[60] The exhibition extended across walls, floors and ceilings into an upstairs flat, the bathroom and lavatory. The catalogue featured statements by each of the three artists.

Apart from conflicting stories about the roots and ethos of AIR, the focus on the three artists is misleading. Mike Brown later highlighted the fact that other artists were involved.[61] The excluded 'others' of AIR were women artists – just as women become honorary males in 'larrikin' culture.[62] Women artists such as Magda Kohn played an important role, as did Leonora Howlett.[63] Howlett, in particular, has attempted to redress this imbalance, arguing that others' and her contribution had been marginalised by Lanceley with his portrayal of AIR as 'daring young subversives' and his 'typically male modernist approach'.[64] More importantly, Howlett felt that AIR's work had been trivialised by Lanceley's denial that there was any 'theoretical basis' behind it. In common with Brown, Howlett claimed a more complex political and ideological foundation based on an ethos of collectivity and collaboration.

> A desire that life and art should be one. There was no fixed point of reference – any time, place, culture was an acceptable departure point, or all together or none at all. Directness of expression as opposed to conscious construction. Authenticity to time place and materials and our own place in the Pacific world as the centre of our universe. Admiration for indigenous art and the use of materials at hand for their work. The conviction that collaboration in group works could combine the spiritual forces of the participants and be more powerful than the isolated individual.[65]

The AIR exhibits in Melbourne bemused viewers and critics. The satirical tone was picked up by some reviewers: Arnold Shore described the concoctions of junk as funny and vital, picking out Brown's *Aunt*

Belladonna with its real biscuit and Japanese dolls for its 'intelligence, artistry and sheer joi de vivre'.[66] Whereas Bill Hannan remarked:

> There is some wit among the dross, and a few patches of good-natured, bumptious satire, but on the whole its a fizzer … no funnier than a bad abstract, though it has the redeeming feature of being rather less ugly … [67]

John Reed could not resist responding to Hannan's lack of humour and failure to notice

> … a very successful revolt against conventional artforms, and the pomposity, preciousness and sheer phoniness which are undoubtedly associated with many displays of painting … [68]

As a conglomeration of raw and daubed junk, in his review for *The Nation*, Hughes highlighted its vernacular, tacky banality:

> Gaudy plastic toys from Woolworths, tin cans, powder-puffs, Holden wind-deflection, cigarettes, toy rayguns. And this poses a problem for the taste merchant. He has built his conception of art around art as a refuge from the vulgarities, the snazzy hideousness of folk culture … [69]

Some of the works were collaborative whilst others were by named artists. *Glad Family Picnic*, the largest single piece in the show, was created by Lanceley. Crothall and Brown helped with its title, which refers to christening ceremonies. Its 'glowering presence' was created through a mixture of bits of torn posters salvaged from Sydney's railway tunnels and various objects daubed with gaudy house paint.[70] Deborah Edwards describes it as 'vintage Imitation Realism' for its rough and ready approach, with street rubbish hastily nailed, glued, but also more often than not daubed with painting, as she indicates.

> Painting featured in the combination of 'trash and tribal' which was the means by which Sydney's own 'urban primitives' sought an authentic presence in their work … '[71]

Between the two AIR exhibitions, all three artists collaborated in paint and collage on the Café Balzac Mural, which was commissioned by Georges and Mirka Mora and created on-site at the Balzac restaurant in March 1962.[72] The collaboration was short-lived though and AIR split later that year.

Irreverent Outsiders or Conduits of Hybridity?

The AIR installations can be read as a critique of consumerism. Alternatively, in the mid-1980s, Margaret Plant situated their vulgarity within an

Australian tradition of irreverence, arguing 'it is foremost an art of play, of ingenuous and ingenious effects'.[73] But the objects have a particular naivety which goes beyond playfulness and draws on ethnic knowledge. Were the AIR artists merely 'urban primitives', or did they have a more complex relationship with indigenous cultures?

Jean Dubuffet's graffiti-style, obsessive calligraphic line and notion of the naif is important here as the AIR artists knew his 1950s series of Corps de Dames.[74] AIR statements stressed their isolation from the rest of the artworld and guarded their 'outsider' status. In 1976, Gary Catalaneo warned against accepting this viewpoint, pointing out that the artist John Olsen, a dominating figure on the art scene who taught at Sydney Art College, was a conduit for a range of European influences. Olsen had spent time in Europe in the 1950s, and his work bore the influence and admiration of Dubuffet's naive, untutored approach:

> ... in the hands of the Imitation Realists, his stylistic legacy – a flattened all-over composition with numerous centres of interest – became an instrument for a more concerted recovery of various kinds of primitivism. They even began to work in a like manner to the archetypal primitive.[75]

But as Terence Maloon has argued, the main impetus was not Western but 'tribal art'.[76] Equally, Plant identified a strong element of 'primitive practice', relating some of the work to marked, carved fetish figures. In Crothall's *Woman Driver*, she cites an uncanny resemblance to New Guinea bioma figures. *Mug Lair*, by Crothall and Brown, is remarkably similar to the kind of idol figures found in Bathurst Island carved sculpture. One of the largest pieces was a six-and-half-feet figure with a torso labelled 'How are you?' which appeared in installation photos beside the *Horrible Lousy Chicken Coop*.[77]

Sailing to Byzantium (1961) was probably the most important, and one of the largest, collaborative pieces (Fig. 31). Hughes referred to it as a piece of 'street-scavenging poetry' akin to the work of Arthur Dove, Schwitters and Rauschenberg (none of whose work could be seen in Australia at the time) but 'fussier, more home-made, filled with slang, caricature and literary references and encrusted with coarse details ... '[78] He argued it had more to do with 'folk art' than with the high tradition of modernism.[79] Reflecting back in the later 1960s, Hughes tried to articulate equivalent work:

> ... there was an element of violence, discontent and social commitment in the Imitation Realist show which is foreign to Rauschenberg; it was perhaps closer to the convulsive black humour of a West-coast artist like Kienholz.[80]

AIR was not primarily an isolated one-off anti-institutional statement; neither was it merely Dubuffet-inspired naivety. Their work needs to be seen as a complex engagement with indigenous and ethnic cultural forms and as an event grounded in its own time and place. AIR reflected an interest in the indigenous cultural artforms of New Zealand and Papua New Guinea rather than in Australian indigenous artforms.[81] This might be seen not merely as a nostalgic reference to a lost innocence or as a patronising Westernised version, but as a real engagement with cultural exchange at a time of cultural flux. Reviewing the AIR work in 2006 raised questions that are just as valid in a contemporary global context.[82]

Undoubtedly, Brown had a deep interest in cross-cultural politics, but it is clear that Brown regarded Crothall as the main instigator and innovator of AIR. In an interview in 1995, Brown explained how Crothall had introduced him to Maori culture. He talked about Crothall's obsessive personality and an eye for visual idiosyncrasies: he had a particular liking for collecting amateur signs, especially ones with odd spellings and irregularities.[83]

Arriving in Sydney in 1958, Crothall, who described himself as 'a confirmed eclectic',[84] brought with him 'an intimate knowledge of Polynesian and Maori culture'[85] partly through being taught by Theo Schoon in New Zealand.[86] Colin McCahon, a fellow New Zealand artist was also an important influence on Crothall.[87] McCahon, compared with Asger Jorn and often described as a highly religious 'visionary' artist, is known for the 'obsessive iconography' of his 'word' and 'number' paintings which he worked on during and since the 1960s.[88] The reference to repetitive tendencies and obsessive working with language and signs resonates with Brown's comments and with Crothall's works, such as *Car Wreckage* of 1961[89] with its ball-point scribbles and expressive, rough approach. Howlett aptly described Crothall as a 'semantic solipsist'.[90]

Brown had direct connections with Papua New Guinea and a familiarity with Sepik art before he was involved with AIR. In 1959, he had worked for the Australian Government's Commonwealth Film Unit in Papua New Guinea.[91] At that time, the notion of ethnographic film-making was in its infancy. The Film Unit was largely engaged in producing films which were directed by the demands of physical anthropologists and natural scientists and the yielding of accurate quantitative data – rather than the cine camera being used as a 'living camera' or 'social probe'.[92] At the end of the 1950s, there was an explosion of artistic and commercial interest in the artwork of Papua New Guinea – and especially in the work of the Sepik region. The mysterious disappearance, in 1961, of Michael Rockefeller, son of the New York governor, whilst in Papua as part of a university expedition, precipitated an article in *Sydney Morning Herald*, which provided the background to the 'big market for New Guinea Art'. It reported that at least 100 tons of 'primitive art objects' were being shipped to New York from Port Moresby every year – and that dozens of anthropologists and collectors were flooding into the Sepik. The National Government of Australia was trying – and failing – to prevent the indiscriminate looting of art that was going on.[93]

So, it is significant that while AIR was showing at MoMA in Melbourne, concurrently Barry Stern was exhibiting a huge collection of bark paintings and carvings from the Sepik area of Papua New Guinea and the Trobriand Islands at his Paddington gallery in Sydney. In *The Nation*, Hughes urged people to see the 'staring, grimacing masks, the formalised birds, reptiles and fish'.[94] Another extensive collection of work was on show in Castlereagh.[95] Viewers at the AIR exhibitions would have recognised common motifs.

AIR was part of a narrative of hybridity and cultural exchange. Brown and Crothall's interests were in Papua New Guinea as a contemporary cultural and increasingly urbanised form. Indeed, it was the incorporation of contemporary trash into the material culture of Papua that was the inspiration for Brown (Fig. 33). Craft traditions and contemporary consumerism merged as bottle-tops, buttons, coins, fabrics, glass and plastic were used in place of cowrie shells.[96] This serendipitous approach to creating everyday artefacts which imported objects and images from Western culture was characteristic of Papua culture from the 1960s onwards.[97] Independence brought a renewed valuing of traditional cultural forms, but it also established the professionalisation of art through art education, display and dealing based on the European pattern of art as self-expression.[98] Ironically, peculiar hybrid forms of art – akin to AIR – emerged in Papua in the 1970s: such as the work of Gikmai Kundun and Benny More, who exhibited their junk works in 1978 in *Garbage*, held at the National Arts School in Port Moresby.

> The materials and formal qualities of Gikmai Kindun's sculpture shows shared aesthetic appreciation with western late modernism. In working with scrap metal and found objects from urban rubbish dumps, the materials as well as the forms of his sculpture comment on the impact of industrialisation and capitalism on Papua New Guinea.[99]

Brown, Crothall and Lanceley after Air

> Where do they go from here? Dada clichés appear, and a few of the assemblages are little more than thin arabesques. Soon there will be that old problem when the taste-merchants make anti-taste into new good taste … [100]

So, as Hughes pondered in 1962, was AIR absorbed, assimilated and digested? Did their work generate other *makeshift* approaches to materials and culture? Did the three main protagonists continue to work with cross-cultural themes?

There is little evidence that it had much immediate impact. A large survey show of Australian art at the Tate in 1961 focused on painting and the commentary identified no classifiable 'schools'. AIR artists were not included but they did get a mention:

> … not that the 'collage environment' of some of the world's sprawlingest, untidiest cities is without its pioneers. Only last year three young artists in their mid-twenties called themselves the Imitation Realists and showed assemblages of objects taken from the plastic Byzantium of the chain stores and the gaudy resorts … [101]

The different motivations of the three key artists determined their development. Crothall left only the mere traces of life and work and, as Anthea Gunn has commented, 'inhabited the peripheries of the art historical discourse' of the period.[102] In the catalogue for a solo exhibition in 1966 at the New Vision Gallery in New Zealand, Crothall articulated solidarity with those viewed as ethnic 'outsiders':

> We are, as a people of Maori, Pakeha and Immigrant influences, largely ignorant of own cultural wealth. We live in a rapidly changing culture but also at a crucial time.[103]

One press photo shows him holding up one of his assemblages – a battered car door festooned with bottle-tops, random lettering and paper clippings – Crothall, with a vacant expression and a tall dunce's cap embossed with 'RC Crotall Ecclectic' [*sic.*]. Like some anachronistic futurist event, he is quoted as saying, 'If I'm expected to be a clown I'll be one'.[104] Oddly, the word 'fear' is just visible above the door. After that he is believed to have slipped into schizophrenia and is presumed to have committed suicide around 1968. Whilst Crothall's work was episodic and incidental, he contributed something significant in positioning himself in the interstitial space between cultures at a transitional point in postcolonial histories.

Of the three artists, Lanceley took the most conventional route to international artistic success. Following the path of many fellow Australian artists in the early 1960s,[105] Lanceley travelled to the UK with perhaps a view to capitalising on the recent interest in Australian art generated by recent exhibitions at the Tate and the Whitechapel.[106] He settled in London, where an introduction to Jasia Reichardt at the Marlborough Gallery led to his first solo exhibition.[107] He continued to work with rubbish, surrounding his work with a rhetoric of 'transformation' and 'alchemy'. The artist became guardian of a more ethical approach to life, as here in 1967,

> ... By rescuing their waste from oblivion, I comment on the civilisation of the taste-makers ... [108]

Lanceley undoubtedly shared the others' interest in the irrational mix of objects in Melanesian sculpture and the desire to create hybrid fetishistic symbols.[109] For him, the 'collage' approach became a fundamental means of revealing meaning slowly, 'layer by layer'.[110]

In 1967, he wrote of his concern to create hybrid artforms that were 'directly opposed to the modernist tendency towards complete flatness of surface and rejection of spatial depth'.[111] In an early monograph, Charles Spencer listed Lanceley's influences as a combination of early modernists Mondrian, Arp, Miro and Ernst, an interest in the surrealists' irrational mix of objects and in the 'function of art in Oceanic cultures'.[112] A fascination with the creation of a 'poetic sensibility' in visual form has been a persistent personal quest.[113] Looking back in 2001, using the anachronistic language, rhetoric and tropes of modernism, Lanceley commented that his references to the real world were always via 'visual poetry' and that his search for his own visual language grew out of the 'authenticity of painting'.[114] The poetic and collage ethos was exemplified, for him, in the work of the composer Bela Bartok and, primarily, the writings of T.S. Eliot.

> As a collagist myself, I was drawn to his poetry because of the way he was able to bring disparate images together into a cohesive whole via a powerful poetic sensibility.[115]

He shared a keen interest in Eliot with fellow artist-scavenger Robert Klippel, described by Deborah Edwards as 'a quiet raider of large loads of archaic machinery and assemblage kits' and a 'purist junk sculptor'.[116] Between October 1963 and June 1964, the two of them shared a cache of wooden machinery parts which they had discovered in the basement of a disused Balmain store,

> crammed to its collapsing ceiling with thousands of obsolete dusty spider-webbed wooden patterns once made for sand-casting maritime machine-parts, arbors and axles, camps and poppets, rotors, pinions and flywheels ... [117]

Before leaving Australia in 1965, this treasure trove of junk provided Lanceley with the materials for a major triptych of relief assemblages, *The Dry Salvages* (Fig. 32),[118] which represented a direct attempt to

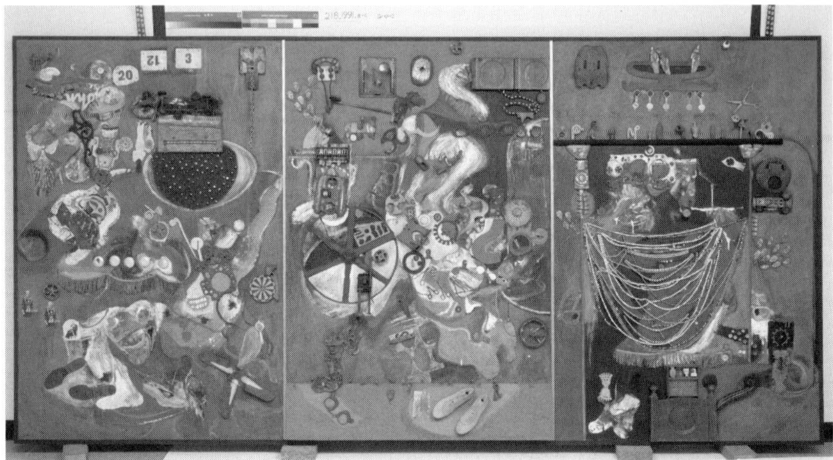

Fig. 32 Colin Lanceley, *The Dry Salvages*, 1963–4, oil and mixed media collage on ply-wood, triptych, 187.6 cm × 374.4 cm × 18.0 cm overall (approximately). Purchased 1991. Collection: Art Gallery of New South Wales © Colin Lanceley. Kind permission of the artist.

materialise a section from Eliot's *Four Quartets*, where the central meta-phor for life is a great American river. For Lanceley, Eliot views life through its objects, flotsam and jetsom, floating and cast ashore at flood tides.[119] Barry Pearce wrote about the way in which Lanceley felt that through his reconstructions of jumbled detritus – broken toys, beads, trinkets, pho-tographs and found objects – he was echoing Eliot's literary exploration of 'a new era of visual pollution as potentially fertile territory'.[120] Later work brings together a continuing working-through of a collage approach – a reflection of the feeling that he had always lived in 'a jumble of collector's detritus'[121] and of being 'fascinated by histories that cling to battered objects, that seemed to adhere to the edges of old things, things that have some kind of previous life, a previous history'.[122]

In Lanceley's early 1960s works, such as *Big Wheel of the Top Brass*, the junk was more exposed. This frenzy of *kitsch* jewellery and flags, fes-tooned with braids and military regalia, echoes the work of Peter Blake or Enrico Baj, whilst his *The Greatest Show on Earth* (1963) was a clut-tered exploration of the vulgarity of the urban circus. Later the junk is still there but the approach to materials and to the process of collage is de-cidedly painterly. Although he continues to describe his work as a kind of 'rough poetry',[123] Lanceley, described by John McDonald as a 'modern-ist diehard',[124] is more concerned with the hybridity of form than culture.

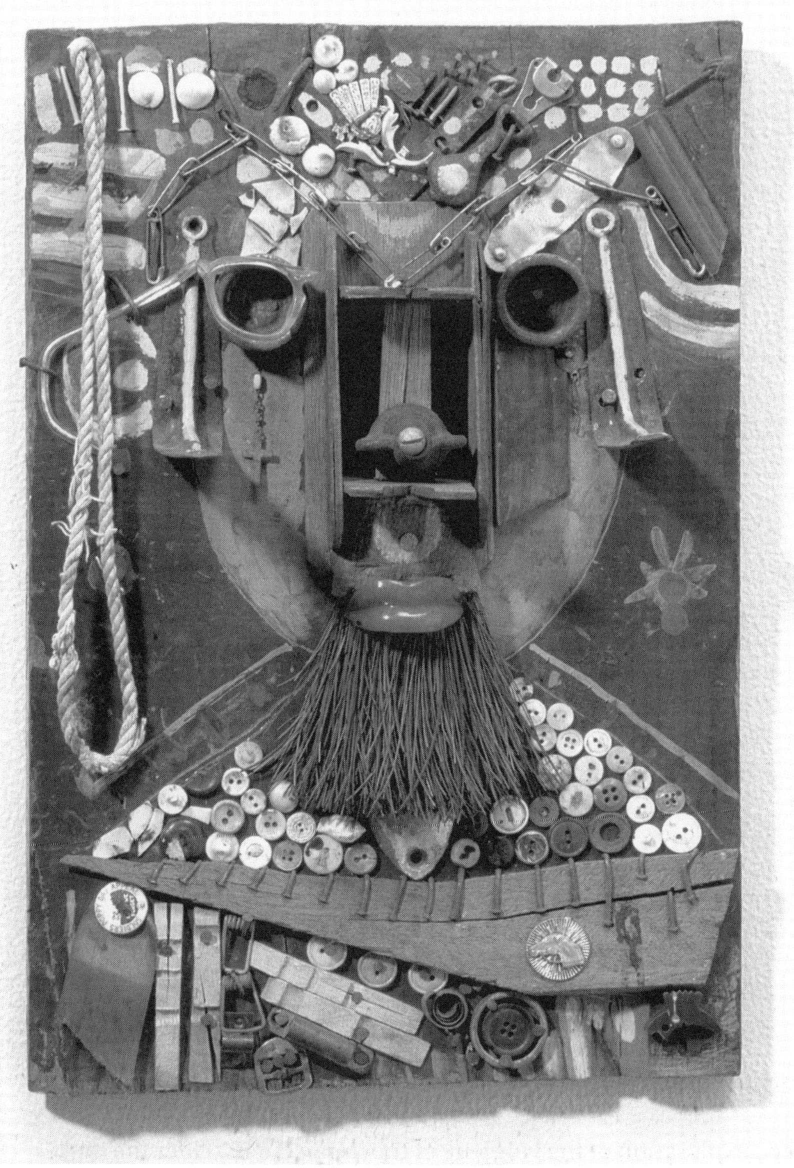

Fig. 33 Mike Brown, *The Little King*, 1961, mixed media on wood panel, 43 cm × 29.2 cm, Heide Museum of Modern Art, Melbourne, Gift of the Trustees of the Museum of Modern Art and Design of Australia to the National Gallery of Victoria, 1981. Transferred to Heide Museum of Modern Art by the Council of Trustees of the National Gallery of Victoria 2005 © Estate of Mike Brown.

In contrast to Lanceley, Mike Brown's outlandish work, characterised by impromptu sampling and eclecticism, might be described as proto-postmodern. In the 1960s, Brown described himself as 'at home with chaos',[125] something which he persistently reiterated as a core principle.[126] Brown's art was self-consciously subversive and confrontational, born of a detestation of elitism in art and a core belief in 'the dissolving of art into everyday life'.[127] He was an artist who, as Barry Pearce noted, 'maintained the rage of provocation until his death in 1997 but was largely marginalised by the establishment'.[128] In 1964 his artwork, *The Kite*, acquired notoriety for embodying a verbal critique of the Australian art establishment. He persistently refused to indulge in the 'art game', flitting from one style and media to another:

> I can assure visitors to this exhibition that the painting on show contains no hidden depth … not because I think simplicity is a virtue but because sophistication for its own sake is a bore … [129]

For Brown, 'trash' was both medium and ethos. In 1983, Brown developed *What Now??* – a large-scale installation of everyday objects and materials gathered with the help of artists and friends and presented at Heide Park and Art Gallery.

Clearly, the fictive accounts of AIR provided by the different artists reflected their differing fundamental and ideological perspectives. Lanceley's efforts in the early 1990s, to ally AIR with a surrealist heritage and Western modernism, aggravated Brown into responding with a diatribe against capitalism and the atomisation of society. For Brown, 'a most tenacious champion of the collectivist ethic',[130] collaboration had not been a 'one-off' but was part of a political ethos which rejected the 'ideology of pure individualism',[131] and he was in various groups and artists' collectives for the rest of his life.[132] For Brown, cultural exchange had also been a key aspect of AIR. He had a personal affinity with Eastern philosophy and Zen Buddhism, but in terms of AIR, he stressed a non-European inspiration, with Maori and Australian indigenous cultural forms being the paramount influence. He argued that they had been engaged in a 'makeshift tribal art', describing Crothall and himself as 'de-tribalised, decultured wanderers in the Annandale Wasteland' and that AIR stood for 'the collaged culture(s) of the ordinary people of Annandale'.[133] Significantly, this reference to the 'makeshift' reflects and resonates with Brown's discovery in Port Moresby of urban natives replacing traditional cowrie shells with bottle-tops.

 Brown's courting of unpopularity and hostility was successful as he attracted a range of controversies. Infamously, his collage *The Big Mess* of 1964 and later an exhibition, *Hard, Fast and Deep: A Peepshow of*

Pornographic Filth,[134] were condemned as pornographic and obscene.[135] With works like *Mary Lou*, a centrepiece of the original AIR exhibition, featuring cut-outs from 'girlie mags' and plastic ducks for breasts, Brown was constantly being accused of misogyny whilst claiming his work was a critique of the objectification of women. For him, *Mary Lou*

> … epitomises the totally synthetic woman. She is a woman who is completely taken in by the modern ideal of beauty and modern aids to beauty.[136]

In 1963, Brown's reworked *Mary Lou as Miss Universe* was refused inclusion in the *Australian Painting Today* exhibition. Following a series of such incidents, Brown left Sydney for New Zealand in 1968.[137] Interviewed in 1995 about the critical reception of *Mary Lou*, again he reiterated it 'arose from the notion of modern dross and rubbish … ' and was meant to be viewed ironically.[138] The misunderstandings that surrounded Brown were irrelevant as, into the 1990s, he shifted into different forms of practice. In particular, he is known for a series of graffiti murals created at night in Fitzroy, Melbourne, and for defending the right of others to make street art. Brown did not make art but engaged in praxis. His dialogic objects participated in the nascent discourses about the polysemic cultural framework of 'Australian' art and constantly acted as a critique of the contemporaneous scene. His work was inconsistent, interrogative and paradoxical: viewed as populist by some, as serious critique by others. Inadvertently perhaps, one of Brown's incidental but significant contributions has been to contemporary folk culture as Melbourne develops as a vibrant stencil and graffiti art capital.

Contemporary Legacies and Current Practice

Reviewing AIR works in a twenty-first century Australia in which the visual arts remain, as noted earlier, 'inseparable from an unreconciled cross-cultural collision'[139] has a peculiar currency. AIR's clumsy appropriation of found objects and its oblique approach to materials have a resonance with contemporary artforms. When I visited the Mike Brown exhibition at Heide Museum of Modern Art in summer 2006, the AIR works on show displayed an ironic, postmodern, vulgarity more akin to a burgeoning punk aesthetic than to 1960s Pop. The centrepiece was a contemporary reworking of a mural which Brown had painted in Reed's house between 1969 and 1970.[140] Instigating a dialogue with the past, it resulted in a Haring-like graffiti-inflected mural which lacked the indigenous visual language evident in the original AIR exhibits on show such as *Sailing to Byzantium*

(1961), with its Maori- and Sepik-inspired motifs and swirling patterns, shifting between psychedelia[141] and *faux* ethnicity or in a whole range of bizarre figures and daubed effigies, such as the exquisitely fragile *Captain Orpheus* and *Stink Pipe* and the vibrant glow of *The Little King* (1961) (Fig. 33).

Through the 1970s, various artists used found objects and junk as raw materials including what Donald Richardson termed 'skangeroonian funk'. The Australian born ceramics artist Margaret Dodd had been part of the original Californian funk movement as a student between 1965 and 1968.[142] A number of these artists, such as Jenny Barwell, exhibited at Frank Watters Gallery in Melbourne.[143] In 1975, Jenny Barwell's reliefs of found objects exemplified what Gary Catalaneo called 'ocker funk'. Catalaneo found a kinship between Barwell's *kitsch* shrines of pseudo-religious 'relics' and popular sporting memorabilia and the junk tableaux of Edward Kienholz or the 'cool and neutral horror' of Bruce Conner's bric-a-brac assemblages.[144]

Rosalie Gascoigne emerged in the 1980s and quickly became Australia's best-known assemblage artist: her work utilised found objects to explore formal relationships whilst also engaging with the politics of place.[145] Her assemblages evoke the local environment – roadside dumps, farmyards, work depots. Her collected and collated objects are meticulously composed and crafted, reflecting the artist's interest in the minimal artform of Japanese ikebana.[146] Commonplace materials, such as weathered beer-cans, tin pans and road-signs, provide a strong sense of place – primarily they are around Canberra. Deborah Edwards writes of Gascoigne as a frequenter of rural council tips – 'one whose sturdy weathered materials had always to carry the impression of country'.[147] She describes Gascoigne as the self-portrayed bricoleur, for whom the original site of debris is of little relevance as, for her, the material is the 'means to aesthetic ends'.[148] Gascoigne did not share AIR's Dadaistic approach to *objets trouvés* but created ordered arrangements which have a lyrical, contemplative aspect. In *Great Blond Paddocks* (1999), Gascoigne took soft-drink crates and used a bandsaw to cut strips: these were then neatly arranged in a horizontal formation so that the nicks and scratches in the wood and bits of yellow paint were visible. Bronwyn Oliver saw them like furrows in a field, 'the undulations appear like topographical surveys indicating the rise and fall of the ground'.[149] Her assemblages of battered objects evoke memories of domestic rural homesteads, re-presenting the everyday through a curious eye.

A younger generation of junk artists might be linked to a similarly formal aesthetic. Donna Marcus is a Queensland-based artist whose kaleidoscopic abstract arrangements of domestic objects and kitchenware echo

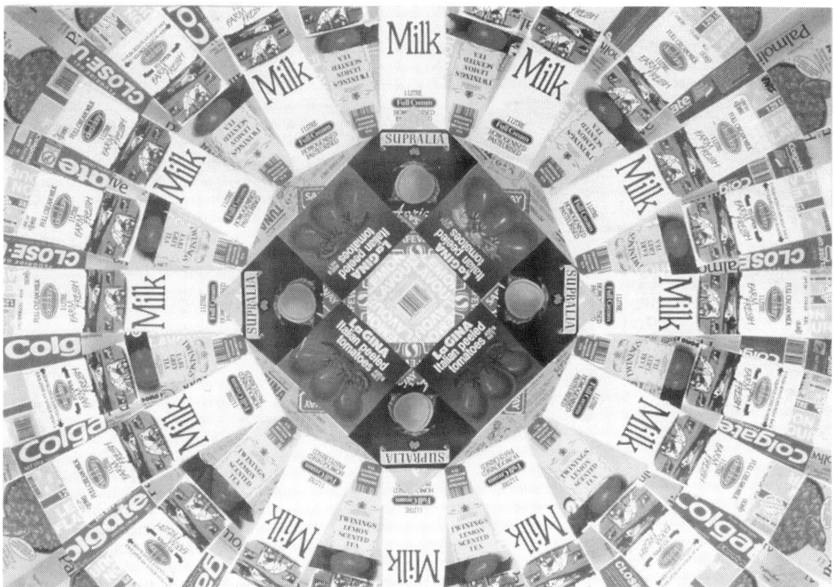

Fig. 34 Elizabeth Gower, *Paper Quilt*, 1978, 64 cm × 90 cm, food packaging on paper. Courtesy of the artist.

Arman's accumulations but also have specific gendered contexts.[150] Elizabeth Gower has been producing collages, quilts and wall hangings based from found materials since the mid-1970s (Fig. 34). Initially, her work engaged with a feminist sensibility, but her continued use of traditional craft techniques, such as pleating, knitting and stitching, has a deeper resonance with the human need to classify and order. Using ephemeral fragments, Gower's practice is dominated by the formal properties of geometry and pattern. With systematically categorised and organised collations of artefacts retrieved from skips, tin-can wrappers and mail-order book catalogues, she is creating a contemporary taxonomy of the mundane 'spam' of everyday life.[151]

Claire Healy and Sean Cordeiro work collaboratively with stacks of objects and belongings. In *Self Storage*, a glasshouse packed tight with an eclectic assortment of objects, organised – as Astrud Mania notes – 'in terms of structural stability and static equilibrium',[152] they echo the piling, fitting, and layering of post-minimalism. But these are their own keepsakes, accrued and stored in a garage whilst they were artists in transit, referencing the universal experience of human migration and global mobility.

Their installations are shaped by the global economic system of this century, within which people, goods, knowledge and information travel, shift and move incessantly.[153]

Cultural hybridity characterises the work of Tom Risley, an improviser with discarded materials from bleached thongs beach-combed from North Queensland to scrap car bonnets from Brisbane car-wreckers and

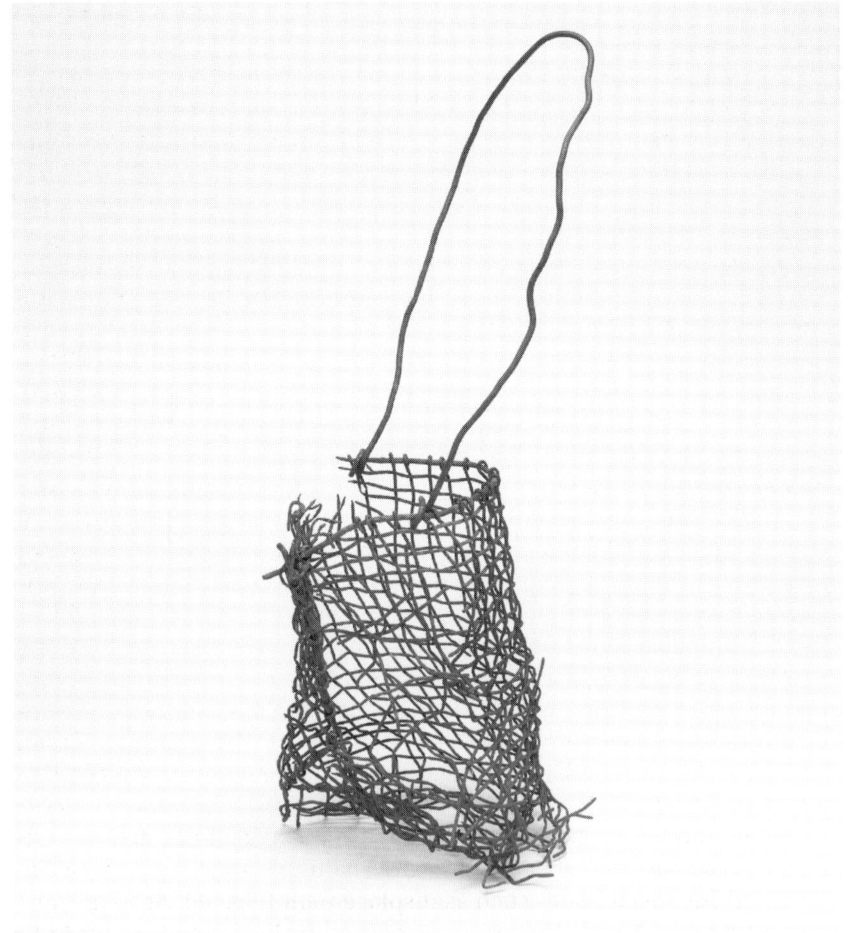

Fig. 35 Lorraine Connelly-Northey, *Narrbong (String Bag)*, 2008, rusted mesh fencing wire, 49.0 cm × 16.0 cm × 15.0 cm. Purchased with funds provided by the Women's Art Group, 2008. Collection: Art Gallery of New South Wales. Kind permission of the artist.

junkyards.[154] His fetishistic totems engage with indigenous Australian and Pacific cultures, yet they reflect an itinerant existence which crosses rural, coastal and urban environments. An exhibition of his work in 1992, *Indigenous Objects and Urban Offcasts*, featured work created since 1983 when he started to collect objects washed up on Cape York beach, developing his own 'colloquial language using found objects'.[155]

Lorraine Connelly-Northey's carefully crafted works echo the kind of hybrid 'urban primitivism' of the earlier AIR objects. She explores her Waradgerie roots and is inspired by the bush environments of north-western Victoria where she grew up.[156] In the 1990s, she began to gather found materials, a resourcefulness she feels she inherited from her Irish father, who encouraged her to work with scavenged materials from rubbish tips. Connelly-Northey uses Aboriginal techniques such as 'coil-weaving' to 'constantly transform the rich repertory of traditional Aboriginal artefacts into contemporary postcolonial objects'.[157] Referring to the traditional forms of *koolimans* (containers) and *narrbongs* (knotted or looped string-bags), her small vessels are intricately crafted with a combination of organic materials – feathers, broken shells and natural grasses – and industrial materials which signify colonial invasion, control and imprisonment – rusty wire netting, corrugated iron and wire mesh.[158] In 2004–5, her large-scale installation – *Hunter-gatherer* – brought together a series of crafted works which drew on indigenous and contemporary material cultures, subverting and interrogating definitions and tropes of each through combining organic found materials and the physical remnants of colonisation. Connelly-Northey's practice represents an amalgamation of artforms and craft traditions which goes beyond simplistic notions of hybridity, producing objects which engage with cultural memory and critique histories.

Any investigation of Australian art of the last 50 years or so reveals a history beset with efforts to define ethnic categories of practice. Artists such as Tracey Moffatt, Gordon Bennett and Lin Onus see themselves as contemporary artists, regardless of their ethnicity. The global art world, whilst it remains mired in a discourse of nationality, is struggling to break down such categories. Cultural hybridity has become a cliché, sometimes underpinned by an uneasy politics of direct action. Ash Keating is a young Australian activist-artist who uses waste as a raw material to address social issues such as displacement (Fig. 36). As Zara Stanhope comments, his work is 'transparently ethical', aiming to contribute 'to socio-political discourse rather than aesthetic pleasure'.[159] In Spring 2006, in a prolonged public performance in Melbourne, Keating gathered Commonwealth Games advertising and publicity materials from skips and

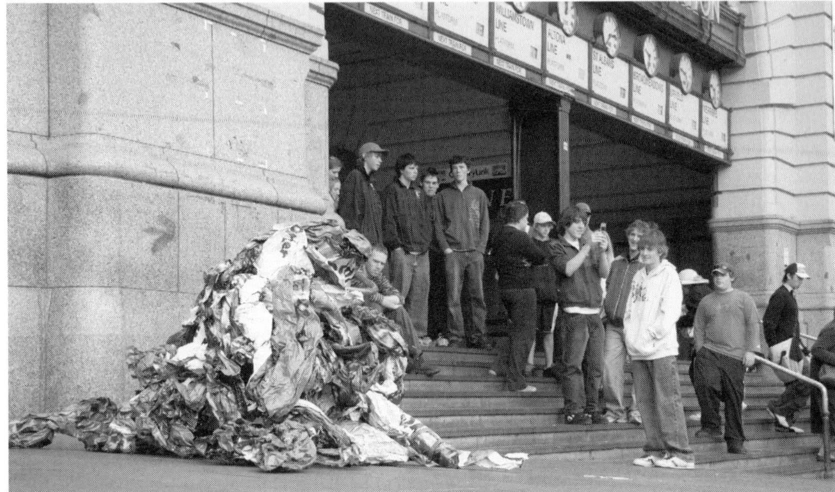

Fig. 36 Ash Keating, *Support Can Make a Difference*, intervention performance with manipulated vinyl sticker advertising at Flinders St Station, Melbourne, 18 May 2006. Photograph Andrew Noble. Courtesy of the artist.

made them into a makeshift shelter, not only to highlight the waste of resources but also to demonstrate the hypocrisy of the notion of 'commonwealth'. Part of the pre-Games 'cleaning up' process had involved the temporary removal of homeless people, a group dominated by indigenous peoples, from Melbourne's public spaces.[160]

Interestingly though, the artist whose work perhaps most reflects cross-cultural dialogues is the Scottish-born 'Australian' Ian Fairweather who was born at the end of the nineteenth century. As Hughes pointed out in 1961, whilst other Australian artists were quick to don the mask of the naive visionary, Fairweather's life was a prolonged flight from Western society.[161] Fairweather's meandering calligraphic line reflects a life of solitary wandering and drifting – in China, South-East Asia and the north of Australia through the 1920s and 1930s. On 29 April 1952, he constructed a raft from debris and floated out of Darwin Harbour, drifted two weeks and washed up on the remote Bribie Island off Timor. In his self-imposed exile, he created a series of paintings with the quasi-religious gravity and spiritual intensity of Rothko. Peter Holbrook describes them as having a 'visionary, transcendental, idealist, or mystical dimension'.[162] By the 1950s, Fairweather had acquired legendary status, his meagre existence known more recently through Robert Walker's remarkable photographs of him painting and reading in his makeshift hut in the 1960s.

Rex Butler, who has written extensively and eloquently on Australia and the hybridity debate, described Fairweather's work as

> … this imagining of a global culture without borders … and it is in the imagining of this syncretic, non-national art … that Fairweather is absolutely an artist of the 21st century, fully the contemporary of Tracey Moffatt and Ricky Swallow.[163]

In 2006, in the context of the 'commonwealth' debate, Butler reminded us that it is time to abandon 'centres and peripheries' and to leave behind, once and for all, the attempt to understand Australian identity in relation to some 'elsewhere' overseas. For Butler, the definition of 'Australian art' is a redundant debate. The real issue, as he indicates, is neither about determining prevailing aesthetics nor about hybridity and appropriation – but it is about a set of localisms. He asks, can we imagine Australian art in another way? Rather than identifying its difference from the rest of the world, perhaps there is a need to reclaim a belonging to it?[164] In place of a disentangling of cultural roots maybe there should be an acceptance of amalgamation. AIR made an episodic, but significant, contribution to initiating this process.

Afterword: Digital Ordure, Leftovers and Leavings

The vectors fly out of the coop. Meanwhile the body passes from moment to moment in real time, until the last intake of breath; language in the process of disintegration tips over the edge. Is this one of the true boundaries where ordure comes into its own?[1]

This book has considered art's use of trash, looking at selected moments through and beyond the twentieth century and the particularities of their specific histories, locations and legacies. The politics of junk is complex and contested: it is tied up with social and cultural histories and with economies and ecologies of human and consumer waste. Meanwhile, the use of trash as a raw material for art-making is currently not just preponderant, it is endemic: from Jean Shin's accumulations of the leftovers of daily life,[2] Tomoko Takahashi's chaotic installations of thrown-away consumer tat[3] to the Ghanaian 'transavantgarde' El Anatsui's enormous hangings of recycled bottle-tops and wire, installed between the majestic columns of the Arsenale in the 2007 Venice Biennale.[4] And, of course, trash is 'cool'. Shin's and Anatsui's creations have popular appeal with rapidly proliferating websites such as everydaytrash.com – 'a closer look at what we throw away' – documenting the re-appropriation and enculturation of our daily domestic discards and the detritus of global capitalism.

> Ghanaian-born/Nigerian-dwelling artist El Anatsui uses all kinds of cool trash in his work: from would-be discarded cassava graters to the caps used to top off local home brew, to milk tins and so on ...[5]

Despite all this, besides providing raw stuff for art-making, trash provides a metaphor which continues to signify cultural radicalism and political subversiveness. In 2009, Michael Cataldi and Nils Norman set up the University of Trash at the SculptureCenter in New York, creating an installation from recycled and found materials which then functioned as a temporary space for hosting a programme of lectures, workshops and events (Fig. 37).[6] In the spirit of the critical pedagogical writings of Paolo Freire and countercultural experiments in the 1960s, the 'school' was open and free to all, potentially creating a TAZ – temporary autonomous zone[7] – a

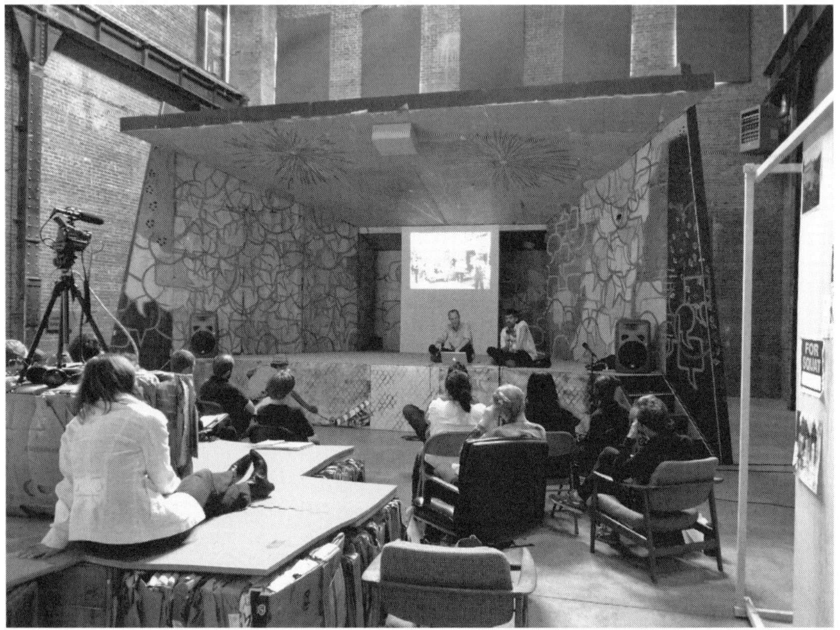

Fig. 37 *The Baltimore Development Cooperative at University of Trash* at the SculptureCenter, New York, 10 May–3 August 2009, project by Michael Cataldi and Nils Norman. Photo by Michael Cataldi, reproduced with kind permission of Michael Cataldi and Nils Norman.

space for radical ideas and activism, utilising a makeshift aesthetic and the ethics of mutual aid.

So, readings of junk depend on our own subjectivities but also they are shaped by trash's situated histories as well as a multiplicity of other contexts encapsulated by Doreen Massey's 'time–place' particularities, highlighted at the outset of this study. Widespread does not equal homogeneous or universal. There is no *mere* trash.

This rumination started with the dirty, sticky affective stuff and it ends there too – with the physical matter with which Mierle Laderman Ukeles, one of Jo Anna Isaak's 'garbage girls',[8] has worked for over 30 years.

> We need holistic inter-connected perceptual models of how we connect and how we add up ...[9]

In 2006, I interviewed Ukeles in her office in New York's Sanitation Department where she has been unpaid artist-in-residence since 1977. She talked eloquently about her early 'maintenance' projects, scrubbing the streets, swilling gallery steps and museum floors, pioneering practices which highlighted the gendered nature of 'cleaning' and were part of a contemporaneous feminist critique and reclamation of social and cultural discourse in the 1970s.[10] Continually though, she returned to the question of the political significance and social value of 'hidden' labour more generally. Many of her projects, aiming to reveal and erase the boundaries between citizen and waste, have extended and expanded over a number of years: *Touch Sanitation*, the ritualistic and celebratory performative piece in which, over 11 months, she shook the hands of New York City's 8,500 sanitation workers, and *Flow City*, 'a radical penetration of art into the workplace',[11] a project based at the 59th Street Marine Transfer Station on the Hudson River, designed to incorporate waste-processing into the fabric of the building's structure, enabling New Yorkers to experience their own garbage being processed around them as they move through transparent passages and walkways (Fig. 38).

> I want visitors to feel the extreme diversity in different materials... I want visitors to see the materials in a kind of hovering state of flux: thrown out, not yet back. I want the visitors to pass through a state of potentiality.[12]

Furthermore, Ukeles' ongoing work on the Freshkills project on Staten Island, to transform what was once the world's largest garbage landfill site, has been described as a 'meditation on sanitation, garbage and tragedy'. Following 9/11, hundreds of thousands of tons of debris, including human ash, was deposited there. Inevitably, as *Village Voice* noted, this added 'a layer of tragedy to a site that was already contested, fragile, enormous, resented and political'.[13] Mindful of the complex political issues surrounding the project, Ukeles also argues that garbage is a powerfully affective and commemorative substance which signifies both the vital and mortal aspects of being human.

> In this 50 year-old social sculpture we have all produced, of four mountains made from 150 million cubic yards of the un-differentiated, unnamed, no-value *garbage*, whose every iota of material identity has been banished, the memorial, graveyard – or whatever it is – needs to be created out of an utterly opposite kind of social contract... a chasm-change in attitude is required, one of very deliberate differentiating, of naming, of attentive reverence for each mote of dust from each lost individual. Thus remembered. This must become a place that returns identity to, not strips identity from, each perished person.[14]

Perhaps though, one of the greatest ecological concerns of the twenty-first century will be virtual waste, cybertrash and spam. Or maybe it will be the escalating accumulations of lethal electric and electronic items

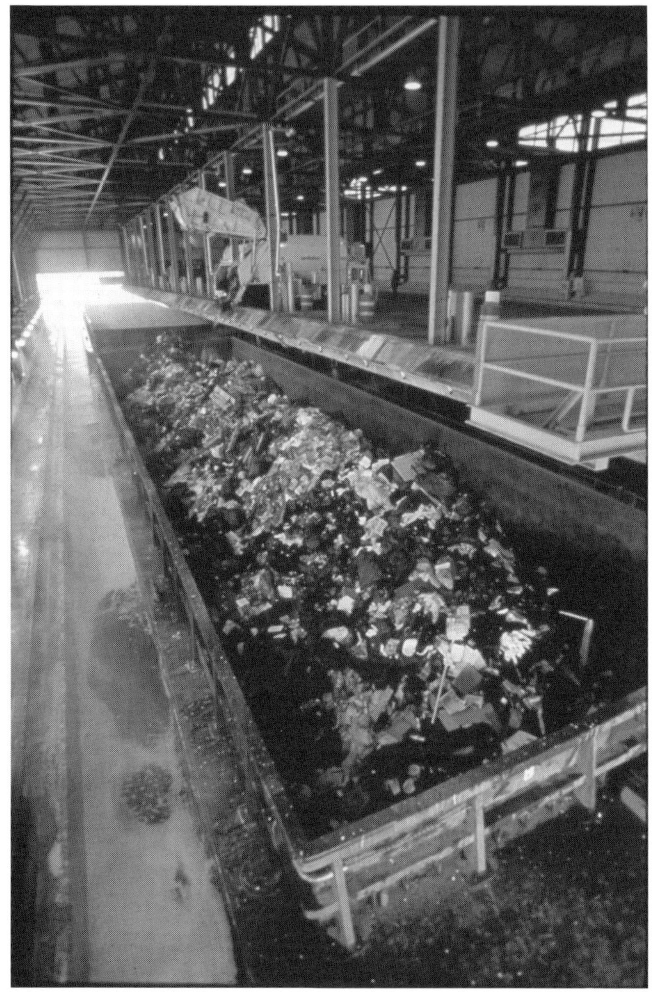

Fig. 38 Mierle Laderman Ukeles, *Flow City*, 1983–1990. Courtesy Ronald Feldman Fine Arts, New York.

and components – *e-waste* – with which artists and activists such as the Australian-based Slow Art Collective have been working.[15]

For over 30 years, the British artist Stuart Brisley has been concerned with waste in all its manifestations – dirt, excrement, pus, pollution – creating visceral performances in the 1960s and 1970s which had powerful political contexts. As a committed scavenger, Brisley has long been fascinated by the 'rubbish dump' and his practice derives from both his

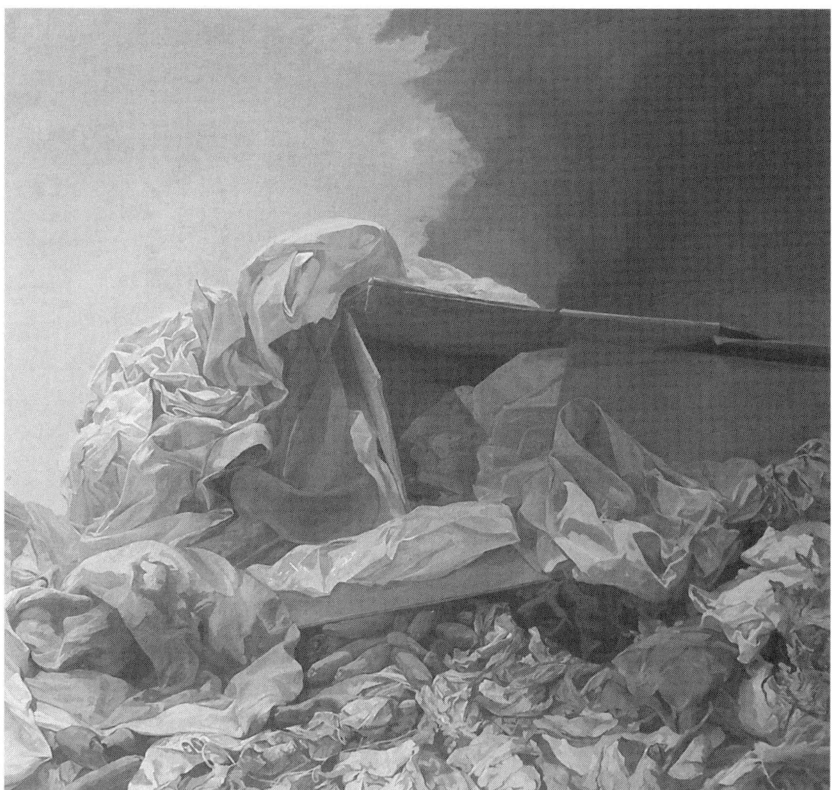

Fig. 39 Stuart Brisley, *Dead-Line*, 2006, oil on canvas 48 × 48 in. © Stuart Brisley/ Photograph courtesy of England & Co Gallery, London.

understanding of the 'symbolic power of the discarded object or displaced artefact'[16] and his association of ordure with global capitalism. His co-foundation of the Museum of Ordure, an online project which presents the process of digital decay – 'bit rot' – explores cyberspace as a site where language and imagery disintegrate just as in the physical world.[17]

Paradoxically, the digital word returns us, eternally, to the real. Brisley's recent series of paintings of old rags and crushed cardboard collected from the streets around Spitalfields in East London mark a return to the theatrical materiality of waste (Fig. 39). The forms express a baroque extravagance, but their fragmentary nature has poignancy. Inevitably, they resonate with the crumpled belongings of the homeless in shop-doorways but, within the folds, there is a lyrical and elegiac sense of belonging and loss.

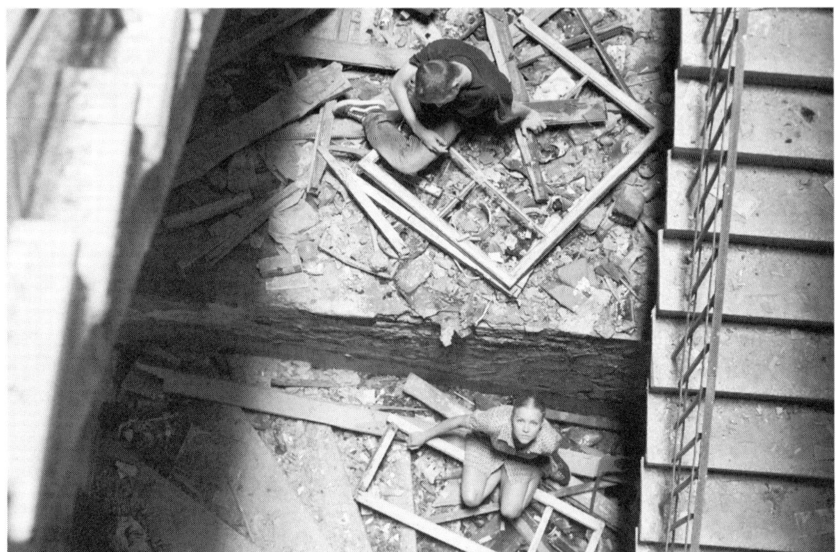

Fig. 40 Alexey Salmanov, *All God's Children Can Dance* 2008, photograph. Ukrainian artist, Salmanov, worked with a classical dancer, Alyona Shoptenko, and a break-dancer, Maxim the Cat, in destroyed buildings in Kiev. Courtesy of the artist.

So, the poetics of remaindered matter, the real physical stuff, persists. Abandoned and discarded objects feed the imagination: like the single crimson suede stiletto shoe I found on West 27th St in New York in September 2009, triumphantly parked in the middle of the pavement beside the neatly stacked cardboard and the bulging black garbage sacks awaiting collection. Or the cheap white plastic rosary beads which someone had dropped in haste on Columbus Avenue, retrieved as I ran across the road and, now, sitting by my computer as I type. These evocative objects have their own stories to tell, yet they accrue new meanings and narratives.

And where there is industrial and architectural dereliction, in the midst of war or urban decay, the flowers of evil blossom and lyric poetry *is* written.[18] A final visual note. With the wreckage of Kiev as a backdrop, the young Ukrainian artist, Alexey Salmanov, produces a series of sublime images (Fig. 40). Aesthetically entrancing, they portray the vulnerability of the body as well as the vitality of the human spirit. The politics and poetics of trash goes on.

NOTES

PREFACE

1. The 'rag and bone' chorus line from *Any Old Iron* made famous in the early twentieth century by Harry Champion and composed c. 1911 by Chas Collins, Fred Terry and E.A. Sheppard.

2. Sillitoe, Alan, *The Ragman's Daughter* [first published 1963] (London, 1966).

3. Benjamin, Walter, 'The Paris of the second Empire in Baudelaire', in C. Baudelaire (ed.), *A Lyric Poet in the Era of High Capitalism* [first published in English 1973] (London, 1993), p. 19.

4. My PhD research also contributed to a monograph *Assembling the Absurd: George Fullard 1923–1973*, London: Lund Humphries/Henry Moore Foundation, 1998 and two exhibitions – *A Fastidious Primitive: George Fullard*, Bothy Gallery, Yorkshire Sculpture Park, 1997 and *Playing with Paradox*, Mappin Art Gallery, Sheffield and Kettle's Yard, Cambridge, 1998. Related research papers include *Junk, funk and empty space: trashing material values in the 50s and 60s* (Association of Art Historians conference April 1999), *An evening of cross-'Beats', cut-ups and rubbish: British and American assemblage in the Sixties* (PMSA public lecture series 2002), *Radical rooting and street pickings: San Francisco Bay Area assemblage then and now* (Henry Moore Institute, Leeds 2006) and *Scavenging from margins to mainstream: artist as bricoleur in the 21ˢᵗc* (Centre André Chastel, Paris 2008). Also see my website www.bricolagekitchen.com a multi-faceted project space for creative-critical practice and collaborations with visual, performance artists, soundsmiths and wordmongers in an exploration of the ideas, narratives and processes of improvisation and the makeshift.

5. Denzin, Norman K. and Lincoln, Yvonna S., *Handbook of Qualitative Research* (London, 1994), p. 3.

6. Kendall, Tina and Koster, Kristin, 'Critical Approaches to Cultural Recycling', *Other Voices* 3/1 (May 2007) http://www.othervoices.org/3.1/guesteditors/index.php

INTRODUCTION

1. *Dieter Roth/Martin Kippenberger* at Hauser & Wirth's Coppermill, 92–108, Cheshire Street (London, 26 May–27 August 2006).

2. Searle, Adrian, 'Dust to dust', *The Guardian*, 30 May 2006, p. 18.

3. Searle: *The Guardian*, p. 19.

4. Robinson, Julia, 'The Voracious Vernacular', in *Assemblage*, New York: Zwirner & Wirth (11 November 2003–31 January 2004).

5. See Vincentelli, Allessandro (ed.), *Edward Kienholz and Nancy Reddin Kienholz*, exhibition catalogue, Gateshead: Baltic Centre for Contemporary Art (14 May–29 August 2005) and Sydney: Museum of Contemporary Art (16 December–5 March 2006).

6. Coppermill had been home to four generations of a local family-run business in the 'rag trade'. Press release May 2006, Hauser & Wirth.

7. Massey, Doreen, *World City* (London, 2007), p. 4.

8. Ali, Monica, *Brick Lane* [orig. 2003] (London, 2004), p. 55.

9. A bricoleur is a '…jack of all trades or a kind of professional do-it-yourself person'. Lévi-Strauss, Claude, *The Savage Mind* (1966), p. 17.

10. Rowe, Colin, 'Collage city', *The Architectural Review* CLVIII/942 (August 1975), p. 66–91, argues for an urban architecture of organic growth – a 'culturalist bricolage' – rather than the uniformity of 'total architecture' schemes.

11. Massey, Doreen, *Space, Place and Gender* (London, 1994), p. 249.

12. Watts, Jonathan, 'Invisible city', *Guardian Unlimited*, 15 March 2006. www.guardian.co.uk/china

13. Packard, Vance, *The Waste Makers* [orig. 1960] (Harmondsworth, 1961).

14. Girling, Richard, *Rubbish! Dirt on Our Hands and Crisis Ahead* (London, 2005), p. 2.

15. Rogers, Heather, *Gone Tomorrow: The Hidden Life of Garbage* (New York, 2005), p. 2. This represents 236 million tons annually of municipal solid waste (EPA website www.epa.gov/epaoswer/non-hw/muncpl/facts.htm). Other studies give higher figures, e.g., Scott Kaufman gives 369 million tons or 7 pounds per day in 'National Garbage Survey Highlights Opportunities for Americans to Move from Being Waste-Full to Waste-Wise', Earth Institute News, www.earthinstitute.columbia.edu/news/2004/story 01-23-04.html

16. Rogers: *Gone Tomorrow: The Hidden Life of Garbage*, p. 2.

17. Between the start of Deng Xiaoping's market-orientated reforms in 1978 and 2005, the annual growth rate of national income, according to World Bank data, averaged 9.7 per cent – a 12-fold increase. See Reddy, Sanjay, 'Death in China', *New Left Review*, 45 May/June 2007, p. 49.

18. In *Planet of Slums*, London, 2006, Mike Davis provides extensive statistics on the escalating global production of rubbish and the incapacity of respective authorities to deal with it, e.g., he reports that in Kabul in 2002, the city planning director noted that every 24 hours, 2 million people produced 800 cubic meters of solid waste and, if 40 of their trucks made three trips per day, they could only transport 200 or 300 cubic meters out of the city.

19. Zayek, aged 12, an e-waste recycling worker living in Anup Vihar, Delhi, quoted in Gerrard, Sophie, 'Cyberjunk', *The Guardian Weekend*, 30 June 2007, p. 38.

20. See the Traders Manifesto of July 2007 at www.plasticbagfreehebdenbridge.co.uk

21. See, for example, *Well Fashioned – Eco Style in the UK*, exhibition at the Crafts Council Gallery, London: (23 March–4 June 2006) at www.craftscouncil.org

22. A key study was the 1973 University of Arizona's Garbage Project, set up as an archaeological exercise but one which evolved into 'a multipurpose enterprise whose interests include diet and nutrition, food waste, consumerism, socioeconomic stratification, resource management, recycling and source reduction, and the inner dynamics of landfills'. See Rathje, William L. and Murphy, Cullen, *Rubbish! An Archaeology of Garbage* (Arizona Press, Tucson, 2001); University of St Andrews AHRC project on waste; Scanlan, John, *On Garbage* (London, 2005); Knechtel, John (ed.), *Trash* (MIT, Cambridge, MA, 2007); Royte, Elizabeth, *Garbage Land: On the Secret Trail of Trash* (New York, 2005); Girling, Richard, *Rubbish! Dirt on Our Hands and Crisis Ahead* (London, 2005); Rogers, Heather, *The Hidden Life of Garbage*

(New York, 2005); Strasser, Susan, *Waste and Want: A Social History of Trash* (New York, 1999).

23. Gignac's NYC garbage boxes – and boxes from other cities – at www.nycgarbage.com

24. Shoat, Ella and Stam, Robert, 'Narrativising visual culture – toward a polycentric aesthetics', in N. Moerzoeff (ed.), *The Visual Culture Reader* (London, 1998), pp. 42–3.

25. Bourriaud, Nicolas, *Postproduction* [first published 2002] (New York, 2005) (second edition with new preface 2005), p. 28.

26. See de Certeau, Michel, *The Practices of Everyday Life* [trans. Steven Rendall, first published 1984] (Berkeley/Los Angeles and London, 1988).

27. Sachs, Tom, *Space Program*, exhibition at Gagosian Gallery, Los Angeles: (8 September–13 October 2007).

28. See Bloemink, Barbara, 'The Continuum between and Transformations of, Art and Design', in B. Bloemink et al. (eds), *Design=/Art: Functional Objects from Donald Judd to Rachel Whiteread* (Merrell/Cooper-Hewitt National Design Museum, London/New York, 2004). In 2000, Sachs organized *American Bricolage* an exhibition of work by American artists at Sperone Westwater, New York.

29. Seitz, William, *The Art of Assemblage*, exhibition catalogue, New York: Museum of Modern Art (1961).

30. For example, see Sariff, S. (ed.), *Recycled Reseen: Folk Art from the Global Scrapheap* (New York, 1996).

31. For other studies devoted to that kind of work see, for example, Collischan, Judy, *Welded Sculpture of the Twentieth Century* (London, 2000).

CHAPTER 1

1. O'Hagan, Andrew, 'The things we throw away', *London Review of Books* 29/10 (24 May 2007), p. 3

2. O'Hagan: 'The things we throw away', in which O'Hagan accompanies Alf and Freegans on a night-time tour of North London.

3. The *karang guni* collect and sell rubbish in Singapore.

4. Photograph reproduced in *Financial Times*, 21 August 2006.

5. Ferrell, Jeff, *The Empire of Scrounge: Inside the Urban Underground of Dumpster Diving, Trash Picking and Street Scavenging* (New York, 2005), pp. 1–2.

6. Ferrell: *The Empire of Scrounge*, p. 3.

7. For a discussion of the term and use of mongo, see Vergine, Lea, *When Trash became Art: Rubbish, Mongo* (Milan, 2007).

8. Botha, Ted, *Mongo-Adventures in Trash* (Bloomsbury, London, 2004).

9. Phillips, Tom, 'Favela hotels serve up a different view of Rio', *The Guardian*, Monday, 6 March 2006.

10. For *Dumped* (first broadcast 2 September 2007) see www.channel4. com/lifestyle/green/dumped.html

11. O'Hagan: 'The things we throw away', p. 5.

12. Shoat, Ella and Stam, Robert, 'Narrativising visual culture – toward a olycentric aesthetics' in N. Mirzoeff (ed.), *The Visual Culture Reader* (London, 1998), pp. 42–3.

13. Davis, Mike, *The Planet of Slums* (London, 2007) p. 48.

14. Strasser, Susan, *Waste and Want: A Social History of Trash* (New York, 1999), p. 3.

15. Girling, Richard, *Rubbish! Dirt on Our Hands and Crisis Ahead* (London, 2005), p. 3. Also see Strasser, Susan, *Waste and Want: A Social History of Trash* (New York, 1999); Rogers, Heather, *The Hidden Life of Garbage* (New York, 2005); Rathje, William L. and Murphy, Cullen, *Rubbish! An Archaeology of Garbage* (Arizona Press, Tucson, 2001); Scanlan, John, *On Garbage* (London, 2005); Royte, Elizabeth, *Garbage Land: On the Secret Trail of Trash* (New York, 2005).

16. Rodgers, Heather, *Gone Tomorrow, The Hidden Life of Garbage* (New York, 2005), p. 31.

17. Anon., cutting from *The Builder* (Sheffield Archives and Local Studies Library, 21 September 1861).

18. *Report on the Sanitary Condition of the Borough of Sheffield* (Sheffield, 1848), p. 30, Sheffield Archives and Local Studies Library.

19. Lee, William, 'Report on highways', in *2nd Report on the State of Large Towns and Populous Districts*, Vol. 2 (1843), Sheffield Archives and Local Studies Library.

20. Strasser: *Waste and Want*, p. 6.

21. Girling: *Rubbish! Dirt on Our Hands and Crisis Ahead*, p. 15.

22. Mayhew, Henry, *London Labour and the London Poor Volume 2* (Griffen, Bohn and Company, Stationer's Hall Court, London, 1851), p. 139, at http://www.perseus.tufts.edu/

23. Strasser: *Waste and Want*, p. 18.

24. Baudelaire, Charles, 'The Ragpickers' Wine' [trans. C.F. MacIntyre], in M. Mathews and J. Mathews (eds), *The Flowers of Evil* (New York, 1989 [1857]), pp. 136–7.

25. McNeil, Tony, 'Baudelaire's Theory of Poetry', University of Sunderland (1999) at http://www.sunderland.ac.uk/~os0tmc/19/ baud4.htm

26. Arendt, Hannah, 'Introduction. Walter Benjamin: 1892–1940', in W. Benjamin (ed.), *Illuminations* (London, 1973), p. 47. Also see Benjamin's essay 'On some motifs in Baudelaire' in the same volume; also Gilloch, Graeme, *Myth and Metropolis: Walter Benjamin and the City* (Cambridge, 1996) and Benjamin, Walter, *Charles Baudelaire: A Lyric Poet in the Era of Capitalism* [trans. Harry Zohn] (London, 1997).

27. Eiland, Howard and McLaughlin, Kevin, 'Translators' foreword', in W. Benjamin (ed.), *The Arcades Project* [after *Das Passagen-Werk* edited Rolf Tiedemann, 1982] (Cambridge, MA/London, 1999), p. ix.

28. Strasser: *Waste and Want*, p. 116.

29. *Steptoe and Son* (Alan Simpson/Ray Galton, first broadcast 1962) revolved around the status of junk-collecting. Son Harold aspired to escape working-class roots and equated the rag and bone business with antique-dealing but was continually humiliated by his father whom he perceived as uncouth, uncultured and a continual reminder that they were on the social and economic margins of society.

30. 'Rag and Bone' is a track on the album *Icky Thump* released by The White Stripes on Warner Bros/XL in 2007.

31. Useful sources on 'eco-friendly' design include Fuad-Luke, A., *The Eco-Design Handbook* (London, 2004); Datschefski, E., *The Total Beauty of Sustainable Products* (Rotovision, London, 2001); Wines, James, *Green Architecture* (Cologne, 2000); Papanek, V., *The Green Imperative* (London, 1995); Burrell, P., *Green Design* (Design Council, London, 1991). See Centre for Sustainable Design at www.cfsd.org.uk

32. See WOBO house in Woodham, Jonathan, *Twentieth-Century Design* (Oxford, 1997), p. 234.

33. See Woodham: *Twentieth-Century Design*, p. 234. However, one of the most remarkable alternative living projects of the 1960s was Drop City, a commune of self-built Buckminster Fuller-style domes constructed from found materials and waste, founded in May 1965 in Colorado. See Felicity Scott, 'Episodes in the Refusal of Work' and Richard Kallweit, 'Dropped Out City' in *Archis* Volume 24, Counterculture, 2010, pp. 30–33 and pp. 34–38.

34. E.F. Schumacher's *Small is Beautiful* [1973] concluded Western economic structures based on large-scale production and labour specialization were economically inefficient, inhumane and creating an environmental crisis for future generations.

35. Papanek, Victor, Preface (dated 1963–71), *Design for the Real World: Human Ecology and Social Change,* [1971] (St Albans, Paladin, 1974), p. 13.

36. Papanek: *Design for the Real World*, p. 287.

37. Bramwell, Anna, *Ecology in the 20th Century: A History* (Yale University Press, New Haven and London, 1989), p. 4.

38. Bramwell: *Ecology in the 20th Century*, p. 243.

39. Rathje quoted in Coleen P. Popson, 'Museums: the Truth is in our Trash', a review of an exhibition, *Fresh Kills: Artists Respond to the Closure of the Staten Island Landfill,* held at Snug Harbor Cultural Centre, Staten Island in 2002, in the Archaeological Institute of America's journal, Vol. 55, No. 1, January/February 2002 at http://www.archaeology.org/0201/reviews/trash.html

40. See Dawson, J., *Ecovillages: New Frontiers for Sustainability* (Green Books, Totnes, 2006) and Tinsley, S. and George, H., *Ecological Footprint of the Findhorn Foundation and Community* (Sustainable Development Research Centre/UHI Millennium Institute, 2006) available at http://www.sustainableresearch.com/research/env2.htm

41. Strasser: *Waste and Want*, p. 16.

42. Strasser: *Waste and Want*, p. 18.

43. A common marketing ploy perhaps, but one anecdotal example might be the cover of Girling's *Rubbish! Dirt on Our Hands and the Crisis Ahead* which features a quote from the British 'celebrity' eco-comic, Ben Elton, 'Be scared. Be very scared. But be sure to read this book'.

44. The seven-page article 'What a load of old rubbish…' appeared in *The Guardian*, 11 June 2007. A series of 'experts' – Mark Barthel from the government-funded Waste and Resources Action Progamme (WRAP), Chris Davey from Recycle Now (a national consumer campaign run by WRAP) and Joy Blizzard of the Local Authority Recycling Advisory Committee – examined contents of each person's waste to see what could have been diverted from the waste-stream/landfill cycle by composting, recycling or reusing.

45. See http://www.lohas.com/ – an organisation for businesses and companies who want to develop, produce and market LOHAS products. Providing guidance about 'greening' your event, service or production processes – including waste diversion and energy-offsetting. It proclaims 'LOHAS is an acronym for *Lifestyles of Health and Sustainability, a market segment focused on health and fitne*ss, the environment, personal development, sustainable living, and social justice'.

46. According to Natural Marketing Institute, 16 per cent or 35 m people in the US are considered to be potential LOHAS customers, see http://www.nmisolutions.com/

47. HMV advertisement in *The Guardian Guide*, 25 August 2007.

48. Royte, Elizabeth, *Garbage Land- On the Secret Trail of Trash* (New York, 2005), p. 253.

49. Girling's book is entitled *Rubbish! Dirt on Our Hands and Crisis Ahead*, London, 2005.

50. In Jean-Paul Sartre's *Les Mains Sales* (Dirty Hands) (1948) the central character, undergoes a prolonged and profound moral crisis – in the end, the 'dirt on his hands' cannot be erased whichever path of action he takes.

51. Malcolm Bull, guest editor of 'Special issue on globalisation and biopolitics', *New Left Review*, 45 May/June 2007, p. 5.

52. Monbiot, George, *Heat: How to Stop the Planet Burning* (London, 2007).

53. See Hamilton, Clive, 'Building on Kyoto' (p. 91–103) and Monbiot, George, 'Environmental feedback – A reply to Clive Hamilton' (p. 105–113) in *New Left Review*, 45 May/June 2007.

54. Stanley Cohen popularised this term in *Folk Devils and Moral Panics*, London, 1972.

55. See Preface, Rathje, William and Murphy, Cullen, *Rubbish! The Archaeology of Garbage* [1992] (Tucson/Arizona, 2001). In sum, the 'percentage paradox' is whereby even though there is actually more recycling going on in terms of tons of paper, etc., the sheer volume of discarded paper continues to rise and more is sent to landfill than ever before – 'the percentage paradox can convey an illusion of progress even as we fall farther and farther behind'. They conclude that there are no simple solutions and a wide range of responses and processes need to be developed, alongside public awareness campaigns and environmental education programmes.

56. According to figures from the UK's Environment Agency for 2004–5, the East of England which traditionally takes large amounts of London's waste, has only three years' landfill capacity at current rates of disposal, London has four years, Wales five years. See *The Guardian*, 11 June 2007 and www.environment-agency.gov.uk

57. See Rathje and Murphy, *Rubbish! The Archaeology of Garbage*, preface.

58. *Online Etymology Dictionary* at www.etymonline.com

59. Mickler, Ernest Matthew, 'Introduction', *White Trash Cooking* (Berkeley, 1986), pp. 4–5.

60. E.g., see 'What a load of old rubbish…' in *The Guardian*, 11 June 2007 and Strasser: *Waste and Want*, p. 5.

61. Douglas, Mary, *Purity and Danger: An Analysis of Concepts of Pollution and Taboo* (London/New York, 1966), p. 165. Douglas cites the mourning rituals of the Nyakyusa tribe of Central Africa in which mourners have rubbish swept on them. The Nyakyusa normally associate dirt with madness but the mourners are said to do this to retain their sanity.

62. Berger, John, 'A load of shit' ['Muck and its entanglements', *Harper's Magazine*, May 1989], *Keeping a Rendezvous* (London, 1993), pp. 38–9.

63. Berger: 'A load of shit', p. 40.

64. See Douglas: *Purity and Danger*, 1966.

65. McClintock, Anne, 'Soft-Soaping empire, commodity racism and imperial advertising', in Nicholas Mirzoeff (ed.), *The Visual Culture Reader* (London, 2005), p. 506–18.

66. Laporte, Dominique, *The History of Shit* [*Histoire de la merde (Prologue)* 1978] (Cambridge, Mass/London, 2000).

67. Rodolphe el-Khoury: 'Introduction' in Laporte, p. viii.

68. Laporte: *The History of Shit*, pp. 34–5.

69. Kristeva, Julia, 'Approaching the Abject', in *Powers of Horror: An Essay on Abjection* [trans. Leon S. Roudiez] (New York, 1982), pp. 3–4.

70. Kristeva: 'Approaching the Abject'.

71. Scanlan, John, *On Garbage* (London, 2005), p. 43.

72. See Bois, Yve-Alain and Krauss, Rosalind, *Formless: A User's Guide* (MIT Press, 2000).

73. Georges Bataille, 'Formless' from *Documents*, 7, 1929, translated from the French by Dominic Faccini, *October*, 60, Spring 1992, quoted in *Undercover Surrealism: Georges Bataille and Documents*, exhibition catalogue, MIT: Hayward Gallery (2006), p. 240.

74. Trocchi, Alexander, *Cain's Book* [1960] (London, 1992), p. 59.

75. See Boyle, Jimmy, *A Sense of Freedom* (London, 1977). Whilst serving sentences for murder, he was part of a pioneering unit which enabled prisoners to explore their creativity and has since become a well-regarded sculptor.

76. See Steve McQueen's film, *Hunger*, 2008.

77. Dubuffet, Jean, quoted from the catalogue of the Dubuffet retrospective exhibition, Musée des Arts Décoratofs, 1961, in Seitz: *The Art of Assemblage*, p. 94.

78. Suzuki, Shunryu, *Zen Mind, Beginner's Mind* [1970], (New York/Tokyo, 1999), p. 121.

79. Wabi-sabi has influenced product design and contemporary crafts in the last decade or so. For example, see Koren, Leonard, 'A Culture of Simplicity', *Resurgence* 203 November/December 2000.

80. See, for example, a discussion of 'bricolage' in Newman, Michael, 'Revising modernism, representing postmodernism: Critical discourses of the visual arts', in L. Appignanesi (ed.), *Postmodernism ICA Documents* (London, 1989), pp. 133–4.

81. Connor, Steven, *Postmodernist Culture* (Oxford, 1997), p. 214.

82. See 'Introduction' in Cartmell, D., Hunter, I.Q., Kaye, Heidi and Whelehan, Imelda, *Trash Aesthetics – Popular Culture and its Audience* (London, 1999), pp. 1–11.

83. See seminal essay Greenberg, Clement, 'Avant-garde and Kitsch' (originally published 1939). Available at http://www.sharecom.ca/greenberg/kitsch.html

84. See Kulka, Thomas, *Kitsch and Art* (Pennsylvania, 1996).

85. For example, *kitsch* and *schlock* are listed in a lexicon of postmodern paradigms in Wheale, Nigel, *The Postmodern Arts: An Introductory Reader* (London, 1995), pp. 48–9.

86. Roberts, John, 'Oh I love trash...', *Variant* Issue 1, 1984 at www. variant.org.uk

87. Roberts: 'Oh I love trash...'.

88. Roberts: 'Oh I love trash...'.

89. Roberts: 'Oh I love trash...'.

90. Rancière, Jacqucs, *The Politics of Aesthetics* [*Le Partage du sensible: Esthétique et politique*, 2000] [trans. and introduction Gabriel Rockhill] (London/New York, 2006), p. 60–1.

91. Laporte: *The History of Shit*.

92. For a feminist analysis of work by Laderman and other artists linked to 'new genre public art' in the 1980s, see Isaak, Jo Anna, 'Trash: Public art by the garbage girls', in S. Adams and A.G. Robins (eds), *Gendering Landscape Art* (Manchester, 2001).

93. Laderman has been artist-in-residence with the New York Sanitation Department since 1977. Author's interview with Mierle Ukeles Laderman, January 2006.

94. Ibid. Apart from a few key works, Hadolt argues that there is still a scarcity of serious cross-cultural research on shit, citing the following as seminal: Loudon 1977, Laporte 1978, Dundes 1985, Ndonko 1993, Faber 1999.

95. As Kolig notes in 'Shit and politics – The case of the Kolig debate in Austria', *Medische Antropologie* 11/1 (1999), pp. 179–96 – 'Shit – as the topic of sexuality perhaps was in academia thirty years ago – is dirty and sticky matter and as such is prone to spoiling one's (academic) 'symbolic capital' (Bourdieu 1984). One colleague even warned me not to get linked with the topic of shit, so as not to share Kolig's fate. In the preface to *Life is Like a Chicken Coop Ladder* about the role of shit in German culture, Alan Dundes (1985) also notices his colleagues' disapproval of shit as subject-matter for research. Shit thus obviously has 'infectious' properties – and not only from a physiological point of view', p. 181.

CHAPTER 2

1. Seitz, William C., *The Art of Assemblage*, exhibition catalogue, New York: Museum of Modern Art (1961), p. 89. The exhibition was presented at the Museum of Modern Art, New York, 2 October–12 November 1961, touring to The Dallas Museum for Contemporary Arts, 9 January–11 February 1962 and San Francisco Museum of Art, 5 March–15 April 1962.

2. See Appadurai, Arjun et al., *The Social Life of Things: Commodities in Cultural Perspective* (Cambridge, 1986).

3. These questions indirectly refer to Alfred Gell's *Art and Agency: An Anthropological Theory* (Oxford, 1998) and Latour, Bruno, *Reassembling the Social: An introduction to Actor Network Theory* (Oxford, 2005).

4. Seitz: *The Art of Assemblage*.

5. Letter dated 7 November 1960 from Seitz to George Cullen, Director of San Francisco Museum of Art regarding the possibilities of them taking the exhibition.

6. Rancière, Jacques, *The Politics of Aesthetics* [*Le Partage du sensible: Esthétique et politique*, 2000] [trans. and introduction Gabriel Rockhill] (London/New York, 2006).

7. From the French verb, *coller*, to glue or stick together. See Taylor, Brandon, *Collage: The Making of Modern Art* (London, 2004).

8. From the French verb, *monter*, to mount. Seitz also draws on the German meaning of *montieren* as mounting/assembling machinery.

9. Eisenstein, Sergei, *Notes of a Film Director* (Moscow, 1947), p. 63. For him, montage was a poetic as well as a cinematographic technique, e.g., he refers to Myakovsky's work.

10. See Gysin, Brion, 'First Cut-ups' (1959) and 'About the Cut-ups' (1964), in W. Jason (ed.), *Back in No Time: The Brion Gysin Reader* (Connecticut, 2001).

11. Lawrence Alloway's terms in 'Collage explosion', *The Listener*, LXVII/1723 (5 April 1962), pp. 603–5.

12. Kaprow in Seitz, p. 90, and similar comments in *New Forms – New Media*, exhibition catalogue, Martha Jackson Gallery, New York, October 1960.

13. Ashton, Doré, 'High tide for Assemblage', in *Studio International* 165/837, (January 1963), p. 25.

14. Eight of Duchamp's thirteen exhibits were designated 'readymades', including *Bicycle Wheel* (1951 replica of lost original), *Bottle Dryer*, 1960, and *Fountain*, 1917 (1950 replica).

15. Useful are Waldman, Diane, *Collage, Assemblage and the Found Object* (London, 1992) and Wheeler, Daniel, 'Assemblage, environments, happenings', in *Art Since Mid-Century* (New York/London, 1991). Also *Assemblage* with essay by Robinson, Julia, Zwirner & Wirth (New York, 11 November 2003–31 January 2004), Vergine, Lea (and various authors), *Trash. From Junk to Art*, exhibition catalogue, Museo di Arte Contemporanea di Trento e Rovereto (1997) and Vergine, Lea, *When Trash became Art: Rubbish, Mongo* (Milan, 2007).

16. Iverson Margaret, 'Readymade, found object, photograph', *Art Journal*, Summer 2004.

17. See Waldman: *Collage, Assemblage and the Found Object*, pp. 8–9.

18. Ashmolean Museum opened to the public in 1683. See www.ashmolean.org

19. See Mauries Patrick, *Cabinets of Curiosities*, (London, 2002).

20. See Colleen J. Sheey, *Cabinet of Curiosities, Mark Dion and the University as Installation*, (Minnesota, 2006).

21. Cummings, Neil and Lewandowska, Marysia, *The Value of Things* (Birkhauser, Basel, 2000).

22. Jeremy Deller and Alan Kane presented *Folk Archive* at the Barbican in 2005.

23. Stewart, Susan, *On Longing, Narratives of the Miniature, the Gigantic, the Souvenir, the Collection* [first published 1984] (Duke University Press, Durham/London, 1993), p. 151.

24. Stewart, *On Longing, Narratives of the Miniature, the Gigantic, the Souvenir, the Collection*, p. 135.

25. Stewart is drawing on Freud, Sigmund, *Standard Works* [trans. James Strachey] (London, 1953), Vol. 7, pp. 153–5 and Vol. 21, pp. 150–7.

26. See image in Seitz, *The Art of Assemblage*, p. 28. Waldman doubts that Boccioni's work predates Picasso's constructions of 1912 though.

27. Boccioni, Umberto, 'Futurist painting: Technical manifesto' (1910), in C. Harrison and P. Wood (eds), *Art in Theory 1900–1990: An Anthology of Changing Ideas* (Oxford, 1992), p. 149–52.

28. E.g., Paris-based Ukrainian émigrés, Vladimir Baranoff-Rossiné and Alexander Archipenko.

29. Picasso continued to develop assemblage processes: *La Chèvre* of 1950 (Musée Picasso, Paris) is one of a series in which he assembled a variety of found objects – toys, domestic utensils and ceramics, basketware, old metal tools – and then cast the whole into bronze, a technique also used by Eduardo Paolozzi in the 1950s. See various authors, *Picasso: Sculptor/Painter*, exhibition catalogue, Tate Gallery, London, 1994.

30. From Schwitters' *Merz 20* (1927) in Bowness, Alan (intro.), *Kurt Schwitters* (Lord's Gallery, London, October–November 1958).

31. The word derives from *kommerz* which appeared in an early assemblage, *Merzbild* 1919. See Elderfield, John, *Kurt Schwitters* (London, 1985)

32. Coplans, John, 'Schwitters' [1968], in S. Morgan (ed.), *Provocations – Writings by John Coplans* (London Projects, London, 1997), p. 67.

33. See Bowness: *Kurt Schwitters*.

34. Coplans: 'Schwitters', p. 70.

35. See Dietrich, Dorothea, 'The fragment reframed: Kurt Schwitters's Merz-column', *Assemblage*, No. 14, April 1991, pp. 82–92.

36. Vere explores scatological aspects of the Hannover Merzbau and the numerous grottoes dedicated to individuals (e.g., Hannah Hoch, Hans Richter, Naum Gabo) which included personal belongings and body fluids in Bernard Vere, 'Its all crap': Scatalogical elements in Kurt Schwitters's Hannover Merzbau, 'in Nina Pearlman (ed.) *Arcade* (London, 2002). Vere refers to Freud's classic essay, 'The sexual aberrations' in *Three Essays on the Theory of Sexuality* (Hogarth Press, London, 1962), in which he discusses such fetish objects as the human foot and hair.

37. In the 1961 exhibition, Seitz included Man Ray's *Le Cadeau*, a flat iron set with tacks.

38. From *Les Chants de Maldoror* [1868], by Isidore Ducasse (Comte de Lautréamont).

39. van Eyck, Aldo, *Tajiri Shinkichi Sculpture*, exhibition catalogue, Amsterdam: Stedelijk Museum (2 March–2 April 1960).

40. Waldman, *Collage, Assemblage and the Found Object*, p. 180.

41. Iverson, Margaret, 'Readymade, found object, photograph', *Art Journal* (Summer 2004), p. 45.

42. The exhibition, *Undercover Surrealism*, Hayward Gallery, 2006, explored the role of Bataille and the Surrealist magazine *Documents*. See the AHRC-funded collaborative project www.surrealismcentre.ac.uk

43. Iverson, ibid., quotes from Breton's writings in 'Surrealist Situation of the Object' (1935).

44. See Iverson's discussion of Hal Foster's positioning of the Surrealist object as in *Compulsive Beauty* (Cambridge, Mass., 1993).

45. See Read, Herbert, 'A nest of gentle artists', *Apollo* 77/7 (September 1962), pp. 536–42. In 1957, Ede remodelled some existing cottages and the house and collections were opened to visitors.

46. See Barassi, Sebastiano, Curator of Collections, Kettles Yard, *The Collection as a Work of Art – Jim Ede and Kettle's Yard*, University Museums of Scotland Conference, 2004.

47. Hamilton Finlay's comments when invited to make work to celebrate the gallery's centenary in 1995.

48. Alloway, Lawrence, 'Junk Art', *Architectural Design* 31/3 (March 1961), pp. 123–33.

49. *Junk* was slang for 'narcotics' in the 1920s. It was also the working title for William Burroughs' first published novel (1953), *Junkie*, about heroin addiction.

50. See Polsky, Ned, *Hustlers, Beats and Others* (Harmondsworth, 1971).

51. Alloway was a key figure in the Independent Group, a group of artists, architects, designers and writers based at the Institute of Contemporary Arts in London in the 1950s. See Massey, Anna, 'The Expendable Aesthetic and America', in *The Independent Group, Modernism and Mass Culture in Britain, 1945–59* (Manchester, 1995), p. 72–95.

52. Alloway, Lawrence, *New Forms – New Media*, exhibition catalogue, New York: Martha Jackson Gallery (October 1960).

53. Alloway, *New Forms – New Media*. The extensive range included work by Americans Lee Bontecou, Bruce Conner and Rauschenberg, Europeans Scarpitta and Takis and British artists Henry Moore and John Latham.

54. See Rauschenberg, Robert, *Combines*, exhibition catalogue, New York: Metropolitan Museum (20 December 2005–2 April 2006). He reiterated his much quoted

comment as here – 'I want my paintings to be reflections of life ... your self-visualization is a reflection of your surroundings' – in Rose, B., *An Interview with Robert Rauschenberg* (New York, 1987), p. 72.

55. Allan, Kaprow, *Assemblage, Environments and Happenings* (New York, 1966).

56. See Frank Popper's survey, *Art, Action and Participation*, London, 1975.

57. Seitz: *The Art of Assemblage*, p. 86.

58. Elderfield, John (ed.), *Essays on Assemblage, Studies in Modern Art 2* (Museum of Modern Art, New York, 1992).

59. Elderfield, *Essays on Assemblage* and Hapgood, Susan, *Neo-Dada, Redefining Art 1958–1962*, exhibition catalogue, New York: American Federation of Arts (1994). More recently, Julia Robinson described it as a landmark exhibition in 'The Voracious Vernacular', in *Assemblage* (Zwirner & Wirth, New York, 11 November 2003–31 January 2004).

60. See Ashton, Doré, 'High tide for Assemblage', in *Studio International* 165/837 (January 1963), p. 25.

61. Roger Shattuck cites Ashton's book, *American Art Since 1945* (New York, 1982). See Shattuck, Roger, 'Introduction: How Collage Became Assemblage', in J. Elderfield (ed.), *Essays on Assemblage, Studies in Modern Art 2* (Museum of Modern Art, New York, 1992), p. 119.

62. William Seitz (b. 1914 Buffalo New York) originally trained as an artist and later taught at Princeton University. Appointed as Associate Curator at MoMA, New York, in 1960, other important exhibitions include *The Responsive Eye*. In 1965, he became Professor of Fine Arts at Brandeis University and Director of the Rose Art Museum. See 'Seitz, William C., Art scholar, dies; ex-curator at the modern taught at Princeton critic in residence became associate curator', *New York Times* 28 October 1974, p. 34.

63. Seitz was the main organiser of the show and wrote the majority of the catalogue but Selz was also involved in planning and selecting for the exhibition.

64. Peter Selz (b. 1919 Munich), after leaving Germany for the States with his Jewish family in the 1930s, studied at Columbia University and also in Paris and Chicago. He pioneered research into German Expressionism and its political contexts. In 1958, Selz became a Curator in the Department of Painting and Sculpture exhibitions at MoMA, New York, where he curated key events such as Jean Tinguely's *Homage to New York* in 1960 and a series of important retrospectives. In 1965, he became Director of the University of California's art museum at Berkeley. See Selz, Peter, interviewed by Karlstrom, Paul (1999). Tapes and transcriptions, American Archives of Art, Smithsonian Institute.

65. Seitz's 'collection' included catalogues such as *Art and the Found Object*, exhibition catalogue, Arts Club of Chicago, June 1959 and various from Galleria Schwarz, Milan.

66. Undated typed statement (probably early 1960) by Seitz on proposed exhibition, 'Collage and Object', in William Seitz papers, MoMA archives, New York.

67. Janis and Blesh (early patron/collector of modern art and co-director of the Sidney Janis Gallery, New York) proposed the term 'Factualism'. See Janis, Harriet and Blesh, Rudi, *Collage – Personalities, Concepts, Techniques* (London, Philadelphia and New York, 1962), p. 243. Also see Hapgood, S., *Neo-Dada, Re-defining Art 1958–1962* (New York, 1994).

68. Seitz: *The Art of Assemblage*, p. 87.

69. Shattuck refers to Helen Comstock's use of the term in her article on Arthur Dove for *Art News*, No. 23, 14 March 1925, p. 5. See Shattuck, Roger, 'Introduction: How Collage Became Assemblage', in J. Elderfield (ed.), *Essays on Assemblage, Studies in Modern Art 2*, p. 119.

70. Cooke, S.J., Planque J. and Schjeldahl, P., *Jean Dubuffet, 1943–1963, Paintings, Sculptures, Assemblages* (Hirshhorn Museum and Sculpture Garden/Smithsonian Institute Press, Washington DC, 1993).

71. Elderfield, John, 'Preface', in J. Elderfield (ed.), *Essays on Assemblage, Studies in Modern Art 2*, p. 7.

72. Seitz's concerns were justified. The legacy of the earlier Brancusi 'fiasco' lingered on as Seitz had considerable problems in establishing the status of assemblage as 'art' with US. In a letter dated 7 April 1961 to Leo Castelli, Seitz asks him to send a note to the 'customs appraiser' supporting the view that Arman's works are artworks so they can enter the US 'duty free'. Alfred Barr also provided evidence that works were 'art' for customs purposes: in a letter dated 15 May 1961, he argued 'these are "neo-realists" and their subject matter is the external world'. Correspondence files, *Art of Assemblage* papers, MoMA archives, New York.

73. Letter from William Seitz to artists/dealers, sent out in May 1961. Correspondence files, *Art of Assemblage* papers, MoMA archives, New York.

74. Exhibition installation photographs reveal a conventional orderly arrangement. Work was largely displayed in 'white cube' rooms – interestingly, the Schwitters' room was an exception as his work was displayed against bluey grey walls. Swatches of paint colour are included in the installation files in the *Art of Assemblage* papers, MoMA archives, New York.

75. Seitz: *The Art of Assemblage*, p. 6.

76. Letter dated 27 March from Seitz to Herta Wescher. Correspondence files, *Art of Assemblage* papers, MoMA archives, New York. Wescher provided Seitz with addresses of various artists and galleries in Europe.

77. Letter dated 6 December 1960 from Seitz to George Cullen. Correspondence files, *Art of Assemblage* papers, MoMA archives, New York.

78. Seitz: *The Art of Assemblage*, pp. 84–5.

79. Dorothy Millar's term for Bruce Beasley (b. 1939 Los Angeles). Millar, a curator at MoMA, New York, urged Seitz to include him in the exhibition. Subject files, MoMA Archives, New York.

80. Baxter, John, (b. 1912 San Francisco), see Seitz: *The Art of Assemblage*, p. 154. See Baxter, John, exhibition catalogue, San Francisco Museum of Art (22 August– 19 September 1967).

81. Seitz corresponded with many Paris galleries including Galerie 'J' on Rue Montfaucon regarding Dufrêne and Galerie Rive Droite at Faubourg Saint-Honore, regarding works by Arman, Dufrene, Hains and Villeglé. He visited Galleria L'Attico in Rome, Galleria Shwarz in Milan and had a lengthy correspondence about potential exhibits with Dietrich P Mahlow, Director of Staatliche Kunsthalle, Baden-Baden.

82. Seitz made visits to Paris, including one in early February 1961. Selz also visited artists' studios and galleries, making a special trip to San Francisco in November 1960.

83. Seitz: *The Art of Assemblage,* p. 88. Seitz was not able to obtain some works for a complex array of reasons. For example, Roland Penrose was unable to supply a piece by Andre Breton as he felt it was too fragile to travel. Correspondence files, *Art of Assemblage* papers, MoMA archives, New York.

84. Seitz followed up and acted upon many of Wescher's suggestions. Peter Selz visited Enrico Baj's studio in 1960. Correspondence files, *Art of Assemblage* papers, MoMA archives, New York.

85. Letter dated 19 May 1961 from Walter Goodhue to William Seitz. Correspondence files, *Art of Assemblage* papers, MoMA archives, New York.

86. Seitz wrote directly to Paolozzi and Denny but Irwin's collage came from the Chicago collector, Arnold H. Maremont.

87. Alley may have responded but no reply is archived at MoMA. Correspondence files, *Art of Assemblage* papers, MoMA archives, New York.

88. For example, Victor Musgrave, who ran Gallery One in London.

89. Some were selected by Alicia Legg for a touring show organised in 1963–4 which featured 39 artworks by largely US artists, including Bruce Conner, Gloria Graves, Nelson Howe, Ed Kienholz, Marisol, Mary Shore, Robert Watts and Mary Wilson. File on circulating exhibition of assemblage, MoMA archives, New York.

90. For example, Arnold H Maremont lent works by Cornell, Miro and Dubuffet.

91. Letter dated 26 August 1960 from Director of Carnegie to Seitz. *Art of Assemblage* papers, MoMA archives, New York.

92. By the mid-1960s, various 'assemblage' collections had emerged: e.g., by 1964, the Albright-Knox Gallery had an extensive collection. Oscar Bailey, Assistant Professor at State University College, Buffalo, wrote to Seitz saying they had an enormous collection of 'preformed and manufactured fragments, objects and materials', ranging from tiny bits of wood to large doors, which they presented and had catalogued as 'found objects'. Letter dated 20 November 1964 from Oscar Bailey to William Seitz. Correspondence files, *Art of Assemblage* papers, MoMA archives, New York.

93. Letter dated 12 January 1961 from Seitz to George Cullen, Director of San Francisco Museum of Art. Correspondence files, *Art of Assemblage* papers, MoMA archives, New York. Works by Jess and Herms were subsequently included in the show.

94. Bruce Conner papers, Box 5, Bancroft Library, University of California, Berkeley.

95. www.wattstowers.org

96. Seitz: *The Art of Assemblage,* p. 73.

97. Practices in Latin America and Japan were explored in the exhibition (and accompanying publication) *Out of Actions: Between Performance and the Object, 1949–1979,* originating in February 1998, at the Museum of Contemporary Art in Los Angeles and travelling to Europe and Japan.

98. van Eyck, Aldo, *Shinkichi Tajiri Sculpture,* exhibition catalogue, Amsterdam: Stedelijk Museum (2 March–2 April 1960).

99. One artwork by a Canadian artist based in London was included on the recommendation of the British art critic and writer, Herbert Read. He suggested that Seitz include work by Austin Cooper (b. 1890, Manitoba), comparing his torn scrap-paper collages to the work of Schwitters. See Read, Herbert, introductory essay, *Austin Cooper,* exhibition catalogue, Gimpel Fils Gallery (1961).

100. For example, Dorothy Cameron's Here and Now Gallery in Toronto sent Seitz photographs of a range of work by Yosef Drenters (b. 1930, Netherlands), who, at the time, was considered by critics to be one of Canada's foremost contemporary artists.

101. Symposium and correspondence files. *Art of Assemblage* papers, MoMA archives, New York.

102. See The Intermedia Society archive at http://www.michaeldecourcy.com/intermedia/intro.htm

103. Wallace, Kevin, *Rezoning: Collage and Assemblage*, exhibition catalogue, Vancouver Art Gallery (19 October 1989–1 January 1990).

104. Wallace cites, as contributory factors, the large influx of 'Vietnam escapists' and 'artistic politicos', many of them moving up from California and the Pacific Coast.

105. See Wallace: *Rezoning: Collage and Assemblage*.

106. Wallace: *Rezoning: Collage and Assemblage*, p. 4.

107. See *Al Neil Project* at the Grunt Gallery, Vancouver (15 October–25 November 2005), www.bruntmag.com

108. Neil quoted in www.bruntmag.com/issue1/neil.html

109. For 40 years, Itter has continued to extend a cabin which Neil started as a junk assemblage at Burrard Inlet at Dollarton, British Columbia in the 1960s. Surrounded by huge cedar trees and facing the beach and ocean, and at 40 feet long, Itter comments that 'sometimes it feels like my life's work'. Author's email correspondence with Carole Itter – 26 September 2007.

110. Al Neil in conversation with Bill Smith, *Coda Magazine*, 1970, extracts available at http://vancouverjazz.com/billsmith/03.shtml

111. Typical of his mid-1960s performances was *Horse Opera*, a spontaneous narration with live improvised playing and turntable sampling with references to icons of contemporary popular culture such as Bela Lugosi, Roy Roger's horse *Pegasus* and *Rintintin*. Turner, Michael, 'Al Neil', *Bruntmag*, Issue 1, 2005.

112. In the 1950s and 1960s, Neil collaborated with artists, musicians and poets such as Art Pepper and Kenneth Patchen on various projects. He created what Glenn Alteen (www.bruntmag.com) has termed 'aural collage' using text, sound, light projections and electronic media.

113. *The Art of Assemblage* symposium was held at MoMA, New York, on 19 October 1961. Tapes, transcription and actual audience question slips are included in the symposium files in *Art of Assemblage* papers, MoMA archives, New York.

114. Feedback on visitor numbers suggested the show had generated great excitement – particularly when it toured to San Francisco. Letter dated 3 May 1962 from San Francisco Museum of Art to William Seitz. *Art of Assemblage* papers, MoMA archives, New York.

115. Comments made November 1961 by Hirsch, Paul, News Editor of High School of Music and Art, New York, quoted in *New York Times*, November 1961.

116. Letter dated 17 October 1961 from Philip Johnson to Seitz. *Art of Assemblage* papers, MoMA archives, New York.

117. Max Kozloff, *The Nation*, 11 November 1961.

118. Seldis, Henry, 'The art of assemblage – The power of negative thinking', *Los Angeles Times*, 18 March 1961.

119. Mr Hess's comment in *Art News* provoked Seitz into a written response in a later issue. Undated cutting, *Art of Assemblage* papers, MoMA archives, New York.

120. The defence of modernist critique and practice against 'de-stabilising' practices such as assemblage is conveyed in a series of seminal essays in *American Sculpture of the Sixties*, exhibition catalogue, Los Angeles County Museum of Art (1967) – for example, see James Monte's 'Bagless Funk' and Doré Ashton's 'Assemblage and Beyond'.

121. Letter dated 31 October 1961 from Allan Kaprow to Seitz. *Art of Assemblage* papers, MoMA archives, New York.

122. Letter dated 6 November 1961 from Seitz to Kaprow. *Art of Assemblage* papers, MoMA archives, New York.

123. Letter dated 21 February 1962 from Pierre Restany to Seitz. *Art of Assemblage* papers, MoMA archive, New York.

124. For example, see Rasmussen, Harry and Grant, Art, *Sculpture from Junk* (Reinhold, New York, 1967) and D'Amico, Victor and Buchman, Arlette, *Assemblage: A New Dimension in Creative Teaching in Action* (Museum of Modern Art, New York, 1972).

125. D'Amico, Victor and Buchman, Arlette, *Assemblage: A New Dimension in Creative Teaching in Action* (Museum of Modern Art, New York, 1972), p. 2.

126. From essay by Robinson, Julia, *Assemblage*, exhibition catalogue, New York: Zwirner & Wirth (11 November 2003–31 January 2004).

CHAPTER 3

1. I interviewed Lucy Puls at her studio in April 2006. Tanner, Marcia, 'Lucy Puls: Rapere Flanneum (Taking the Veil)', *Lucy Puls*, exhibition catalogue, San Francisco: Stephen Wirtz Gallery (5 October– November 1994), p. 7.

2. Jeff Kelley, 'Memory improper' in *Lucy Puls*, p. 21.

3. Puls quoted in Tanner, *Lucy Puls*, p. 21.

4. Tanner, *Lucy Puls*, p. 12.

5. Massey, Doreen, *Space, Place and Gender* (London, 1994), p. 121.

6. See Massey, *Space, Place and Gender*, pp. 121–122. Also see my earlier references to Massey's points on this in the Introduction.

7. See Starr, Sandra Leonard, *Lost and Found in California: Four Decades of Assemblage Art*, exhibition catalogue, Santa Monica, California (1988); Ayres, A. *Forty Years of California Assemblage*, exhibition catalogue, Los Angeles: UCLA (1989–90); Phillips, Lisa (ed.), *Beat Culture and the New America: 1950–1965*, exhibition catalogue, New York: Whitney Museum of American Art (1995); Solnit, Rebecca, *Secret Exhibition, Six Californian Artists of the Cold War Era* (San Francisco, 1990); Johnstone, Mark and Holtzman, Leslie Aboud, *Epicenter: San Francisco Bay Area Art Now* (San Francisco, 2002). Various exhibitions at Oakland Museum include *Hello again: A New Wave of Recycled Art and Design* in 1997 and *Bay Area Sculptors, Exhibition V: The Object,* 1999. Since 1990, San Francisco's Sunset Scavenger Solid Waste Transfer and Recycling Center has run an Artist-In-Residence Programme, providing artists with a large onsite well-equipped studio space to utilise waste as a resource, see http://www. sunsetscavenger.com/AIR/aboutus.htm

8. For example, see Donald Factor's comments on the 'mushrooming' of assemblage in California, 'Assemblage', *Artforum* II/12 (Summer 1964), p. 38.

9. Coplans, John, 'Circle of styles on the West Coast', *Art in America* 52/3 (June 1964), pp. 36–7.

10. Coplans: 'Circle of styles on the West Coast'.

11. *Artforum* set up 1962 in San Francisco, shifted to Los Angeles 1964–7, then New York. Plagens was West Coast Editor. His *Sunshine Muse, Art on the West Coast 1945–70* [1974, re-issued with introduction 1999] is an invaluable survey published at the time, when critics largely ignored the West Coast art scene – a point still being reiterated by Stephen Wirtz. Author's interview with Wirtz at Stephen Wirtz Gallery, April 2006.

12. Plagens: *Sunshine Muse, Art on the West Coast 1945–1970*, p. 74.

13. Plagens: *Sunshine Muse, Art on the West Coast 1945–1970*, p. 75.

14. Transcription of Bruce Conner interview with Meredith Tromble, 1988; Bancroft Library, University of California, Berkeley, Bruce Conner papers, Box 5.

15. Press release, *A Look at Recent Bay Area Painting and Sculpture*, exhibition at San Francisco Museum of Art (8 September–9 October 1960) which featured 50 works by 20 artists. SFMOMA archives.

16. *On Looking Back 1945–1962*, SFMOMA, exhibition (10 August– 8 September 1968), SFMOMA exhibition file notes. Other exponents of the 'Bay Area Neo-dada revolution' were listed as Roy de Forest, Seymour Locks, Robert Hudson, Manuel Neri, Joan Brown, Jess and William Wiley.

17. See Ayres, A. *Forty Years of California Assemblage*, exhibition catalogue, Los Angeles: UCLA, 1989–90; Starr, Sandra Leonard, *Lost and Found in California: Four Decades of Assemblage Art*, exhibition catalogue, Santa Monica, California (1988); Solnit, Rebecca, *Secret Exhibition, Six Californian Artists of the Cold War Era* (City Lights, 1990); Phillips, Lisa, *Beat Culture and the New America: 1950–1965*, exhibition catalogue, New York: Whitney Museum of American Art (1995). Smaller exhibitions include *Assemblage and Collage in California in the 1960s* at San Francisco: 871 Fine Arts, Geary Street (16 June–31 August 2005).

18. For a recent broad re-assessment of the artistic and cultural scene of Los Angeles, see Grenier, Catherine (ed.), *Los Angeles 1955–1985* (Centre Pompidou, 8 March– 17 July 2006).

19. Candida Smith described it thus in Candida Smith, Richard, *Utopia and Dissent: Art, Poetry and Politics on California* (Berkeley/Los Angeles, 1995), pp. 110–13.

20. Albright, Thomas, *Art in San Francisco Bay Area 1945–1980* (Berkeley/Los Angeles, 1985), p. 42.

21. Candida Smith: *Utopia and Dissent*, p. 112.

22. For example, see Murdock, Robert M., 'Assemblage: Anything and Everything, Late 1950s', in *Poets of the Cities – New York and San Francisco* (Dallas Museum of Fine Arts, 1974), p. 37. Factor, Donald, had referred to this exhibition in his article 'Assemblage', *Artforum* II/12 (Summer 1964), p. 38. Plagens also described it as 'seminal' in 1974.

23. The origins, interpretations and histories of the term 'Beat' are all contested and problematic. As the American sociologist Polsky, Ned, noted in 1961 in 'The village beat scene: Summer 1960', *Dissent* 8/3 (Summer 1961), pp. 339–59, the term obscures as much as it illuminates. Kenneth Baker articulated his notion of 'Beat ethos' in a review of an exhibition of Californian assemblage at Geary Street in May 2006. Featuring the work of Herms, Conner, Berman and Jess, he noted that the works 'exude the true Beat spirit of bemused, bewildered disgust with

American culture's favourite drugs: hypocrisy and materialism'. Review from *San Francisco Chronicle*, www.sfgate.com

24. An extensive popular and nostalgic literature on the Beats preceded more recent academic studies and research. For more recent scholarship on Beat culture, including conferences/publications, online resources and archive links, see http://www.wooster.edu/beatstudies/index.html. The Beat Studies Association was set up in 2004 and, affiliated to the American Literature Association, it is devoted to developing scholarship on the Beats. Also see Skerl, Jennie (ed.), *Reconstructing the Beats* (New York, 2004).

25. See Solnit, Rebecca, *Secret Exhibition, Six Californian Artists of the Cold War Era* (San Francisco, 1990) – the six were Wallace Berman, Jess, Bruce Conner, Jay DeFeo, Wally Hedrick and Georg Herms.

26. Besides staging poetry readings, the Six Gallery also showed the assemblages of Ed Kienholz, Bruce Conner, Joan Brown and Robert Arneson. Phillips, Lisa (ed.), *Beat Culture and the New America 1950–1965* (Whitney Museum of Modern Art, New York, 1995). The show toured from Whitney Museum of Modern Art to the Walker Art Center, Minneapolis and M.H. de Young Memorial Museum, The Fine Arts Museums of San Francisco.

27. Solnit: *Secret Exhibition*, p. ix.

28. Solnit: *Secret Exhibition*, p. ix.

29. Plagens: *Sunshine Muse, Art on the West Coast 1945–1970*, p. 87.

30. Peter Selz's iconic *Funk* exhibition was held at the University Art Museum, Berkeley, 18 April–29 May 1967. In March 1967, 'Sweet land of funk' was published in *Art in America* by the artist, Harold Paris. Also see T. Albright, *Art in San Francisco Bay Area 1945–1980*, p. 81. Albright's book includes a chapter focusing on the Beat Era and Bay Area Funk. He argues that by the time 'Funk Art' had gained currency as a term, it had largely vanished as a genre and that Peter Selz's show 'brought together a few remnants of the real thing'. Ceramicists played a key role in Funk. Conner is often cited as the best known and most powerful practitioner, though he insisted on maintaining a distinction between 'funky' and 'Funk'. For Conner, 'funky art' grew out of the authentic Beat movement of mid-late 1950s, whereas 'Funk' crystallised in the mid-1960s, arose from bohemian underground but was never a coherent style.

31. See Monte, James, 'Bagless Funk' and Ashton, Doré, 'Assemblage and Beyond', in *American Sculpture of the Sixties*, exhibition catalogue, Los Angeles County Museum of Art (1967).

32. Plagens: *Sunshine Muse*, p. 87.

33. Starr: *Lost and Found*, p. 13.

34. Starr: *Lost and Found*.

35. Herms in Starr: *Lost and Found*.

36. In March 2007, as part of its aim to become a 'green city', San Francisco became the first US city to ban plastic bags. Other strategies include developing city-wide 'green' public transport systems. See http://www.independent.co.uk/environment/green-living/san-francisco-bans-plastic-shopping-bags-442326.html

37. SFMOMA artists files. In 1968, Grant listed himself as teaching art and 'sensory awareness'. He had solo shows at Spatsa Gallery in 1958 and 1959 and was, for example, part of the *Junk Art* exhibition at Vancouver Art Gallery in 1968. In the

1960s, Grant wrote various books on junk art such as *Sculpture from Junk* and *Art from Found Materials.*

38. Pritkin, Renny, Artistic Director, Visual Arts, *Fabricators; New Bay Area Sculpture* (Center for the Arts, Yerba Buena, San Francisco, 5 September–1 October 1995), p. 4.

39. Pritkin: *Fabricators; New Bay Area Sculpture.*

40. Conner showed at Robert Fraser Gallery, London 1964.

41. In Stephen Wirtz's view, the East–West Coast polarity still dominates the art scene. Author's conversations with Stephen Wirtz, San Francisco, 2006.

42. Rancière, Jacques, *The Politics of Aesthetics* [*Le Partage du sensible: Esthétique et politique,* 2000] [trans. and introduction Gabriel Rockhill] (London/New York, 2006), pp. 60–1.

43. Rancière: *The Politics of Aesthetics.*

44. de Certeau, Michel, *The Practice of Everyday Life* [trans. Steven Rendall] (Berkeley/Los Angeles/London, 1984), p. xviii.

45. De Certeau: *The Practice of Everyday Life,* p. 27.

46. De Certeau: *The Practice of Everyday Life.*

47. See *Poets of the Cities – New York and San Francisco* (Dallas Museum of Fine Arts, 1974).

48. A phrase usually sourced to Stephen Dedalus's enlightenment in James Joyce's *Portrait of the Artist as a Young Man.*

49. See Davies, Lana, 'Robert Rauschenberg and the Epiphany of the Everyday', in *Poets of the Cities – New York and San Francisco* (Dallas Museum of Fine Arts, Dallas, 1974), p. 40–55.

50. From Jack Spicer's 'After Lorca', in R. Blaser (ed.), *The Collected Books of Jack Spicer* (Los Angeles, 1975), p. 33–4.

51. See preface of Meltzer, David (ed.), *San Francisco Beat – Talking with the Poets* (San Francisco, 2001), p. v – a revised and expanded version of the earlier classic, *The San Francisco Poets.*

52. Starr, Kevin, 'Preface', in P. Polledri (ed.), *Visionary San Francisco* (San Francisco Museum of Modern Art/Munich, 1990), p. 14.

53. Editors' preface in Brook, James, Carlsson, Chris and Peters, Nancy J. (eds), *Reclaiming San Francisco: History, Politics, Culture* (San Francisco, 1998).

54. In the popular imagination, San Francisco's counterculture is well-known, though there remains plenty of scope for serious academic research as Clinton R. Starr indicated in his doctoral thesis on 'New Bohemianism', 2005, and in J. Skerl (ed.), *Reconstructing the Beats* (New York, 2004).

55. In 1947, Harpers published *The New Cult of Sex and Anarchy* by Mildred Brady which looked at art and cultural life of the Bay area. Brady identified two camps of Bohemians – the devotees to Henry Miller at Big Sur 'embroiled in sexualism, surrealism and anarchism' and the other group based around Rexroth, reading Kropotkin and Willhelm Reich. Brady comments that both groups 'glorified the irrational' and 'counted their orgasms'. Brady's article is discussed in Peters, Nancy, 'The Beat Generation and San Francisco's Culture of Dissent', in B. Carlsson and N. Peters, *Reclaiming San Francisco* (San Francisco, 1998) p. 205.

56. Rexroth, Kenneth, 'The Making of the Counterculture', 1965–7 at http://www.bopsecrets.org/rexroth/essays/counterculture.htm

57. Rexroth's essay, *Communalism: From its Origins to the Twentieth Century* [1974] included a chapter on the Diggers and Gerald Winstanley.

58. Rexroth's comments are made in 'San Francisco letter', in *Evergreen Review* 1/2 (1957), p. 6. The whole issue was devoted to the San Francisco poetry scene.

59. Rexroth in *American Poetry in the Twentieth Century* (New York, 1971), p. 137.

60. Rexroth, Kenneth, 'San Francisco's mature bohemians', *The Nation* 184/8 (1957), p. 159.

61. Converging poet-writers included Jack Kerouac from industrial Massachusetts, Allan Ginsberg from Patterson New Jersey, Gregory Corso from Greenwich Village, Charles Olson from Massachusetts, Robert Duncan from California, Lawrence Ferlinghetti from New York, Kenneth Koch from Cincinnati, Philip Lamantia from San Francisco.

62. Meltzer writes of the Beats' 'fictive history' in the preface to Meltzer, *San Francisco Beat: Talking with the Poets*, p. v.

63. James Brook remarks on the 'poetic transformation' of San Francisco in Brook, Carlsson and Peters, *Reclaiming San Francisco*, p. 125.

64. Davidson, Michael, *The San Francisco Renaissance – Poetics and Community at Mid-Century* (Cambridge, 1989), p. xi. The San Francisco Renaissance was from c. 1955–1965. Ginsberg's reading of *Howl* in October 1955 is seen as marking the beginning of the San Francisco Renaissance. Previously, the 1940s was dominated by three poets, Kenneth Rexroth, Brother Antoninus and Robert Duncan. In the mid-1950s, a younger generation joined them, including Gary Snyder, Lawrence Ferlinghetti, Michael McClure, Philip Whalen, Philip Lamantia and Bob Kaufman, to create a vital and productive artistic community, whose identity was strengthened by its geographical distance from New York. They were a disparate group; some looked to nature, others to Asia and Eastern philosophy and religion for inspiration. They spawned the fashion for reading poetry in coffeehouses to the accompaniment of jazz. See Steven Watson's essay for the exhibition, *Rebel Painters and Poets*, National Portrait Gallery, Smithsonian Institute, 1996, http://www.npg.si.edu/exh/rebels/ index2.htm

65. Davidson: *The San Francisco Renaissance – Poetics and Community at Mid-Century*.

66. Davidson: *The San Francisco Renaissance – Poetics and Community at Mid-Century*, p. xi.

67. Davidson: *The San Francisco Renaissance – Poetics and Community at Mid-Century*, p. 2.

68. In 'A Pig-headed father and the New Wood' in *London Magazine*, December 1962, Vol. 2, No. 9, Eric Mottram reviewed Donald Allen's 1960 anthology of *New American Poetry 1945–60*. Mottram identified the lines of descent of these dissenting poets – from Whitman, through Carlos Williams to Olsen, Creeley, Duncan, Ashberry, Meltzer, Whalen, Ginsberg and Corso, noting they replaced 'academic kitsch' with the violent, brutal, illiterate and the hysterical. 'Protest poems, committed poems, and poems of desperate privacies are resolving into a new and distinctly American poetry for the first time since Whitman', p. 73.

69. Selz, Peter, *The Art of Engagement, Visual Politics in California and Beyond* (Los Angeles, 2006).

70. See Davidson, *The San Francisco Renaissance*, p. 27. Duncan's essay represents a pioneering discussion of the political role of the homosexual individual at a time of draconian censorship and obscenity laws.

71. The period of coalescence and collaboration was brief. In 1956, Ginsberg, Burroughs and Kerouac all left San Francisco.

72. The Diggers were named after the seventeenth-century English radical agrarianists and communists, led by Gerard Winstanley and William Everard, who cultivated commonland to feed themselves and the poor and believed that private property was the cause of 'all wars, blood-shed, crime and enslaving laws …'. In the 1960s Diggers distributed their ideas through *The Digger Papers*, some available online at http://www.diggers.org/digger_papers.htm

73. See Emmett Grogan's memoir, *Ringolevio* [first published 1972] (Edinburgh, 1999).

74. Grogan: *Ringolevio*, p. 329.

75. Grogan: *Ringolevio*, p. 375.

76. Grogan: *Ringolevio*, pp. 320–1.

77. 'Garbage and nothing', *Digger Papers*, August 1968 at http://www. diggers.org/digpaps68/garbage.html

78. A misleading conflation as, according to Grogan at least, the Diggers espoused opposition to the LSD-induced transcendental experience. The San Francisco Diggers (there was a group in New York also) were a reaction against other organs of the underground which they felt catered to the new 'hip' moneyed classes – especially the Haight Independent Proprietor (HIP) merchants association. See Grogan, p. 299.

79. The New York Diggers also created a free shop, distributing free food in Tompkins Square and forming the East Side Service Organisation to help homeless people.

80. See Starr: *Lost and Found in California.*

81. Gordon Wagner interviewed by Richard Candida Smith, 1989, tapes and transcriptions held in Bancroft Library, University of California, Berkeley. Wagner (b. 1915, Redondo Beach California) had various solo and groups shows in California, including a retrospective exhibition at Angel's Gate Cultural Centre in 1987. He spent time in Paris in the 1930s under the wing of painter Norman Chamberlain.

82. Wagner described trips to Red Mountain dump, an abandoned gold-mining town in Red Rock Canyon in the Mojave Desert which was bulldozed over by the early 1970s. Wagner tapes transcription, Bancroft Library, University of California, Berkeley, p. 155.

83. Wagner referred to the exhibition, *Sixty Six Signs in Neon*, organised by Noah Purifoy, artist and co-founder/director of Watts Tower Centre in the 1960s. The exhibition travelled to various universities in California. See exhibition, *Noah Purifoy: Outside and in the Open*, African-American Museum, Los Angeles, 25 January–27 July 1997.

84. Wagner's beliefs in Zen were reflected in his work. He talked of his 'inner calmness and taoism' in his interview with Richard Candida Smith when quizzed about the significance of Buddhism to his work. Wagner tape transcription, Bancroft Library, University of California, Berkeley, p. 208.

85. Wagner tapes transcription, Bancroft Library, p. 88.

86. Wagner tapes transcription, Bancroft Library, pp. 223–36.

87. Undated cutting, *Times Herald*, Valejo, 1 June 1969, on *Just Yesterday* at San Francisco Museum of Modern Art, an exhibition of 60 works including Voulkos, Anderson and Paris. SFMOMA artist files (Fred Martin).

88. Plagens: *The Sunshine Muse,* p. 89.

89. This featured in *A Look at Recent Bay Area Art,* 14 September–9 October 1960, SFMOMA exhibition files.

90. Featured in the *San Francisco Art Association 24th Annual Drawing, Painting and Sculpture exhibition,* 2 February–3 May 1961 which also included Bruce Conner's *Resurrection.*

91. Grant, Art, *Junk Art,* exhibition catalogue, Vancouver Art Gallery (October 1968).

92. DeFeo, Hedrick and McLure lived at 2330 Fillmore Street. Herms lived in Larkspur, 1960–2.

93. Coplans, John, 'Circle of styles on the West Coast', *Art in America* 52/3 (June 1964), p. 36. In 1957, police closed the Berman exhibition at the Ferus Gallery in Los Angeles and Berman was arrested, convicted and fined for obscenity and lewdness. Later, he produced *Semina,* and was an early publisher of Burroughs, Meltzer and McLure. In 1968, his house in Beverley Canyon was dislodged by rain and collapsed, destroying much of his work. Herms died in a car accident in 1976. On Berman, see Michael Duncan and Kristine McKenna, *Semina Culture, Wallace Berman and His Circle,* Santa Monica Museum of Art, 2005.

94. Wagner tapes, Bancroft Library, University of California, Berkeley, pp. 205–6. Herms' work featured in the survey exhibition *Los Angeles 1955–1985 Birth of an Art Capital,* Centre Pompidou, 8 March–17 July 2006.

95. Subsequently, Herms moved to 'Topanga Canyon (Greenwich Village in a ravine) and then to isolation near Malibu in a totally permissive environment called Tap City Circus'. Plagens: *The Sunshine Muse,* p. 86.

96. Anonymous cuttings in artists files, SFMOMA.

97. Plagens: *The Sunshine Muse,* p. 86.

98. As noted in *Georg Herms, The Prometheus Archives: A Retrospective Exhibition of the Works of George Herms,* exhibition catalogue, Newport Harbor Art Museum, Newport Beach, California, The Oakland Museum and Seattle Art Museum, 1979.

99. Conner's period as a junk assembler was short – in 1964, he turned to other media such as drawing and film-making, to avoid being compartmentalised and identified with the idiom. In an *Artforum* interview in 1984, Conner commented that he still viewed himself as an 'outsider'.

100. According to Conner, he didn't sign work from 1960 to 1964, stopped making collages and assemblages from 1964 to 1967 and quit 'all the art business until 1971'. Conner interviewed by Paul Karlstrom, 1974; transcription and tapes available at Archives of American Art, Smithsonian Institution.

101. Bruce Conner papers, Box 3, Bancroft Library, University of California, Berkeley.

102. Bruce Conner, notes 1960, SFMOMA, artists files. Conner maintained that approach since: in a letter dated 1 April 1983 to Julia Brown at Museum of Contemporary Art, Los Angeles, Conner insisted on 'political' being replaced by 'social' with reference to comment on his films in association with an exhibition.

103. Press release for the Bruce Conner show which was the inaugural exhibition at Batman Gallery, 3 November 1960.

104. Conner interviewed by Paul Karlstrom, 1974; transcription and tapes available at Archives of American Art, Smithsonian Institution.

105. Conner's single exhibit was in the *79th Annual Painting and Sculpture Exhibition,* 24 March–24 April 1964 at SFMOMA. That year, the annual show for open

submissions received 1444 submissions from which 173 paintings and 79 sculptures were selected.

106. Conner's comment in interview with Karlstrom, 1999; transcription and tapes available at Archives of American Art, Smithsonian Institution.

107. Leider, Philip, 'Bruce Conner: A new sensibility', *Artforum* 1/6 (November 1962), p. 30–1.

108. See Boswell, Peter, Bruce Jenkins and Joan Rothfuss, *2000 BC: The Bruce Conner Story Part II* (Walker Art Center, Minneapolis, 1999–2000), p. 41.

109. Solnit: *Secret Exhibition,* p. 61.

110. See Boswell, Peter, Bruce Jenkins and Joan Rothfuss, *2000 BC: The Bruce Conner Story Part II* (Walker Art Center, Minneapolis, 1999–2000), pp. 44–53 for Peter Boswell's references to assemblages made whilst in Mexico, 1961–2. Also, Conner discusses this in his interview with Karlstrom.

111. Selz: *Art of Assemblage* papers, p. 8.

112. See Natsoulos, John, *The Spatsa Gallery 1958–1961,* exhibition catalogue, Davis: Natsoulas/Novelozo Gallery (11 January–3 February 1991) and also various essays in Howard, Seymour et al., *The Beat Generation Galleries and Beyond* (John Natsoulas Press, Davis, 1996).

113. Howard et al.: *The Beat Generation Galleries and Beyond.*

114. Conner's comment is made to Peter Boswell in an interview, 15 June 1983, quoted in Boswell, Jenkins and Rothfuss: *2000 BC: The Bruce Conner Story Part II*, p. 41.

115. John Natsoulos in *The Spatsa Gallery 1958–1961,* exhibition catalogue, Davis: Natsoulas/Novelozo Gallery (11 January–3 February 1991), p. 13.

116. See *2000 BC: The Bruce Conner Story Part II.*

117. Bruce Conner, quoted in unpublished interview with Dan Tucker, 1972, in Peter Plagens, *The Sunshine Muse,* p. 78.

118. Chadwick, Whitney, *Working It Out – Joan Brown and Manuel Neri 1958–64,* exhibition catalogue, Wiegand Gallery, College of Notre Dame (21 March–29 April 1995).

119. For Carlos Villa (b. San Francisco 1936), an exploration of Chicano identity is at the heart of his practice, later through objects and performances of fetishistic body rituals. See, for example, *Carlos Villa New Works*, exhibition catalogue (26 September–9 November), SFMOMA.

120. Joan Brown donated *Fur Rat* to the University of California, Berkeley collection in 1970. Bancroft Library has a large collection of Brown's cards, many of which feature fur, cats and rats.

121. Solnit: *Secret Exhibition,* p. 61.

122. For Meltzer, they had ceased to sing 'true songs'. Meltzer's comments are recounted in Candida Smith: *Utopia and Dissent,* p. 207.

123. Peter Selz and Susan Landauer, in Selz: *Art of Assemblage* papers.

124. Candida Smith: *Utopia and Dissent.*

125. Puls and Spence both exhibit with Stephen Wirtz Gallery, see http://www.wirtzgallery.com/main.html. I interviewed Puls and Spence in their studios, April 2006.

126. Jess and Duncan lived here in the 1950s when it hosted a diverse community of artists such as Conner, Lamantia , Berman, Hedrick and de Feo.

127. Author's interview with Spence, April 2006.

128. In the 1980s, activists organised demonstrations and sit-ins to highlight the plight of the large numbers of homeless, especially around Berkeley and the civic centre.

129. Craigs List, set up by Craig Newmark in San Francisco in 1993, still operates from there with a small workforce. The e-mail circular developed into a community exchange and networking site. As Newmark recently commented, '…effectively we are a flea market and flea markets are more about socialising than about commerce'. *The Guardian*, 4 November 2006.

130. See Bourriaud Nicolas, *Relational Aesthetics* (Paris, 1998) and *Postproduction* (New York, 2002).

131. Massey: *Space, Place and Gender,* p. 5.

132. Ibid.

133. Solnit, Rebecca, *Hollow City* [first published 2000] (London/New York, 2002), p. viii.

CHAPTER 4

1. Alloway, Lawrence, 'Junk Culture', *Architectural Design* 31/3 (March 1961), pp. 123–33.

2. Freud, Sigmund, *The Joke and Its Relation to the Unconscious* [trans. Joyce Crick with introduction by John Carey] [*Der Witz und seine Beziehung zum Uberwufton,* Leipzig and Vienna 1905] (London/New York, 2003), p. 175.

3. Lyrics from *My Old Man's a Dustman*, recorded by Lonnie Donnegan, 1960.

4. Berger, Peter L., *Redeeming Laughter, The Comic Dimension of Human Experience* (Berlin/New York, 1997), p. 207.

5. See Molon, Dominic and Rooks, Michael, *Situation Comedy: Humour in Recent Art* (New York: ICI, 2005). Also see www.southbankcentre.co.uk for *Laughing in a Foreign Language*, exhibition at The Hayward (Southbank Centre, London, 25 January–13 April 2008).

6. See, for example, Paul McCarthy's exhibition, *LaLa Land Parody Paradise*, at the Whitechapel Gallery, London, 23 October 2005– 8 January 2006, and *Caribbean Pirate Project* installed at Coppermill, Hauser & Wirth, 2005–6, and Jason Rhoades' installation *Black Pussy*, shown at Hauser & Wirth, London, 2005.

7. Molon and Rooks: *Situation Comedy: Humour in Recent Art,* p. 50.

8. See, for example, Niebylski, Dianna C., *Humoring Resistance: Laughter and the Excessive Body in Contemporary Latin American Women's Fiction* (New York, 2004).

9. See Cixous, Hélène, 'The laugh of the medusa', in R.R. Warhol and D.P. Herndl (eds), *Feminisms: An Anthology of Literary Theory and Criticism* (New Jersey, 1991).

10. See Isaak, Jo Anna, *Feminism and Contemporary Art – The Revolutionary Power of Women's Laughter* (London, 1996). This book reflects back on an exhibition Isaak organised in 1982 with the same title.

11. See Isaak, Jo Anna, 'Introduction', *Laughter, Ten Years After,* an electronic exhibition catalogue, http://academic.hws.edu/art/exhibitions/laughter/index.html

12. Isaak: 'Introduction'.

13. See Cardeña, Ivette and Littlewood, Roland, 'Humour as resistance: deviance and pathology from a ludic perspective', *Anthropology and Medicine* 13/3 (December 2006), pp. 285–96.

14. Berger: *Redeeming Laughter*, pp. 206–7.

15. Žižek, Slavoj, 'The Christian-Hegelian comedy', in F. Lunn and H. Munder (eds), *When Humour Becomes Painful* (Zurich, 2005), p. 56.

16. Berger: *Redeeming Laughter*, p. 207.

17. Alloway, Lawrence, 'Junk culture', *Architectural Design* 31/3 (March 1961), p. 123–33. Alloway (1926–90), English art critic, curator and writer, was a significant figure in the postwar artworld: a great supporter of abstract art in the 1950s (see Alloway, Lawrence (ed.), *Nine Abstract Artists* (London, 1954)) such as the Constructionist group (with Kenneth Martin and Victor Pasmore) he was a founding/leading figure in the Independent Group at the Institute of Contemporary Arts, London, where he was Assistant Director (1955–60). In 1961, he moved to New York where he was Senior Curator at the Guggenheim Museum. At the time of writing, there is no major published study on Alloway.

18. Jarry's absurdist character, Ubu, first appeared in marionette performances in the late 1880s and was later central in various written and performed versions of *Ubu Roi*. See Jarry, Alfred, *The Ubu Plays* [trans. by Cyril Connolly and Simon Watson Taylor] (Methuen, London, 1968). Critchley explores farting in *Molloy* and Beckett's references to *risus purus* – 'the mirthless laugh' – at some length. See Critchley, *On Humour* (London, 2002), pp. 47–50.

19. Critchley, Simon, 'Did you hear the joke about the philosopher who wrote a book about humour?', in F. Lunn and H. Munder (eds), *When Humour Becomes Painful* (Zurich, 2005), p. 51.

20. *Steptoe and Son*, first broadcast BBC television 1962.

21. *The Dustbinmen* was a series written for British television by Jack Rosenthal, first broadcast in the 1970s.

22. Recorded by Lonnie Donnegan, 1960.

23. 'Hysteria' has a complex history which has been extensively critiqued in feminist literature. Suffice it here to refer back to a counterposing text, Jo Anna Isaak's, *Feminism and Contemporary Art – The Revolutionary Power of Women's Laughter* (London, 1996). On the contagion of mirth and where it can lead, see Gutwirth, Marcel, *Laughing Matter: An Essay on the Comic* (Ithaca and London, 1993), p. 12–13, for his account of a Laurel and Hardy film in which it turns out that Hardy has been laughing uncontrollably for no reason at all.

24. See http://www.markmcgowan.org/

25. Critchley, Simon, *On Humour* (London, 2002), p. 68.

26. Berger: *Redeeming Laughter*, p. 205.

27. Billig, Michael, *Laughter and Ridicule: Towards a Social Critique of Humour* (Sage, London, 2005), p. 5.

28. Gutwirth, Marcel, *Laughing Matter: An Essay on the Comic* (Cornell University Press, Ithaca and London, 1993). Billig also cites three commonly articulated categories of humour as related to superiority, incongruity and release theories.

29. Gutwirth: *Laughing Matter: An Essay on the Comic*, pp. 2–3.

30. Gutwirth: *Laughing Matter: An Essay on the Comic*, p. 16.

31. Two recent controversies show the complexities at play with *ethos* and *ethnos*: the satirical drawings of the Muslim prophet Muhammad first published in the Danish newspaper *Jyllands-Posten* in September 2006 and the 'offensive' telephone messages left by Russell Brand and Jonathan Ross for Andrew Sachs on the *Russell Brand* show on BBC Radio Two in October 2008.

32. Billig: *Laughter and Ridicule*, p. 2.

33. 'Positive' forms might be the 'healing' power of laughter, its appearance in popular self-help genres, its role in mental health and stress relief; 'negative' might include bigotry, causing humiliation/offence, mockery, lampooning.

34. Billig: *Laughter and Ridicule*, p. 47.

35. Billig cites Locke's discussion of wit in *An Essay Concerning Human Understanding*, first published in 1690.

36. Billig: *Laughter and Ridicule*, p. 86.

37. See Bergson, Henri, 'Essay on the meaning of the comic' and *Le rire* and Freud, *The Joke and its Relation to the Unconscious.*

38. Billig: *Laughter and Ridicule*, p. 111.

39. Bergson's phrase discussed in Billig: *Laughter and Ridicule*, p. 134.

40. See Freud: *The Joke and its Relation to the Unconscious.*

41. Billig: *Laughter and Ridicule*, p. 159.

42. Billig: *Laughter and Ridicule*, p. 161.

43. Freud: *The Joke and its Relation to the Unconscious*, p. 175.

44. Billig: *Laughter and Ridicule*, p. 175.

45. Billig: *Laughter and Ridicule*, pp. 175–6.

46. Gutwirth: *Laughing Matter: An Essay on the Comic*, p. 136.

47. Gutwirth: *Laughing Matter: An Essay on the Comic*, p. 137.

48. Gargantua and Pantagruel are the subject of five books by Francois Rabelais published in the seventeenth century. See Mikhail Bakhtin's classic study, *Rabelais and his World* (Bloomington, 1941).

49. A useful survey here is Mey, Kirstin, *Art and Obscenity* (London, 2007).

50. Berger: *Redeeming Laughter*, p. 176.

51. The definitive work on the 'absurd' tradition, a key figure in which is Eugene Ionesco (1912–94), is Martin Esslin's *The Theater of the Absurd*, first published in 1961. See Berger: *Redeeming Laughter,* pp. 176–7.

52. Berger: *Redeeming Laughter*, p. 179.

53. Berger: *Redeeming Laughter*, p. 182.

54. See Berger: *Redeeming Laughter*, p. 13 for a discussion of humour and play offering an *intermezzo* from daily life. A key study of the phenomenon of 'play' is Huizinga, Johan, *Homo Ludens: A Study of the Play Element in Culture* (Boston, 1955).

55. Alloway, Lawrence, 'Paolozzi and the comedy of waste', *Cimaise*, Series VII, No. 4 (October–December 1960), p. 122.

56. In the mid-1960s, Reichardt assisted her husband Tony Reichardt who ran the Marlborough New London Gallery: Fullard and Lacey had solo shows at the Marlborough in the 1960s. Jasia Reichardt was later curator of the iconic exhibition *Cybernetic Serendipity* at the Institute of Contemporary Arts in 1968. Author's interview with Jasia Reichardt, 12 November 1997.

57. Alloway, Lawrence, 'Collage explosion', in *The Listener*, Vol. LXVII, No. 1723 (5 April 1962), pp. 603–5.

58. Bowness, Alan (intro.), *Kurt Schwitters*, exhibition catalogue, London: Lord's Gallery (October–November 1958). The exhibition of Duchamp's work to a wider audience in the early 1960s was also significant; a major retrospective in the United States in 1962 had an international impact.

59. From Schwitters' *Merz 20* (1927), quoted by Bowness: (intro.), *Kurt Schwitters* (exhibition catalogue).

60. Alloway, Lawrence, 'Paolozzi and the comedy of waste', *Cimaise*, Series VII, No. 4 (October–December 1960), p. 122.

61. Interestingly, Paolozzi was one of the eight sculptors who showed in the British Pavilion at the 1952 Venice Biennale – others were Robert Adams, Kenneth Armitage, Reginald Butler, Lynn Chadwick, Geoffrey Clarke, Bernard Meadows and William Turnbull. At the time, they became associated with the 'geometry of fear' – a comment made by Herbert Read who identified a formal, if tenuous, unity in their work, arguing it reflected a collective wave of Cold War existentialist anxiety. See Read, Herbert, 'New aspects of British Sculpture', in *The XXVI Venice Biennale, British Pavilion* (British Council, London, 1952) and Burstow, Robert, 'The geometry of fear: Herbert Read and British Modern Sculpture after the second world war', in D. Thistlewood and B. Read (eds), *Herbert Read – A British Vision of World Art* (Leeds/London, 1993).

62. Caro's new work was exhibited at *New London Situation*, Marlborough New London Gallery in 1961 but the first major showing was at the Whitechapel Art Gallery, London in 1963. See, for example, Robertson, Bryan, 'A revolution in British Sculpture', in *The Times* (9 March 1965), p. 15 and Hodin, J.P., 'The Avant-Garde of English Sculpture and the Liberation from the Liberators', in *Quadrum* XVIII (1965), p. 55. As Director of the Whitechapel, Robertson was responsible for creating seminal exhibitions of the new abstract work of Caro and his followers as well as 'hyping up' a groundswell of ecstatic critical opinion. See note on the 'New Generation' below.

63. See transcript of Lawrence Alloway's interview with Caro in *Gazette*, 1961, No. 1, p. 1.

64. See Robertson, Bryan, 'Preface', in *The New Generation: 1965*, exhibition catalogue, London: Whitechapel Art Gallery, 1965, p. 8. The 1965 exhibition was made up of the work of nine young sculptors: David Annesley, Michael Bolus, Philip King, Roland Piché, Christopher Sanderson, Tim Scott, William Tucker, Isaac Witkin and Derrick Woodham, many of whom had been Caro's students at St Martins.

65. Cooke, Lynne, 'New abstract sculpture and its sources' in S. Nairne and N. Serota (eds), *British Sculpture in the Twentieth Century* (London, 1981), p. 183. Of course, since the 1980s, a much expanded range of British sculptural practice has been researched and included in exhibition surveys and published accounts but even in the mid-1990s, an identifiable 'canon' of British sculpture could be identified as one dominated and shaped by the respective modernisms of Herbert Read and Clement Greenberg.

66. Alloway, Lawrence, 'Paolozzi and the comedy of waste', *Cimaise*, Series VII, No. 4 (October–December 1960), p. 122.

67. For a discussion of the work of Hamilton and Alloway, see Massey, Anna, *The Independent Group, Modernism and Mass Culture in Britain, 1945–1959* (Manchester,

1995). Also see Alloway, Lawrence, 'The development of British pop', in L. Lippard (ed.), *Pop Art* [1966], third revised edition (London, 1970), pp. 27–67.

68. See Massey, *The Independent Group, Modernism and Mass Culture in Britain, 1945-1959* and Robbins, David (ed.), *The Independent Group: Postwar Britain and the Aesthetics of Plenty* (MIT Press, Cambridge, Massachusetts and London, 1990) and Spencer, Robin (ed.), *Eduardo Paolozzi, Writings and Interviews* (Oxford, 2000). The Krazy Kat Arkive, now held by the Victoria and Albert Museum, contains Paolozzi's extensive collection of ephemera, collages, scrapbooks and objects, including a series of screen prints for *Bunk* which was first staged at the ICA in 1952.

69. In 1971, Alloway published an essay entitled 'Anthropology and art criticism'. See Alloway, Lawrence [edited/commentary Richard Kalina], *Imagining the Present: Context, Content and the Role of the Critic* (London, 2006).

70. Spencer, Robin, 'Word and image in Paolozzi's art', *Things – Assemblage, Collage and Photography since 1935*, exhibition catalogue, Norwich Gallery, Norwich School of Art and Design (12 January–1 July 2000), p. 62.

71. Spencer: 'Word and image in Paolozzi's art', p. 64.

72. Paolozzi's script notes quoted in Finch, Christopher, *Image as Language, Aspects of British Art 1950-1968* (Harmondsworth, 1969), p. 50.

73. Alloway, Lawrence, 'Paolozzi and the comedy of waste', *Cimaise*, Series VII, No. 4 (October–December 1960), p. 120.

74. For a survey of Fullard's work and his use of assemblage, see Whiteley, Gillian, *Assembling the Absurd: The Sculpture of George Fullard* (London, 1998).

75. Before the exhibition, *Picasso: Sculptor/Painter*, held 16 February–8 May 1994, the Tate Gallery had staged three major shows of Picasso's work: an important exhibition in 1960; an exhibition organised by Roland Penrose in 1967 devoted solely to his sculpture and the 1988 show, *Late Picasso: Paintings, Sculpture, Drawings, Prints 1953-1972*.

76. Watts, Alex, 'Paris commentary', in *Studio*, Vol. 146, No. 726 (September 1953), p. 88–90.

77. See the exhibition catalogue with introduction by Roland Penrose for *Picasso*, Arts Council of Great Britain, Tate Gallery, London, 6 July–8 September 1960.

78. Picasso had cast conglomerations of objects, including leaves and twigs, as early as the 1930s. The Picasso exhibition May–June 1955 at Marlborough Fine Art, Old Bond Street, London, had shown 63 drawings and 10 bronzes.

79. Fullard, George, 'Sculpture and survival', in *The Painter and Sculptor*, Vol. 2, No. 2 (Summer 1959), p. 12.

80. Anon., *Quadrum* No. 12 (1961), p. 176.

81. See Victor Musgrave's papers and Gallery One archive held at the Tate Gallery, TGA 8714.

82. Reichardt, Jasia, *Apollo* No. 75 (October 1961), p. 124. Fullard had a solo show at Gallery One's new Mayfair premises in 1961: Bruce Lacey had a solo exhibition there in 1963.

83. Playing and childhood games featured extensively. See Whiteley, Gillian, *George Fullard – A Fastidious Primitive*, exhibition catalogue, Wakefield: Yorkshire Sculpture Park (1997) and *Playing with Paradox: George Fullard 1923–1973*, exhibition catalogue, Cambridge: Mappin Art Gallery, Sheffield/Kettle's Yard (1998).

84. Critchley: *On Humour*, p. 50.

85. Critchley refers to Breton's writings on the great surrealist tradition of l'humour noir' and to Breton's book, *Anthologie de l'humour noir* (Jean-Jacques Pauvert, Paris, 1966), first published 1939. Interestingly, despite its contemporaneity, 'black humour' predates Breton and goes back to Jonathan Swift writing in the eighteenth century. Critchley: *On Humour*, p. 10.

86. Breton, André, 'Introduction', in A. Breton/M. Polizzotti (ed.), *Anthology of Black Humor* [trans. Mark Polizzotti] (San Francisco, 1997), p. vi.

87. Although many refer to WW1, during WW2 Fullard served in 17/21st Lancers and was blown up in a tank at Monte Cassino where he received near-fatal injuries.

88. The 17/21st Lancers were popularly known as the 'death or glory' boys and this was reflected on the regimental badge which features a skull and cross-bones.

89. Reichardt, Jasia, 'George Fullard and the menacing baby saint', in *Metro* No. 9 (1965), pp. 27–8.

90. A descriptor Robert Melville used in a review of Fullard's Marlborough exhibition. See 'Junk war', in *New Statesman*, 20 November 1964, Vol. 68, No. 1758, p. 800–1.

91. Henri, who became Assistant Director of Liverpool College of Art in 1964, had his first solo exhibition at the Institute of Contemporary Arts, London, in 1968.

92. Henri, Adrian, *Environments and Happenings* (London, 1974). Henri devotes a section to British practice, covering significant provincial developments. He includes, for example, the 'Festival of anarchy' organised by John Arden and John Fox in Kirbymoorside in 1963, a multi-media event that attracted artists from London, Liverpool and the North of England. See Henri, *Environments and Happenings*, pp. 111–28. Henri's personal archive shows an extensive network of fellow artists, poets, writers assisted him with information to compile the book: e.g., the performance artist Roland Miller, who worked with Shirley Cameron and also with Jeff Nuttall's *People Show*, sent Henri a long list of names and contact addresses including Al Beach, Jeff Nuttall, Albert Hunt, Roger Coleman and John Fox of Welfare State International. Adrian Henri Archive and Papers, University of Liverpool.

93. The 'Kitchen Sink' painters (coined by the critic, David Sylvester in an article for *Encounter* for their focus on ordinary domestic interiors) were Jack Smith, Edward Middleditch, Derrick Greaves and John Bratby. See Spalding, Julian (ed.), *The Forgotten Fifties*, exhibition catalogue, Sheffield: Graves Art Gallery (1984). The 'sink' in Smith's painting, *Mother Bathing Child,* was actually in Fullard's studio-flat in Chelsea which, at the time, Smith shared. Author's discussions with Irena Fullard, 1996.

94. Henri's comments quoted in Milner, Frank, 'Introduction', *Adrian Henri, Paintings 1953–1998*, exhibition catalogue, Liverpool: Bluecoat Press/Walker Art Gallery (2000), p. 10.

95. Henri, Adrian, Milton Keynes Festival, 1979. Notes in Adrian Henri Archive and Papers, University of Liverpool.

96. From Henri's manuscript notes, c. 1967. Adrian Henri Archive and Papers, University of Liverpool.

97. See author's texts for *The Life and Works of Jeff Nuttall*, MidPennine Art Gallery, Burnley and Lanternhouse, Ulverston, 2005. Also author's papers including *Situating the insurgent imagination: Jeff Nuttall, Bomb Culture and British countercultural practice* (Belfast, 2007) and *The 'subversive thread of imagination' and affect:*

Jeff Nuttall and 1968 (Austin, Texas, 2008) will form the basis of a forthcoming publication.

98. 'Cut-ups' refers to the collage technique with text used by Burroughs and others. Nuttall met Burroughs on his visit to London in 1964. Nuttall, Jeff, *Bomb Culture* [1968] (London, 1970), pp. 142–5.

99. Nuttall: *Bomb Culture*, pp. 225–6. Nuttall's book, an autobiographical account of the early 1960s by a resolutely subversive figure, remains a valuable source of information on countercultural activities and events.

100. See Lacey, Bruce, *40 Years of Assemblage, Environments and Robots*, exhibition catalogue, London: Whitechapel Art Gallery (25 February–6 April 1975). In 2007, Norwich Arts Centre celebrated Lacey's 80th birthday with a retrospective exhibition, *Bruce Lacey: My Life in Therapy*, a 'happening' and film screenings including *Every Body's Nobody*, made with John Sewell in 1960.

101. 'British Rubbish' toured the UK and also went to Brussels and San Francisco. Author's discussions with Bruce Lacey, 16 May 2000. Also see author's extensive interviews with Lacey for the British Library's *Artists' Lives* project as part of the National Sound Archive, 2000, abstracts available at http://sounds.bl.uk/

102. Letter to author from Jeff Nuttall, 17 February 1999.

103. See Glew, Adrian, 'Bruce Lacey, The Womaniser 1966' in C. Stephens and K. Stout (eds), *Art & the 60s, This Was Tomorrow*, exhibition catalogue, London: Tate Britain (30 June–3 October 2004).

104. Taylor, R., 'Current and forthcoming exhibitions', in *Burlington Magazine* Vol. CVII, No. 742 (January 1965), p. 97.

105. Lacey had great respect for Lenny Bruce and had worked alongside him on his London tour. Lacey and The Alberts were invited to America to tour with the comic but circumstances prevented it going ahead. Author's discussions with Bruce Lacey, May 2000.

106. Nuttall: *Bomb Culture*, p. 117.

107. On Lacey and The Alberts see Seago, Alex, *Burning the Box of Beautiful Things* (Oxford, 1995), p. 86–91.

108. Nuttall: *Bomb Culture*, p. 107.

109. See the chapter entitled 'Sick' in Nuttall: *Bomb Culture*.

110. See Isaak, Jo Anna, 'Introduction', *Laughter, Ten Years After*, an electronic exhibition catalogue at http://academic.hws.edu/art/ exhibitions/laughter/index.html

111. From Jeff Nuttall: *Muscle*, 1982, p. 5.

112. Critchley: *On Humour*, p. 46.

113. See Arnatt, Keith, *Rubbish and Recollections*, exhibition catalogue, London: Oriel Mostyn Gallery, Llandudno/Photographers Gallery (1989).

114. See Tate Gallery, *Starlit Waters – British Sculpture, An International Art 1968–1988*, exhibition catalogue, Liverpool: Tate Gallery (1988). More generally see Marshall C. (ed.), *Breaking the Mould, British Art of the 1980s and 1990s* (London, 1997), Causey, Andrew, *Sculpture since 1945* (Oxford/New York, 1998) and Curtis, Penelope (ed.), *Vol II – A Guide to Sculptors in the Leeds Collections* (Leeds, 2003).

115. An apposite term for an artist driven by a curiosity with objects, coined by Lisa Tickner in 'A strange alchemy: Cornelia Parker', in *Art History* 26/3 (June 2003), p. 364–92.

116. See Hopkins, David, 'Out of it: drunkenness and ethics in Martha Rosler and Gillian Wearing', in *Art History, Special Issue: Difference and Excess in Contemporary Art: The Visibility of Women's Practice* 26/3 (June 2003), pp. 340–64.

117. See Deitch, Jeffrey and Rosenthal, Norman, *Tim Noble and Sue Webster – Wasted Youth* (New York, 2006) published to coincide with their exhibition, *Polymorphous Perverse,* at the Freud Museum, London, 8 December 2006–7 January 2007.

118. Deitch and Rosenthal: *Tim Noble and Sue Webster – Wasted Youth.*

119. Gutwirth: *Laughing Matter,* p. 190.

120. Billig: *Redeeming Laughter,* p. 242.

CHAPTER 5

1. de Certeau, Michel 'Walking in the city', *The Practice of Everyday Life* [trans. Steven Rendall] (Los Angeles, 1984), p. 107.

2. de Certeau, 'Walking in the city', p. 98.

3. Lefebvre, Henri, 'The inventory' [*La Somme et le reste,* Paris, 1959], in S. Elden, E. Lebas and E. Kofman (eds), *Henri Lefebvre, Key Writings* (London/New York, 2003), p. 175. As David Harvey [1991] notes, for Lefebvre, moments are 'revelatory of the totality of possibilities, contained in daily existence…', quoted in Rob Shields, *Lefebvre, Love and Struggle: Spatial Dialectics* (New York/London, 1999) in which Shields devotes a whole section to 'moments', a topic on which Lefebvre wrote extensively.

4. See Gumpert, Lynn (ed.), *The Art of the Everyday: The Quotidian in Postwar French Culture* (Grey Art Gallery New York University, 1997) which accompanied an exhibition curated by Gumpert and Thomas Sokolowski which travelled to Pittsburgh and Atlanta, 1997–8. (Author's note: throughout this chapter, I use quotidien for the orginal French and quotidian for the alternative Anglicised term.)

5. De Certeau: *The Practice of Everyday Life,* p. v.

6. For example see Highmore, Ben, *Everyday Life and Cultural Theory* (London, 2002) and Highmore, Ben, *The Everyday Life Reader* (London, 2002); Roberts, John, *Philosophising the Everyday: Revolutionary Praxis and the Fate of Cultural Theory* (London, 2006) (and his earlier *The Art of Interruption: Realism, Photography and the Everyday* (Manchester, 1998)) and Sherringham, Michael, *Everyday Life: Theories and Practices from Surrealism to the Present* (Oxford, 2006).

7. Shields: *Lefebvre, Love and Struggle: Spatial Dialectics,* p. 61.

8. See Shields comments on Lefebvre and Marx in Shields ibid., p. 61.

9. Key here, amongst Lefebvre's extensive body of writings, are *The Production of Space* [1974] and, of course, *Critique of Everyday Life* [1947, 1961, 1981] and related writings.

10. Shields: *Lefebvre, Love and Struggle: Spatial Dialectics,* p. 66.

11. See Sheringham, 'Introduction', in *Everyday Life: Theories and Practices from Surrealism to the Present,* pp. 1–16, in which he argues for *le quotidien* as a coherent intellectual tradition, outlining its genealogy with 1960–80 representing a phase of active invention and 1980 onwards, a phase of 'practice, variation, and dissemination'.

12. For a thorough exploration of Barthes' relationship to Lefebvre, see Sheringham, *Everyday Life: Theories and Practices from Surrealism to the Present,* p. 175–211.

13. Barthes, Roland, *Mythologies* [1957] (Vintage, London, 1993).

14. Barthes: *Mythologies*, p. 79.

15. Law, Alex, 'The critique of everyday life and cultural democracy', *Variant*, Issue 29 (Summer 2007), at www.variant.org.uk

16. From Vaneigem, Raoul, 'The insignificant signified', in *Revolution of Everyday Life*, Chapter One, full text available at www.bopsecrets.org originally published in 1967 as *Traité de savoir-vivre à l'usage des jeunes générations*. Sheringham outlines the complex dialogue (variously characterised as 'exchange, rivalry and in the end enmity') between Lefebvre and the Situationists in Sheringham, *Everyday Life: Theories and Practices from Surrealism to the Present*, p. 158–74.

17. Sheringham (referring to Jean-Luc Nancy's *Chroniques philosophiques*, Paris: Galilée, 2004), *Everyday Life: Theories and Practices from Surrealism to the Present*, p. 397.

18. Restany, Pierre, 'The new realists', from the catalogue for the exhibition, *Le Nouveau Réalisme à Paris et à New York* (Galerie Rive Droite, Paris, 1961).

19. Restany's role was fundamental but also 'conflictual' throughout: Restany, through Arman whom he had known since 1953, met Yves Klein in 1955, Rotella in 1957, Hains and Dufrene and others in 1959. Restany first used the term 'Nouveau Réalisme' in April 1960 on the occasion of an exhibition of the work of Arman, Dufrêne, Hains, Klein, Tinguely and Villeglé at the Galerie Apollinaire, Milan. For a chronology and documents, see *Le Nouveau Réalisme*, exhibition catalogue, Paris: Galleries Nationales du Grand Palais (28 March–2 July 2007) and Hannover: Sprengel Museum (9 September–27 January 2008).

20. Works by Arman, César, Dufrêne, Hains, Raysse, Rotella, Saint-Phalle, Spoerri, Tinguely, de la Villeglé featured in the 1961 exhibition.

21. See Michel Tapie, *Un Autre Art* published 1952.

22. Cone, Michèle C., '"Métro, Boulot, Dodo": the art of the everyday in France, 1958–72', in L. Gumpert (ed.), *The Art of the Everyday: The Quotidian in Postwar French Culture* (Grey Art Gallery, New York University, Pittsburgh and Atlanta, 1997–8), p. 50.

23. Livingstone, Marco, 'Paris 1960: realism off the shelf', *Nouveau Réalisme*, exhibition catalogue, London: Mayor Gallery (2000), no page numbers.

24. I refer here to Vance Packard's *The Waste Makers* [1960] discussed earlier.

25. Packard: *The Waste Makers*.

26. See Carrick, Jill, 'Le Nouveau Réalisme: un détournement de la profusion des choses' in *Le Nouveau Réalisme*, exhibition catalogue, Paris: Galleries Nationales du Grand Palais (28 March–2 July 2007) and Hannover: Sprengel Museum (9 September–27 January 2008). Previous key exhibitions include *Les Années 60s* at MAMAC, Nice, 1997, MoMA 1999 and Paris MMAM 2001.

27. Carrick, Jill, 'Phallic victories? Niki de Saint-Phalle's *Tirs*', *Art History*, Vol. 26, Issue 5, November 2003, p. 700–29.

28. Thrift, Nigel, *Non-Representational Theory: Space, Politics, Affect* (London, 2008), p. 77.

29. De Certeau's religious interests are well-documented: his doctorate was in the field of religious history, he had personal associations with Jesuit and Ignatian traditions and his work brought together an extensive knowledge of religious philosophies to inter-disciplinary studies.

30. For example, Thrift cites Goodchild, P., *Capitalism and Religion* (London, 2002), Gumbrecht, H.U., *Production of Presence: What Meaning Cannot Convey* (Stanford, 2004) and Braidotti, R., *Transpositions* (Cambridge, 2006).

31. Thrift refers to Santner on 'ensoulment' as in Santner, E.L., *On the Psychotheology of Everyday Life* (Chicago, 2001) – although for other theoretical explorations of affect and soul via Marxism, see Berardi, Franco 'Bifo', *The Soul At Work: From Alienation to Autonomy*, Semiotext(e) (2009).

32. Santner, E.L. *On the Psychotheology of Everyday Life* (Chicago, 2001), p. 9.

33. Baudrillard, Jean, *The System of Objects* [1968] (Verso, London, 2005), pp. 223–4.

34. See Restany, 'The new realists' quoted earlier and also Restany, Pierre, 'Modern nature' [trans. from French by Joachin Neugroschel], *Breakthroughs: Avant-garde Artists in Europe and America 1950–1990* (New York), p. 33.

35. See Leeman, Richard, 'Pierre Restany, théoréticien et historiographe du Nouveau Réalisme', in *Le Nouveau Réalisme*, exhibition catalogue, Paris: Galleries Nationales du Grand Palais (28 March–2 July 2007) and Hannover: Sprengel Museum (9 September–27 January 2008), p. 257–60.

36. Baudrillard: *The System of Objects*, p. 1.

37. Arman quoted in Jaimey Hamilton, 'Arman's system of objects', *Art Journal* (Spring 2008).

38. Baudrillard: *The System of Objects*, p. 222.

39. Robinson, Jeffrey, *Arman, Works from 1955–1989*, exhibition catalogue, London: Mayor gallery (1989), no page numbers.

40. See *Arman, Passage à l'acte* (Paris/Milan, 2001), pp. 70–1.

41. Yves Klein quoted in Stich, Sandra, *Yves Klein, From Blue Monochrome to the Void*, exhibition catalogue, London, Hayward Gallery, p. 140.

42. For an exploration of these ideas in relation to Zen, see Beck, Charlotte Joko, *Everyday Zen: Love and Work* (London, 1997) and Beck, Charlotte Joko and Smith, Steve, *Nothing Special: Living Zen* (San Francisco, 1995).

43. Anne Davy and Sophie Cazé make these comments in the Preface to *Deschamps Retrospective 1956–2003*, Musée de l'Hospice Saint-Rock Issoudun, Musée des Beaux Arts de Dole (2003), p. 5.

44. Deschamps explains his use of the term in an interview with Hélène Kelmachter in *Gérard Deschamps, Homo Accessoirus*, exhibition catalogue, Paris: Fondation Cartier pour l'art contemporain (1998).

45. Pierre Restany on 'Deschamps et le rose de la vie' [1962] in *Deschamps Retrospective 1956–2003*, Musée de l'Hospice Saint-Rock Issoudun, Musée des Beaux Arts de Dole (2003), p. 67.

46. See interview with Kelmachter already cited.

47. See *Gérard Deschamps*, exhibition catalogue, Paris: Galerie Peyroulet (1988).

48. *Gérard Deschamps*, exhibition catalogue, see Michel Giroud, 'The pink is life'.

49. See Blistère, Bernard, *Pneumostructures*, exhibition catalogue, Paris: Galerie Martine et Thibault de la Châtre (2005).

50. Blistère: *Pneumostructures*.

51. Blistère, *Pneumostructures*.

52. Barthes, *Mythologies*, p. 36.

53. Barthes, *Mythologies*.

54. See Jouffroy, Alain, *Raysse*, Fall edition, 1996. Also see *Martial Raysse*, exhibition catalogue, New York, Paris: Galerie Alexandre Jolas (1965), *Martial Raysse 1970–80*, exhibition catalogue, Paris: Centres Georges Pompidou 1981 and *Martial Raysse*, exhibition catalogue, Paris: Galerie Nationale du Jeu de Paume (1992–3).

55. Raysse quoted in *Martial Raysse*, exhibition catalogue, Paris: Galerie Nationale du Jeu de Paume (1992–3), p. 36.

56. Raysse quoted in Brown, Lydie, 'Martial Raysse: Première Partie: l'esthétique', in *Zoom* (Paris, 1971), pp. 63–71.

57. See Brunet, Nathalie and Eschapasse, Maurice, *A propos de Nice*, exhibition catalogue, Centre Georges Pompidou (1977).

58. Claude Rivière's comments were in *Combat*, Monday 22 August 1960.

59. Of course Ben Vautier worked extensively across media with everyday objects and assemblage in the 1960s and since. See his *Bizarre Bazaar* (2002), a whirring conglomeration of found and manufactured objects, displayed at *Shopping: A Century of Art and Consumer Culture*, Tate Liverpool, 2003. Vautier was, and continues to be, a focal figure for Fluxus activities in Nice. See www.ben-vautier. com

60. See *Claude Gilli*, exhibition catalogue, Nice: Musée d'Art Moderne Contemporain (10 April–6 June 1999). Gilli was born in Nice in 1938.

61. Arman in *Nice to Berlin*, exhibition catalogue (1980), quoted in *Claude Gilli*, exhibition catalogue, Nice: Musée d'Art Moderne Contemporain (10 April–6 June 1999), p. 15.

62. See Petersen, Ad, Henri Berend, Willem Jacob, *Sandberg, Designer and Director of the Stedelijk* (010 Publishers, Rotterdam, 2004).

63. Cone, Michèle, '"Métro, Boulot, Dodo": the art of the everyday in France, 1958–72', p. 53.

64. See Snoddy, Stephen, Jackson, Tessa, Gourmelon, Mo, 'An accomplished schemer' in *Annette Messager: Telling Tales*, exhibition catalogue, Bristol: Arnolfini (1992), p. 10. The exhibition, *Annette Messager: The Messengers,* was presented at Centre Georges Pompidou in 2007 and at The Hayward, Southbank Centre, in 2009.

CHAPTER 6

1. Mike Brown, quoted in Sayers, Andrew, *Australian Art* (Oxford, 2001), p. 189.

2. Morgan, Kendragh, *It ain't necessarily so… Mike Brown and the Annandale Imitation Realists*, exhibition notes, Bulleen: Heide Museum of Modern Art (18 July–1 October 2006).

3. Haese, Richard, 'Brought to light', *Australian Art 1850–1965*, p. 286. See Note 132 for more on Haese's writings on Brown.

4. Lynn, Elwyn, 'Pop goes the easel', *Art and Australia* (1963), p. 166.

5. Ross Crothall, quoted in *Sunday Mirror* (20 May 1962). Newspaper clippings NLA, Canberra.

6. Moffatt, Ian, *Sunday Mirror*, 20 May 1962. Press scrapbooks, National Library of Australia, Canberra.

7. Gleeson, James, *The Sun*, 23 May 1962. Press Scrapbooks, National Library of Australia, Canberra.

8. Robert Hughes review appeared in *The Nation*, 16 June 1962.

9. The Assistant Director of the Art Gallery of New South Wales was newly appointed to write a regular art column for the *Sunday Telegraph* – his first article published on 27 May 1962 was devoted to a review of the 2nd AIR exhibition at Rudy Komon Gallery in Sydney.

10. Thomas, Daniel, 'The week in art', *Sunday Telegraph*, 27 May 1962.

11. Catalaneo, Gary, 'The aesthetics of the imitation realists', *Meanjin Quarterly* 35/2 (1976), p. 175.

12. See Elkins, James, *Is Art History Global?* (London, 2006).

13. On AIR and Pop, see Evatt, Clive, *The Imitation Realists and Australian Pop Art*, (Power Department of Fine Arts, University of Sydney, 1972, unpublished). In 1972, Evatt set up Hogarth Galleries, Paddington, Sydney, Australia's oldest established gallery devoted to indigenous art.

14. Lynn: 'Pop goes the easel', p. 167.

15. Lynn: 'Pop goes the easel', p. 168.

16. French, Blair, 'Jonathan Jones', *Adventures with Form in Space*, exhibition catalogue, Art Gallery of New South Wales (9 August–9 September 2006), p. 34.

17. French: 'Jonathan Jones'.

18. Sayers: *Australian Art*, p. 209.

19. On hybridity and the conceptualisation of a 'third space' see Bhabha, Homi, *Location of Culture* (London, 1995) and Bhabha, Homi, 'The third space: an interview with Homi Bhabha', in J. Rutherford (ed.), *Identity, Culture, Difference* (London, 1990), pp. 207–21.

20. Crothall in *Sunday Mirror*, 20 May 1962. Newspaper clippings NLA, Canberra.

21. Butler, Rex, *Contemporary Commonwealth 2006*, exhibition catalogue, National Gallery of Victoria, p. 52.

22. See Hughes, Robert, *The Art of Australia*, Harmondsworth (1966) and revised editions since.

23. Hughes: *The Art of Australia*, pp. 311–15.

24. There has been a significant Chinese presence in Australia since the 1840s but a new wave of Chinese artists settled after 1989, for example, Ah Xian (b. 1960) arrived in Australia in 1990. See Devery, Jane, 'Ah Xian', *Contemporary Commonwealth 2006*, exhibition catalogue, National Gallery of Victoria, pp. 130–4.

25. France, Christine, 'Larrikins in London – an Australian presence in 1960s London', *Art and Australia* 41/3 (Autumn 2004), p. 388.

26. Patrick White's comments in *Sunday Mirror*, 3 December 1961. Press clippings file December 1961–July 1962, AGNSW archive.

27. Hughes, Robert, 'The intellectual in Australia', *Australian Writing Today* (Penguin, Harmondsworth, 1968), p. 298.

28. Alomes, Stephen, *When London Calls: The Expatriation of Australian Creative Artists to Britain* (Cambridge, 1999), p. 7.

29. Gleeson in 1956, quoted in Phipps, Jennifer, *I Had a Dream: Australian Art in the 1960s*, National Gallery of Victoria.

30. Phipps, *I Had a Dream: Australian Art in the 1960s*, p. 8.

31. Robertson advised AGNSW on the acquisition of works by young British contemporaries and, in return, he purchased Australian work. On a lecture tour of

Australia in 1960 he selected work for the *Recent Australian Painting* exhibition held in 1961 at Whitechapel Gallery, although ten of the artists in this show were living in London at the time.

32. Hughes: *The Art of Australia*, pp. 160–1.

33. Hughes: *The Art of Australia*, pp. 160–5.

34. Hughes: *The Art of Australia*, p. 290.

35. Richardson, Donald, *Art in Australia* (Longman, Melbourne, 1988), pp. 149, 188.

36. Plant, Margaret, *Irreverent Sculpture*, exhibition catalogue, Monash University Gallery (1985), p. 30.

37. See Chiu, Melissa, 'Asian Australian artists: cultural shifts in Australia', *Art and Australia* 37/2 (December 1999/January/February 2000), pp. 254–60.

38. Brougher, Kerry, Morphy, Howard and Elliott, David, *In Place (Out of Time): Contemporary Art in Australia*, exhibition catalogue, Oxford: Museum of Modern Art (1997).

39. Hughes: *The Art of Australia*, p. 207.

40. See Sayers, *Australian Art* and Caruana, Wally, *Aboriginal Art* [1993] (London, 2003).

41. See Preston, Margaret, in *Australia: National Journal* 2/6 (May 1941).

42. Sayers: *Australian Art*, p. 141.

43. Plant: *Irreverent Sculpture*, p. 26. Also Brougher, Kerry, Brophy, Howard and Elliott, David, *In Place (Out of Time): Contemporary Art in Australia*, exhibition catalogue, Oxford: Museum of Modern Art (1997).

44. Tony Tuckson, painter and Deputy Director of the Art Gallery of New South Wales, with responsibility of developing the collection of aboriginal art.

45. Others included Yosl Bergner (b. 1920), a European refugee artist who depicted Australian poverty and Arthur Boyd (1920–99) whose powerful landscapes evoked and suggested the distressing conditions of the lives of indigenous peoples.

46. In 1958, Jewish refugee artist, Magda Kohn, who became the partner of Ross Crothall, opened a coffee shop in Taylor Square; later she ran one at 28 Flinders Street.

47. Crothall (b. 1934, New Zealand) studied under Theo Schoon 1954–8, arrived at Sydney in 1958. Lanceley, a New Zealander, and Brown, born in Sydney (both b. 1938). Brown and Crothall studied only briefly at East Sydney Technical College. Olsen was one of the few artist-teachers at the College who gained their common admiration. Author's interview with Lanceley, August 2006.

48. A particularly public spat over the roots, motivations and directions of AIR developed between Brown and Lanceley, chiefly after Lanceley published 'Craven A – surrealism and the Annandale imitation realists', in *Art and Australia* 31/4 (Winter 1994), p. 481–9. Crothall's 'disappearance' in the 1960s precluded his taking part.

49. See Lanceley: 'Craven A – surrealism and the Annandale imitation realists'. There are various accounts and references to 'aesthetic chess', a game they devised using found objects. Lanceley viewed it in a surrealist context whereas Brown felt it symbolised collectivity.

50. Plant: *Irreverent Sculpture*, p. 22. This exhibition included the first significant presentation and critical re-consideration of AIR since 1962.

51. Haese, Richard, in L. Seear and J. Ewington (eds), *Brought To Light: Australian Art, 1850–1965 From the Queensland Art Gallery Collection*, Queensland Art Gallery (1998), p. 286.

52. Described by Mike Brown in an interview in 1972 as 'rows of painting as alike as cigarette packets' in Clive Evatt, *The Imitation Realists and Australian Pop Art*, p. 3.

53. Described thus by Lanceley in 'Craven A – surrealism and the Annandale imitation realists, in S.A. Wallace (ed.), *Art and Australia* 31/4 (Winter 1994), p. 481–9.

54. Haese: *Brought To Light: Australian Art*, p. 286.

55. Haese: *Brought To Light: Australian Art*.

56. AIR's original plans to show at the Terry Clune Gallery in Sydney fell through but Elwyn Lynn arranged for John Reed to visit AIR. Reed got in just ahead of Rudy Komon in Sydney.

57. Daniel Thomas notes this in his review for the *Sunday Telegraph*, 27 May 1962.

58. AIR exhibition catalogue, Museum of Modern Art, Melbourne, 1962.

59. Rudy Komon (d. 1982) an Austrian political refugee who arrived in Australia in the 1930s opened a winebar in Sydney in 1953. In 1959, he converted it into a gallery to show the work of Olsen, Brack, Blackman and Dickerson. Komon's main rival was Kim Bonython's gallery in Adelaide, which had a reciprocal arrangement with Swathe-Burr Gallery in Los Angeles – Bonython arranged a show of 60 Australian artists there in 1961. See Robert Hughes' article on the background to the Komon Gallery in 'Vollard of Woollhara' in the *Nation* (Sydney), 16 December 1961. Also Rudy Komon papers and press scrapbooks, National Library of Australia, Canberra.

60. Private view card, Rudy Komon papers, National Library of Australia, Canberra.

61. See, Mike Brown's comments highlighting the women artists involved in AIR in his article 'Kite II – Part 2', *Art Monthly (Australia)*, November, 1994.

62. For a discussion of women as 'excluded others', see Lloyd, G., 'No one's land: Australia and the philosophical imagination', *Hypatia* 15/2 (Spring 2000), p. 29 – part of a special issue after the conference, *Going Australian: Reconfiguring Feminism and Philosophy*, University of Warwick, 1998.

63. Leonora Howlett (b. 1940, Sydney) studied at Sydney Technical College 1956–60, married Lanceley in January 1961 but the partnership was brief and problematic by the time they were working on the AIR shows. Subsequently, Howlett travelled extensively in Europe and Mexico, returning to Australia where her work has been strongly influenced by non-Western cultures, particularly Arabic patterns and Islamic art. Artists files, AGNSW archives.

64. Letter dated 8 November 2005 from Leonora Howlett, AGNSW archives.

65. Howlett: AGNSW archives.

66. Shore, Arnold, *The Age*, 13 February 1962. Press cuttings file December 1961–July 1962, AGNSW archive.

67. Hannan, Bill, 'Where eggheads peep out', *Sydney Bulletin*, 24 February 1962. Press cuttings file December 1961–July 1962, AGNSW archive.

68. Letter from John Reed, published in *Sydney Bulletin*, March 1962. Press cuttings file December 1961–July 1962, AGNSW archive.

69. Hughes, Robert, *The Nation* (Sydney), 16 June 1962. Press cuttings file, AGNSW archive.

70. Lanceley had a free supply of household paints at the time as he had a job mixing paints for Dulux. Author's interview with Lanceley, 24 August 2006.

71. Edwards, Deborah, 'Colin Lanceley: junk start', in *Colin Lanceley – The Dry Salvages 1963-64 and Gemini 1964*, exhibition catalogue, Sydney: Art Gallery New South Wales (1 January–25 March 2001), p. 7.

72. See Haese: *Brought To Light: Australian Art*, p. 286.

73. See Plant: *Irreverent Sculpture*, p. 22.

74. Plant: *Irreverent Sculpture*, p. 28.

75. Catalaneo, Gary, 'The aesthetics of the imitation realists', *Meanjin Quarterly*, 35/2 (1976), p. 176.

76. Maloon, Terence, 'Colin Lanceley: the man on the dump; sophisticated Lanceley', *Art and Australia* 25/1 (Spring 1987), pp. 65–71.

77. Plant: *Irreverent Sculpture*, p. 28. This large figure was reconstructed for the Crothall exhibition at the New Vision gallery in Auckland in 1966.

78. Hughes, Robert, *Colin Lanceley*, Sydney [1987/1993], p. 9.

79. Hughes: *Colin Lanceley*.

80. Hughes: *The Art of Australia*, p. 307.

81. Australia took over the Southern part, Papua, from the British in 1907. The Western part of the island was controlled by the Dutch until it became an Indonesian province in 1962. Papua New Guinea achieved independence in 1975. Useful cultural accounts/sources include: Crawford, Al, *Sakema Gogodala Woodcarvers*, National Cultural Council, Port Moresby (1975); Craig, Barry, *Art and the Decoration of Central New Guinea* (Aylesbury, 1988); Simons, Susan Cochrane and Stephenson, Hugh (eds), *Luk Luk Gen! Look again! Contemporary Art from Papua New Guinea* (Perc Tucker Regional Gallery, Townsvillle, 1990); *Contemporary Tradition: Material Culture in Papua New Guinea*, exhibition catalogue, University of Tasmania (6 August–6 September 1996); Cochrane, Susan, *Contemporary Art in Papua New Guinea* (Roseville, Sydney, 1997).

82. A number of AIR works were exhibited at Heide in 2006 – see Morgan, Kendragh, *It ain't necessarily so … Mike Brown and the Annandale Imitation Realists*, exhibition catalogue, Bulleen: Heide Museum of Modern Art (18 July–1 October 2006).

83. Brown and Crothall visited New Zealand in 1959. Brown talked about their relationship in some detail in an interview with Helen Topliss, 14 April 1995. Transcription of audio tape held in National Library of Australia, Canberra.

84. Ross Crothall comment in exhibition catalogue, New Vision Gallery, Auckland, New Zealand (11–23 July 1966).

85. Haese: *Brought To Light: Australian Art*, p. 286.

86. For a recent study of Schoon and Crothall see Gunn, Anthea, 'Picturing the space: Theo Schoon, Ross Crothall and visual art in the Pacific', *Double Dialogues*, Issue 7 (Winter 2007). Schoon (b. Java) went to New Zealand in 1939 and probably passed on Maori and Java cultural interest to Crothall. Clive Evatt's unpublished dissertation 'The imitation realists and Australian pop art' refers to this. AIR exhibit 133 (Melbourne) by Ross Crothall was titled, *Self-Portrait with a Pot by Theo Schooner 'My Teacher'*, p. 2.

87. Mentioned in various accounts, e.g., Howlett's letter dated 8 November 2005, to AGNSW. AGNSW archives.

88. See Bloem, Marja and Browne, Martin, *Colin McCahon: A Question of Faith*, exhibition catalogue, Amsterdam: Stedelijk Museum (2002).

89. Exhibited at the New Vision Gallery, Auckland in 1965 – the only other exhibition Crothall did.

90. Howlett's letter dated 8 November 2005.

91. Prior to the arrival of TV in Australia in 1954, the central producer of documentary film had been the News and Information Bureau – in 1956, this became the Commonwealth Film Unit. Before the 1960s, the Unit made a number of films about the welfare of Aboriginal communities. See Bryson, Ian, *Bringing to Light: A History of Ethnographic Filmmaking at the Australian Institute of Aboriginal and Torres Strait Islander Studies* (Canberra, 2002).

92. Bryson: *Bringing to Light.*

93. Anonymous article in *Sydney Morning Herald*, 5 December 1961. Press cuttings file, December 1961–July 1962, AGNSW archive.

94. Hughes, Robert, 'Stern challenge', *The Nation* (Sydney), 10 February 1962.

95. Two hundred exhibits (a private collection) of work from New Guinea featured in 'The art of the primitive man' show at the Newman Gallery, Castlereagh, reviewed in Sydney Daily Mirror, 12 February 1962. Press cuttings file December 1961–July 1962, AGNSW archive.

96. In *Introduction to Art of the Sepik*, Melbourne, 1972, Gloria Stewart notes the 'ingenuity of the craftsmen' in adapting modern materials in order to satisfy the demand for objects and artefacts, particularly in the case of Mwai and Gable masks.

97. An exhibition in 1996 sought to counter the idea of non-western cultures being 'polluted' by western inferences and aimed to show Papua New Guinea culture in an ever-shifting state of amalgamation and dialogue. *Contemporary Tradition: Material Culture in Papua New Guinea*, exhibition catalogue, University of Tasmania: University Gallery (6 August–6 September 1996).

98. For a summary of the developments in art education in the 1960s in Papua New Guinea and its effects on traditional practices see Simons and Stephenson, *Luk Luk Gen! Contemporary Art from Papua New Guinea.* The highly schematised work which relied on line to define mass and infill patterns, of the Port-Moresby-based Naive Group in the later 1960s – Akis, Kauage and Ruki Fame – bears a remarkable resemblance to AIR.

99. Cochrane: *Contemporary Art in Papua New Guinea*, p. 76.

100. Robert Hughes, review of AIR at Rudy Komon Sydney 1962 quoted in *Dry Salvages*, p. 2.

101. Daniel Thomas in Turnbull, Colin, Young, Elisabeth and Thomas, Daniel. *Australian Painting: Colonial; Impressionist; Contemporary*, exhibition catalogue, London: Tate Gallery (24 January–3 March 1963), p. 26.

102. See Anthea Gunn, 'Picturing the space: Theo Schoon, Ross Crothall and visual art in the Pacific' in *Double Dialogues*, Issue 7 (Winter 2007).

103. Crothall, Ross, exhibition catalogue, New Zealand: New Vision Gallery, Auckland (11–23 July 1966). Crothall returned to New Zealand in 1965 but 'disappeared' around 1968.

104. Unidentified press cutting, artist's files, National Gallery of Australia, Canberra.

105. See Alomes: *When London Calls*, p. 78. According to Alomes, the end of the 1950s and early 1960s witnessed the greatest congregation of Australian artists in London

since the turn of the century, e.g., Arthur Boyd arrived in 1959, Charles Blackman and Brett Whiteley arrived in 1960, Leonard French, Martin Sharp later.

106. The Whitechapel had an exhibition of Sydney Nolan's work in 1957 and then an exhibition of Australian work in 1961; the Tate show was in 1963.

107. *Colin Lanceley*, exhibition catalogue, Marlborough Gallery (February 1966). His 'launch' onto the London art scene featured an appearance in the BBC TV series Release, a Studio International article and a meeting with Joan Miro. Not all critics were great fans – Norbert Lynton dismissed Lanceley's work at the Marlborough show as 'fairly average international nonsense' and 'pointless rhetoric'. 1966 cuttings file, AGNSW archive.

108. Lanceley in *Sunday Mirror*, September 1967.

109. All three artists had collections of Melanesian art.

110. Author's interview with Lanceley, 24 August 2006.

111. *Colin Lanceley: Relied Tondos and Wasteland Drawings*, exhibition catalogue, London: Whitechapel Art Gallery (9 September–19 October 1975).

112. Spencer, Charles, *Colin Lanceley* (London), p. 2.

113. Lanceley makes this point emphatically in the *Dry Salvages*, TSE video presentation, 2001, and reiterated this when I interviewed him, 24 August 2006.

114. Lanceley: *Dry Salvages*.

115. 'Colin Lanceley speaks on *The Dry Salvages*' in *Colin Lanceley – The Dry Salvages 1963-64 and Gemini 1964*, exhibition catalogue, Sydney: Art Gallery New South Wales (1 January–25 March 2001), p. 4.

116. Edwards, Deborah, 'Colin Lanceley: junk start', in *Colin Lanceley – The Dry Salvages 1963-64 and Gemini 1964*, exhibition catalogue, Sydney: Art Gallery New South Wales (January–25 March 2001), p. 4.

117. Hughes in Wright, William and Hughes, Robert, *Colin Lanceley* (Sydney, 1987/ 1993), p. 12.

118. The triptych, *The Dry Salvages*, 1963–4, was dismantled and parts sold separately in the late 1960s. Sandra McGrath gave *Gemini* 1964 to the Art Gallery of New South Wales in 1968.

119. Lanceley discusses T.S. Eliot's writings in *Colin Lanceley – The Dry Salvages 1963–64 and Gemini 1964*, exhibition catalogue, Sydney: Art Gallery New South Wales (1 January–25 March 2001), *The Dry Salvages*.

120. Pearce, Barry, *Colin Lanceley – The Dry Salvages 1963-64 and Gemini 1964*, exhibition catalogue, Sydney: Art Gallery New South Wales (1 January–25 March 2001), p. 2.

121. Pearce: *Colin Lanceley – The Dry Salvages 1963-64 and Gemini 1964*, p. 4.

122. Pearce: *Colin Lanceley – The Dry Salvages 1963-64 and Gemini 1964*.

123. Author's interview with Colin Lanceley, 24 August 2008.

124. McDonald, John, 'Spectrum', *Sydney Morning Herald*, 27–8 August 2005. Artists' files, AGNSW archive.

125. Brown's comment in Lynn, Elwyn 'Pop goes the easel', *Art and Australia* (November 1963), p. 172.

126. In 1977, the National Gallery of Australia presented the first major survey exhibition of Mike Brown's work, *Embracing Chaos*. Sixty works were exhibited including slides, video, collage, sculpture, drawings, assemblages – he cited a vast range of sources such as tribal art, pop songs, comics, banal advertisements.

127. McDonald, John, 'Mike Brown obituary', *Sydney Morning Herald*, 11 April 1997.

128. Pearce: *Colin Lanceley – The Dry Salvages 1963-64.*

129. Brown, Mike, *Face Value*, exhibition catalogue (1963–4). Artists files, NGA Research Library. The Kite featured in the Mike Brown exhibition at Heide in 2006 – see Morgan, Kendragh, *It ain't Necessarily so …Mike Brown and the Annandale Imitation Realists*, exhibition catalogue, Bulleen: Heide Museum of Modern Art (18 July–1 October 2006).

130. Pearce: *Colin Lanceley – The Dry Salvages 1963-64.*

131. Brown commenting in undated, unpublished typed sheet of notes entitled 'The history of the southern amorphs', AGNSW archive.

132. For example, in 1982 Brown was at the core of the group, United Artists – it included Martin Sharp, Robert Klippel, Dale Hickey and Ivan Durant – to escape the conventional gallery system and spaces. Richard Haese has written extensively on Mike Brown – see *Power to the People: The Art of Mike Brown*, retrospective exhibition catalogue, National Gallery of Victoria, Melbourne, 1995 (with supplementary essays by Mike Brown and Charles Nodrum); *Rebels and Precursors: Revolutionary Years of Australian Art*, Viking Open Market, 1982, and a forthcoming monograph on Mike Brown.

133. Brown, Mike, 'Kite II – Part 1', *Art Monthly (Australia)* (September 1994), p. 7. Brown followed up this article with 'Kite II – Part 2' in the November 1994 issue of *Art Monthly*.

134. Exhibition held at Charles Nodrum Gallery, Melbourne in 1987.

135. Brown is the only Australian artist to have been successfully charged with obscenity – five works in the exhibition *Painting A-Go-Go* at Gallery A in 1965 were deemed offensive. Frank Watters and Geoffrey Legge, directors of Watters Gallery, organised the 'Mike Brown Appeal find' exhibition in February 1967. Author's interview with Frank Watters, August 2006. From its opening in 1964, the Gallery showed and supported challenging, revolutionary, quirky art by some of Australia's most rebellious artists. They lost the appeal but his three-month custodial sentence was reduced to a fine of $20. Brown's work *Kite* was a response to this. See Lucas, Clay, 'You say you want a revolution', *Art and Australia* 36/2, pp. 238–43.

136. Mike Brown in *Sunday Mirror* (Australia), 1 December 1963, on the occasion that Douglas Pratt, Sydney member of the Commonwealth Art Advisory Board, threatened to withdraw promised financial support if the work was not removed from display. Cutting AGNSW archive.

137. See Morgan, *It ain't necessarily so… Mike Brown and the Annandale Imitation Realists.*

138. Mike Brown's interview with Helen Topliss, 14 April 1995. Transcription of audio tape held in National Library of Australia, Canberra.

139. Blair French's comment provided a starting point for this chapter. French, Blair, 'Jonathan Jones', *Adventures with Form in Space*, exhibition catalogue, Art Gallery of New South Wales (9 August–9 September 2006), p. 34.

140. See Morgan: *It ain't necessarily so…Mike Brown and the Annandale Imitation Realists.* Three contemporary artists, Rob McKenzie, Kain Picken and Nick Selenitsch, were commissioned to re-make the work with materials from Brown's studio. Working from slides, rather than replicating, they produced a mural in the spirit of the original, working in the gallery as part of the exhibition. The

project was supported and assisted by Mike Brown's sons, Zen Lucas and Clay Lucas.

141. AIR's influence on Martin Sharp is evident. Margaret Plant noted 'the obsessive line, the congestion of images in Annandale work declare wittingly or unwittingly a psychedelic partnership'. Plant: *Irreverent Sculpture*, p. 28.

142. Richardson, Donald, *Art in Australia* (Longman, Melbourne, 1988), p. 190.

143. Jenny Barwell (b. 1933), primarily a painter in the 1960s, started to work with found objects in the 1970s. Frank Watters staged a Jenny Barwell retrospective exhibition 24 July–10 August 1985.

144. Catalaneo, Gary, *Ocker Funk*, exhibition catalogue, Sydney: Frank Watters Gallery (1975).

145. Rosalie Gascoigne moved to Canberra in 1943 where she lived and worked. With no formal art training, she first exhibited work in 1974 at the Macquarie Gallery, Canberra. Subsequent exhibitions include Sydney Biennale 1979, 1st Australian Sculpture Triennale at Preston Institute of Technology and La Trobe University, Melbourne, in 1981 and Venice Biennale 1982.

146. Gascoigne's son's art collection included a Rauschenberg assemblage which she caretaked in the 1970s. Obituary, *The Australian*, 29 October 1994. Also see Gascoigne, Rosalie, exhibition catalogue, National Art Gallery (16 December– 12 February 1984).

147. Edwards, Deborah, 'Colin Lanceley: junk start' in *Colin Lanceley – The Dry Salvages 1963-64 and Gemini 1964* (Art Gallery of New South Wales, 2001), p. 7.

148. Edwards, Deborah, 'Rosalie Gascoigne' in Coates, Rebecca and Howard Morphy (eds.) *In Place (Out of Time) Contemporary Art in Australia*, exhibition catalogue, Museum of Modern Art, Oxford, 1997, p. 41.

149. Oliver, Bronwyn, 'Rosalie Gascoigne: great blond paddocks, 1999', *Art and Australia*, Vol. 37, No. 4 (June–August 2000), p. 538.

150. See www.diannetanzergallery.net.au

151. Author's interview with Elizabeth Gower, August 2007. See http://www.sutton-gallery.com

152. Mania, Astrid, 'Self storage', *Adventures with Form and Space, The Fourth Balnaves Foundation Sculpture Project*, exhibition catalogue, Sydney: Art Gallery of New South Wales (9 August–17 September 2006), p. 26.

153. Mania: 'Self storage'.

154. Tom Risley (b. 1947, Rockhampton, Queensland) has no formal art training. Exhibitions include Ray Hughes Gallery and 2nd Australian Sculpture Triennial 1984 at National Gallery of Victoria, Melbourne.

155. Hall, Doug, *Tom Risley: The Indigenous Object and the Urban Offcast*, exhibition catalogue, Queensland Art Gallery (1992), p. 4.

156. Lorraine Connelly-Northey (b. 1962), Swan Hill Victoria. See Judith Ryan, 'Lorraine Connelly-Northey: hunter-gatherer' and Rex Butler, 'View from Australia' in *Contemporary Commonwealth 2006*, exhibition catalogue, National Gallery of Victoria, pp. 50–5.

157. Ryan, 'Lorraine Connelly-Northey: hunter-gatherer', p. 53.

158. See *Gatherer*, exhibition ephemera, Gabriele Pizzi Gallery, Melbourne (25 October– 19 November 2005) and *Landmarks*, exhibition catalogue, National Gallery of Victoria, Melbourne (10 February–11 June 2006).

159. Stanhope, Zara, *Octopus 6: We Know Who We Are*, exhibition catalogue, Gertrude Contemporary Art Spaces (7 July–19 August 2006).

160. Author's correspondence with Ash Keating. His activities are documented in *Octopus 6: We Know Who We Are*, exhibition catalogue, Gertrude Contemporary Art Spaces (7 July–19 August 2006).

161. Hughes: *Colin Lanceley*, p. 291.

162. Ian Fairweather (b. 1891 Scotland, d. 1974) served in the First World War, studied at the Slade in the 1920s, studied Japanese and Chinese languages and culture both formally and informally. Despite his 'outsider' status, he represented Australia in VII Bienal de Sao Paulo in 1963. See Holbrook, Peter, 'Vision and abandonment' in *Ian Fairweather, an Artist of the 21st Century*, exhibition catalogue, Lismore Regional Gallery (2 December 2005–21 January 2006), p. 6.

163. Butler, Rex, 'Ian Fairweather in the 21st century' in *Ian Fairweather, an Artist of the 21st Century*, exhibition catalogue, Lismore Regional Gallery (2 December 2005–21 January 2006), p. 26.

164. Butler, Rex, 'View from Australia' in *Contemporary Commonwealth 2006*, exhibition catalogue, National Gallery of Victoria (2006), p. 52.

AFTERWORD

1. Brisley, Stuart, *Beyond Reason: Ordure*, (London, 2003), p. 5.

2. See www.jeanshin.com

3. A typical installation was Takahashi's *Deep Sea Diving/Dive 3: HQ* 2002, at Kunsthalle Bern, Switzerland. See *Tomoko Takahashi*, exhibition at Serpentine Gallery, London, 22 February–10 April 2005.

4. A major retrospective of Anatsui's work will form the inaugural exhibition at the new Museum for African Art, due to open late 2010 in New York. See www.africanart.org

5. See www.everydaytrash.com

6. Author's interview with Michael Cataldi, September 2009. See www.universityoftrash.org

7. A TAZ is a transitory utopian space which enables the fleeting suspension of usual rules and mores – see Bey, Hakim, 'From TAZ: the temporary autonomous zone', in S. Duncombe (ed.), *Cultural Resistance Reader* (Verso, London, 2002), p. 113.

8. In 'Trash: public art and the garbage girls', Isaak writes about the inter-connections between the production of waste, the production of art and the role of women in those productions and includes Ukeles, Nancy Rubins, Betty Beaumont, Agnes Denes, Nancy Holt, Dominique Mazeaud, Suvan Geer and Christy Rupp. Isaak in Adams, Steven and Robins, Anna G. (eds), *Gendering Landscape Art* (Manchester/ New Brunswick NJ, 2001), pp. 173–85.

9. From Ukeles' 'Sanitation manifesto', quoted in *The Act*, Vol. 2, No. 1 (1990).

10. Author's interview with Mierle Laderman Ukeles, January 2006.

11. Ukeles, Mierle L., *Sculpting with the Environment* (London/ New York, 1995), p. 184. The project remains unfinished. See www.feldmangallery.com

12. Ukeles: *Sculpting with the Environment*, p. 185.

13. Carr, C., 'Fresh kills becomes an urban artwork', *Village Voice*, 20 May 2002, p. 43.

14. Ukeles, Mierle L., 'Leftovers/its about time for fresh kills', *Cabinet, A Quarterly Magazine of Art and Horticulture*, Issue 6, Spring 2002, p. 20. Ukeles continues to work

with landscape designers, engineers, ecologists and others to develop the site's future. See www.freshkillspark.wordpress.com

15. In *TS2*, the Slow Art Collective (Chaco Kato, Ash Keating, Dylan Martorell and Tony Adams) created a large-scale art installation project using tons of e-waste to highlight the excesses of disposable lifestyles and to promote alternatives. *TS2* ran from 19 August to 13 September 2009 in partnership with Moonee Valley City Council Waste Transfer Station and the adjacent Incinerator Arts Complex, Australia. See http://sac-ts2.blogspot.com/

16. England, Jane, 'Introduction' in *Stuart Brisley*, exhibition catalogue, London: England & Co (2006), p. 3.

17. See Brisley, Stuart, *Beyond Reason: Ordure* (London, 2003) and www.museumordure.org.uk

18. A passing but knowing indirect reference to Charles Baudelaire's *Les Fleurs du Mal* (first published 1857) and Adorno's much-quoted comment that 'to write poetry after Auschwitz is barbaric' – see Adorno, Theodor W., 'Culture, criticism and society', in *Prisms* (London, 1967), p. 34.

SELECTED BIBLIOGRAPHY

Adams, Steven and Robins, A. Greutzner (eds), *Gendering Landscape Art* (Manchester, 2001).

Ades, Dawn and Baker, Simon, *Undercover Surrealism: Georges Bataille and Documents*, exhibition catalogue, Hayward Gallery/MIT (2006).

Adrian, Henri, *Paintings 1953–1998*, exhibition catalogue, Liverpool: Bluecoat Press/Walker Art Gallery (2000).

Albright, Thomas, *Art in San Francisco Bay Area 1945–1980* (Berkeley/Los Angeles, 1985).

Ali, Monica, *Brick Lane* [orig. 2003] (London, 2004).

Alloway, Lawrence, 'Paolozzi and the comedy of waste', *Cimaise*, Series VII, 4 October–December 1960.

Alloway, Lawrence, *New Forms –New Media*, exhibition catalogue, New York: Martha Jackson Gallery (October 1960).

Alloway, Lawrence, 'Junk culture', *Architectural Design* 31/3 (March 1961), pp. 123–33.

Alloway, Lawrence, 'Collage explosion', *The Listener* LXVII/1723 (5 April 1962), pp. 603–05.

Alomes, Stephen, *When London Calls: The Expatriation of Australian Creative Artists to Britain* (Cambridge, 1999).

Appadurai, Arjun et al., *The Social Life of Things: Commodities in Cultural Perspective* (Cambridge, 1986).

Ashton, Doré, 'High tide for assemblage', in *Studio International* 165/837 (January 1963), p. 25.

Ayres, A., *Forty Years of California Assemblage*, exhibition catalogue, Los Angeles: UCLA (1989–90).

Barthes, Roland, *Mythologies* [1957] (London, 1993). Baudrillard, Jean, *The System of Objects* [1968] (Verso, London, 2005),

Beck, Charlotte Joko, *Everyday Zen: Love and Work* (London, 1997).

Benjamin, Walter, *Illuminations* [trans. Harry Zohn, edited and with introduction by Hannah Arendt] (New York, 1968).

Benjamin, Walter, 'The Paris of the second Empire in Baudelaire', in C. Baudelaire (ed.), *A Lyric Poet in the Era of High Capitalism* [first published in English in 1973] (London, 1993).

Benjamin, Walter, *The Arcades Project* [after *Das Passagen-Werk* edited Rolf Tiedemann, 1982] (Cambridge, MA/London, 1999).

Berger, John, *Keeping a Rendezvous* (London, 1993).

Berger, Peter L., *Redeeming Laughter, The Comic Dimension of Human Experience* (Berlin/New York, 1997).

Bhabha, Homi, *Location of Culture* (London, 1995).

Billig, Michael, *Laughter and Ridicule: Towards a Social Critique of Humour* (London, 2005).

Blistère, Bernard, *Pneumostructures*, exhibition catalogue, Paris: Galerie Martinet Hibault de la Chatre (2005).

Bloemink, Bernard et al., *Design=/Art: Functional Objects from Donald Judd to Rachel Whiteread* (Merrell/Cooper-Hewitt National Design Museum, London/New York, 2004).

Bois, Yve-Alain and Krauss, Rosalind, *Formless: A User's Guide* (MIT Press, Cambridge, MA, 2000).

Boswell, Peter, Bruce Jenkins and Joan Rothfuss, *2000 BC: The Bruce Conner Story Part II* (Walker Art Center, Minneapolis, 1999–2000).

Bourriaud, Nicolas, *Relational Aesthetics* [1998] (Paris, 2002).

Bourriaud, Nicolas, *Postproduction* [2002] (New York, 2005).

Bowness, Alan (intro) *Kurt Schwitters*, exhibition catalogue, London: Lord's Gallery (October–November 1958).

Bramwell, Anna, *Ecology in the 20th Century: A History* (New Haven and London, 1989).

Breton, André and Polizzotti, Mark, *Anthology of Black Humor* [trans. Mark Polizzotti] (San Francisco, 1997).

Brisley, Stuart, *Beyond Reason: Ordure* (London, 2003).

Brook, James, Carlsson, Chris and Peters, Nancy J. (eds), *Reclaiming San Francisco: History, Politics, Culture* (San Francisco, 1998).

Brougher, Kerry, Morphy, Howard and Elliott, David, *In Place (Out of Time): Contemporary Art in Australia*, exhibition catalogue, Oxford: Museum of Modern Art (1997).

Brunet, Nathalie and Eschapasse, Maurice, *A propos de Nice*, exhibition catalogue, Centre Georges Pompidou (1977).

Bull, Malcolm (ed.), 'Special issue on globalisation and biopolitics', *New Left Review* 45, May/June 2007.

Burrell, P., *Green Design* (Design Council, London, 1991). Rex Butler et al, Contemporary Commonwealth 2006, exhibition catalogue, National Gallery of Victoria, 2006.

Carrick, Jill, 'Phallic victories? Niki de Saint-Phalle's *Tirs*', *Art History*, Vol. 26, Issue 5, November 2003, 26/5, pp. 700–29.

Cartmell, D., Hunter, I.Q., Kaye, Heidi and Whelehan, Imelda, *Trash Aesthetics – Popular Culture and its Audience* (London, 1999).

Caruana, Wally, *Aboriginal Art* [1993] (London, 2003).

Catalaneo, Gary. *Ocker Funk*, exhibition catalogue, Sydney: Frank Watters Gallery (1975).

Causey, Andrew, *Sculpture since 1945* (Oxford/New York, 1998).

Clough, Patricia Ticineto with Halley, Jean, *The Affective Turn, Theorizing the Social* (Durham/London, 2007).

Coates, Rebecca and Howard Morphy (eds.) *In Place (Out of Time) Contemporary Art in Australia*, exhibition catalogue, Museum of Modern Art, Oxford, 1997.

Cochrane Simons, Susan and Stephenson, Hugh (eds), *Luk Luk Gen! Look again! Contemporary Art from Papua New Guinea* (Perc Tucker Regional Gallery, Townsvillle, 1990).

Connor, Steven, *Postmodernist Culture* (Oxford, 1997).

Contemporary Commonwealth 2006, exhibition catalogue, National Gallery of Victoria (2006).

Cooke, S.J., Planque J. and Schjeldahl, P., *Jean Dubuffet, 1943–1963, Paintings, Sculptures, Assemblages* (Hirshhorn Museum and Sculpture Garden/Smithsonian Institute Press, Washington DC, 1993).

Coplans, John, 'Circle of styles on the West Coast', *Art in America* 52/3 (June 1964), pp. 36–7.

Crawford, Al, *Sakema Gogodala Woodcarvers* (National Cultural Council, Port Moresby, 1975).

Creeley, Robert and Chassman, Neil A. et al., *Poets of the Cities – New York and San Francisco* (Dallas Museum of Fine Arts, 1974).

Critchley, Simon, *On Humour* (London, 2002). Cummings, Neil and Lewandowska, Marysia, The Value of Things (Birkhauser, Basel, 2000).

D'Amico, Victor and Buchman, Arlette, *Assemblage: A New Dimension in Creative Teaching in Action* (Museum of Modern Art, New York, 1972).

Datschefski, E., *The Total Beauty of Sustainable Products* (Rotovision, 2001).

Davidson, Michael, *The San Francisco Renaissance – Poetics and Community at Mid-Century* (Cambridge, 1989).

Davis, Mike, *Planet of Slums* (London, 2006).

Dawson, J., *Ecovillages: New Frontiers for Sustainability* (Totnes, 2006). de Certeau, Michel, *The Practices of Everyday Life* [trans. Steven Rendall, first published 1984] (Berkeley/Los Angeles and London, 1988).

Débray, Cecile et al., *Le Nouveau Réalisme*, exhibition catalogue, Paris: Galleries Nationales du Grand Palais (28 March–2 July 2007) and Hannover: Sprengel Museum (9 September–27 January 2008).

Denzin, Norman K., Lincoln, Yvonna S., *Handbook of Qualitative Research* (London, 1994).

Dietrich, Dorothea, '*The Fragment Reframed: Kurt Schwitters's Merz-column*', *Assemblage*, 14 April 1991, pp. 82–92.

Douglas, Mary, *Purity and Danger: An Analysis of Concepts of Pollution and Taboo* (London/New York, 1966).

Duncan, Michael and McKenna, Kristine, *Semina Culture, Wallace Berman and His Circle* (Santa Monica Museum of Art, Santa Monica, 2005).

Duncombe, Stephen (ed.), *Cultural Resistance Reader* (London, 2002).

Elden, Stuart, Lebas, Elizabeth and Kofman, Eleonore (eds), *Henri Lefebvre, Key Writings* (London/New York, 2003).

Elderfield, John, *Kurt Schwitters* (London, 1985).

Elderfield, John (ed.), *Essays on Assemblage, Studies in Modern Art 2* (Museum of Modern Art, New York, 1992).

Elkins, James, *Is Art History Global?* (London, 2006).

Ferrell, Jeff, *The Empire of Scrounge: Inside the Urban Underground of Dumpster Diving, Trash Picking and Street Scavenging* (New York, 2005).

Finch, Christopher, *Image as Language, Aspects of British Art 1950–1968* (Harmondsworth, 1969).

Freud, Sigmund, *Standard Works* [trans. James Strachey] (London, 1953).

Freud, Sigmund, *The Joke and its Relation to the Unconscious* [trans. Joyce Crick with introduction by John Carey, *Der Witz und seine Beziehung zum Uberwufton*, Leipzig and Vienna 1905] (London/New York, 2003).

Gerrard, Sophie, 'Cyberjunk', *The Guardian Weekend* (30 June 2007).

Gilloch, Graeme, *Myth and Metropolis: Walter Benjamin and the City* (Cambridge, 1996).

Girling, Richard, *Rubbish! Dirt on Our Hands and Crisis Ahead* (London, 2005).

Grenier, Catherine (ed.), *Los Angeles 1955–1985* (Centre Pompidou, 8 March–17 July 2006).

Grogan, Emmett, *Ringolevio* [first published 1972] (Edinburgh, 1999).

Gumpert, Lynn (ed.), *The Art of the Everyday: The Quotidian in Postwar French Culture* (Grey Art Gallery, New York University Grey Art Gallery, Pittsburgh and Atlanta, 1997–8).

Gutwirth, Marcel, *Laughing Matter: An Essay on the Comic* (Ithaca and London, 1993).

Hapgood, Susan, *Neo-Dada, Redefining Art 1958–1962*, exhibition catalogue, New York: American Federation of Arts (1994).

Henri, Adrian, *Environments and Happenings* (London, 1974).

Herms, George, *The Prometheus Archives: A Retrospective Exhibition of the Works of George Herms*, exhibition catalogue, Newport Beach, CA: Newport Harbor Art Museum, The Oakland Museum and Seattle Art Museum (1979).

Highmore, Ben, *Everyday Life and Cultural Theory* (London, 2002).

Hughes, Robert, *The Art of Australia* (Harmondsworth, 1966).

Isaak, Jo Anna, *Feminism and Contemporary Art – The Revolutionary Power of Women's Laughter* (London, 1996).

Iverson, Margaret, 'Readymade, found object, photograph', *Art Journal* (Summer 2004).

Janis, Harriet and Blesh, Rudi, *Collage – Personalities, Concepts, Techniques* (London, Philadelphia and New York, 1962).

Johnstone, Mark and Holtzman, Leslie Aboud, *Epicenter: San Francisco Bay Area Art Now* (San Francisco, 2002).

Kallweit, Richard, 'Dropped Out CIty' and Felicity Scott, 'Episodes in the Refusal of Work' in Archis Volume 24, Counterculture, 2010, pp. 30–33 and pp. 34–38. Kaprow, Allan, *Assemblage, Environments and Happenings* (New York, 1966).

Kerouac, Jack et al., San Francisco Issue, *Evergreen Review*, 1/2 (1957).

Knechtel, John (ed.), *Trash* (MIT, Cambridge, MA, 2007).

Kristeva, Julia, *Powers of Horror: An Essay on Abjection* [trans. Leon S. Roudiez] (New York, 1982).

Kulka, Thomas, *Kitsch and Art* (Pennsylvania, 1996).

Lacey, Bruce et al., *Things – Assemblage, Collage and Photography since 1935*, exhibition catalogue, Norwich Gallery, Norwich School of Art and Design (12 January–1 July 2000).

Laporte, Dominique, *The History of Shit* [*Histoire de la merde (Prologue)* 1978] (Cambridge, MA/London, 2000).

Latour, Bruno, *Reassembling the Social: An introduction to Actor Network Theory* (Oxford, 2005).

Lévi-Strauss, Claude, *The Savage Mind* (Chicago, 1966).

Livingstone, Marco, *Paris 1960: Realism off the Shelf, Nouveau Réalisme*, exhibition catalogue, London: Mayor Gallery (2000).

Lunn, Felicity and Munder, Heike (eds), *When Humour Becomes Painful* (Zurich, 2005).

Marshall, C. (ed.), *Breaking the Mould, British Art of the 1980s and 1990s* (London, 1997).

Massey, Anna, *The Independent Group, Modernism and Mass Culture in Britain, 1945–59* (Manchester, 1995).

Massey, Doreen, *Space, Place and Gender* (London, 1994).

Massey, Doreen, *World City* (London, 2007).

Mauries, Patrick, *Cabinets of Curiosities* (London, 2002).

Meltzer, David (ed.), *San Francisco Beat – Talking with the Poets* (San Francisco, 2001).

Mey, Kirstin, *Art and Obscenity* (London, 2007).

Mirzoeff, Nicholas, *The Visual Culture Reader*, second edition (London, 2005).

Molon, Dominic and Rooks, Michael, *Situation Comedy: Humour in Recent Art* (ICI, New York, 2005).

Monbiot, George, *Heat: How to Stop the Planet Burning* (London, 2007).

Morgan, Kendragh, *It ain't Necessarily so … Mike Brown and the Annandale Imitation Realists*, exhibition notes, Heide Museum of Modern Art, Bulleen (18 July–1 October 2006).

Nuttall, Jeff, *Bomb Culture* [1968] (London, 1970).

O'Hagan, Andrew, 'The things we throw away', *London Review of Books* 29/10 (24 May 2007).

Packard, Vance, *The Waste Makers* [orig. pub. 1960] (Harmondsworth, 1961).

Papanek, Victor, *Design for the Real World: Human Ecology and Social Change* [1971] (St Albans, 1974).

Papanek, Victor, *The Green Imperative* (London, 1995).

Perry, Gill et al., *Art History, Special Issue: Difference and Excess in Contemporary Art: The Visibility of Womens' Practice*, Vol. 26, No. 3 (June 2003).

Phillips, Lisa (ed.), *Beat Culture and the New America: 1950–1965*, exhibition catalogue, New York: Whitney Museum of American Art (1995).

Plagens, Peter, *Sunshine Muse, Art on the West Coast 1945–70* [1974], re-issued with introduction (Berkeley, 1999).

Plant, Margaret, *Irreverent Sculpture*, exhibition catalogue, Monash University Gallery (1985).

Polledri, Paolo (ed.), *Visionary San Francisco* (San Francisco Museum of Modern Art/Munich, San Francisco/Munich, 1990).

Polsky, Ned, *Hustlers, Beats and Others* (Harmondsworth, 1971).

Rancière, Jacques, *The Politics of Aesthetics, Le Partage du sensible: Esthetique et politique*, 2000 [trans. and introduction Gabriel Rockhill] (London/New York, 2006).

Rasmussen, Harry and Grant, Art, *Sculpture from Junk* (New York, 1967).

Rathje, William L. and Murphy, Cullen, *Rubbish! An Archaeology of Garbage* (Arizona Press, Tucson, 2001).

Richardson, Donald, *Art in Australia* (Melbourne, 1988).

Roberts, John, 'Oh I love trash…', *Variant*, Issue 1 (1984) at www.variant.org.uk

Roberts, John, *Philosophising the Everyday: Revolutionary Praxis and the Fate of Cultural Theory* (London, 2006).

Robinson, Julia, *Assemblage* (Zwirner & Wirth, New York, 11 November 2003–31 January 2004).

Rogers, Heather, *Gone Tomorrow: The Hidden Life of Garbage* (New York, 2005).

Rowe, Colin, 'Collage City', *The Architectural Review* CLVIII/942 (August 1975), pp. 66–91.

Royte, Elizabeth, *Garbage Land: On the Secret Trail of Trash* (New York, 2005).

Sariff, Suzanne (ed.), *Recycled Reseen: Folk Art from the Global Scrapheap* (New York, 1996).

Sayers, Andrew, *Australian Art* (Oxford, 2001).

Scanlan, John, *On Garbage* (London, 2005).

Seago, Alex, *Burning the Box of Beautiful Things* (Oxford, 1995).

Searle, Adrian, 'Dust to dust', *The Guardian* (30 May 2006).

Seear, Lynne, Julie Ewington (eds), *Brought To Light: Australian Art, 1850–1965, From the Queensland Art Gallery Collection* (Queensland Art Gallery, 1998).

Seitz, William C., *The Art of Assemblage*, exhibition catalogue, New York: Museum of Modern Art (1961).

Selz, Peter, *Funk Art*, exhibition catalogue, Berkeley: University Art Museum (18 April–29 May 1967).

Selz, Peter, *The Art of Engagement, Visual Politics in California and Beyond* (Los Angeles, 2006).

Seymour, Howard et al., *The Beat Generation Galleries and Beyond* (Davis, 1996).

Sheey, Colleen J., *Cabinet of Curiosities, Mark Dion and the University as Installation* (Minnesota, 2006).

Sherringham, Michael, *Everyday Life: Theories and Practices from Surrealism to the Present* (Oxford, 2006).

Shields, Rob, *Lefebvre, Love and Struggles, Spatial Dialectics* (London, 1999).

Shoat, Ella and Stam, Robert, 'Narrativising Visual Culture – Toward a Polycentric Aesthetics', in N. Moerzoeff (ed.), *The Visual Culture Reader* (London, 1998), pp. 42–3.

Sillitoe, Alan, *The Ragman's Daughter* [first published 1963] (London, 1966).

Skerl, Jennie (ed.), *Reconstructing the Beats* (New York, 2004).

Smith, Richard Candida, *Utopia and Dissent: Art, Poetry and Politics on California* (Berkeley/Los Angeles, 1995).

Solnit, Rebecca, *Secret Exhibition, Six Californian Artists of the Cold War Era* (San Francisco, 1990).

Solnit, Rebecca, *Hollow City* [first published 2000] (London/New York, 2002).

Spencer, Robin, (ed.), *Eduardo Paolozzi, Writings and Interviews* (Oxford, 2000).

Starr, Sandra L., *Lost and Found in California: Four Decades of Assemblage Art*, exhibition catalogue, Santa Monica, CA (1988).

Stephens, Chris and Stout, Katharine (eds), *Art & the 60s, This Was Tomorrow*, exhibition catalogue, London: Tate Britain (30 June–3 October 2004).

Stewart, Susan, *On Longing, Narratives of the Miniature, the Gigantic, the Souvenir, the Collection* [first published 1984] (Durham/London, 1993).

Strasser, Susan, *Waste and Want: A Social History of Trash* (New York, 1999).

Suzuki, Shunryu, *Zen Mind, Beginner's Mind* [1970] (New York/Tokyo, 1999).

Taylor, Brandon, *Collage : The Making of Modern Art* (London, 2004).

Thompson, Michael, *Rubbish Theory: The Creation and Destruction of Value* (Oxford, 1979).

Thrift, Nigel, *Non-Representational Theory: Space, Politics, Affect* (London, 2008).

Trocchi, Alexander, *Cain's Book* [1960] (London, 1992).

Vergine, Lea (and various authors), *Trash. From Junk to Art,* exhibition catalogue, Museo di Arte Contemporanea di Trento e Rovereto (1997).

Vergine, Lea, *When Trash became Art: Rubbish, Mongo* (Milan, 2007).

Vincentelli, Allessandro (ed.), *Edward Kienholz and Nancy Reddin Kienholz,* exhibition catalogue, Gateshead: Baltic Centre for Contemporary Art (14 May–29 August 2005).

Waldman, Diane, *Collage, Assemblage and the Found Object* (London, 1992).

Wallace, Keith, *Rezoning: Collage and Assemblage,* exhibition catalogue, Vancouver Art Gallery (19 October 1989–1 January 1990).

Warhol, Robyn R. and Herndl, Diane Price (eds), *Feminisms: An Anthology of Literary Theory and Criticism* (New Jersey, 1991).

Weiss, Jason (ed.), *Back in No Time: The Brion Gysin Reader* (Connecticut, 2001).

Wheale, Nigel , *The Postmodern Arts: An Introductory Reader* (London, 1995).

Wheeler, Daniel, *Art Since Mid-Century* (New York/London, 1991).

Whiteley, Gillian, *Assembling the Absurd: George Fullard 1923–1973* (London, 1998).

Wines, James, *Green Architecture* (Cologne, 2000).

Woodham, Jonathan, *Twentieth-Century Design* (Oxford, 1997).

Index